# ECONOMIC ESSAYS

# ECONOMIC ESSAYS

## ROY HARROD

### SECOND EDITION

### MACMILLAN
### ST. MARTIN'S PRESS

Preface to the Second Edition and Essay 16
© Roy Harrod 1972

First Edition 1952
Second Edition 1972

*Published by*
THE MACMILLAN PRESS LTD
*London and Basingstoke*
*Associated companies in New York Toronto*
*Dublin Melbourne Johannesburg and Madras*

SBN 333 13536 9

*Printed in Great Britain by*
Biddles Ltd, Guildford, Surrey

# CONTENTS

# PREFACE TO THE SECOND EDITION

In 1951 I set myself to collect together a number of essays that I had written before that year, which seemed worthy of publication in a single volume. They were concerned with different aspects of economics. After the volume appeared, I wondered whether I had made a mistake. Would someone interested primarily in, say, imperfect competition be prepared to spend the extra money and occupy the extra bookshelf space just to possess the additional material about population, economic dynamics and Professor von Hayek's fascinating views on individualism? I pleaded on behalf of the book that it all bore on topics in which the general economist has to interest himself.

Since that time specialisation has greatly increased; the interests of each separate economist tend to be more sharply focused on his own theme. I was accordingly delighted and gratified when Macmillan, whose judgement I trust, proposed a new edition of this volume.

There is only one piece that was not in the original volume, namely Essay 16 entitled 'Increasing Returns'. This was first published in the *Essays in Honor of E. H. Chamberlin* (1967). It should be read immediately after Essays 3–10. These nine essays between them give the sole available complete account of my contribution to the theory of imperfect competition; I have never published a separate volume on this subject. Essays 3, 4 and 5 appeared in the *Economic Journal* before Professor Joan Robinson and Professor E. H. Chamberlin published their celebrated works on this subject. Essay 6 supplies my own theoretic solution of the problem of duopoly which holds also for oligopoly, a prevalent condition. Essay 7 was published shortly after the appearance of the Robinson and Chamberlin treatises and I regard its last section (III) as of the first order of importance.

Essay 8 was published more than twenty years after my

original contributions to the subject. Meanwhile my thinking had undergone some change. During the 'twenties, personal field work, which I undertook alone, established that 'increasing returns' were widely prevalent in industry. The original doctrines of imperfect competition implied that this was so. To date there appears to be no reason to modify this tenet. But in certain other respects the theory, as so far evolved, began to seem unsatisfactory, notably as regards the tendency for excess capacity to be built up wherever there was imperfect competition. The theory that each firm would aim at operating at a level that equated its marginal revenue to its marginal cost, entailed that *either* on average the firms, taking good times with the bad, would continue to make supernormal profit, *or* that too many firms would be attracted into the business of producing each article.

When during the 'thirties the Oxford Economists Research group made more systematic enquiries of business men, there was strong resistance to the idea that, in fixing their prices, they would have regard to marginal revenue, a concept that they even found it difficult to understand. And, apart from those enquiries, common sense seemed to suggest to my mind that there was something unrealistic about the idea that, throughout the wide field of imperfect competition, there must either be supernormal profit or a tendency to the build-up of an excessive number of businesses. There must, I thought, surely be some fault in the theory.

The eighth essay, published in this book for the first time (1952), was my attempt to redress the theory, so as to avoid this unrealistic conclusion. I argued that, while the accepted doctrine dealt with the interrelations between short- and long-period costs, on the demand side, only short-period marginal revenue was considered by it. But this was irrational. Any loss of profit in future, consequent on at present charging a price high enough to attract new competitors into invading the market, should be subtracted from short-term marginal revenue in assessing long-term marginal revenue. The intersection of the long-period curves would indicate the right price to charge; this would be lower than if only short-period marginal revenue were taken into account; normally short-period marginal revenue would continue indefinitely to be *below* marginal cost. In many cases the equilibrium price would be equal to full cost (i.e. including overheads and profit). This conclusion was not only theoretically correct, but much more conformable with the testimony of practical people.

Another sixteen years had passed when I was invited to contribute (in some haste) to the Festschrift for Chamberlin. Its sponsors were anxious that Chamberlin, who was then seriously ill, should see the volume. He did see it, but was by then too far gone in sickness to read it. I devised a construction, based on some reasonable, although not logically necessary, assumptions, by which at equilibrium the average cost curve and the long-period average revenue (called in this essay 'average net proceeds') curve are once more tangential. The demand curve, however, intersects downwards at the point of tangency. The price is determined by the point of intersection. The marginal cost curve and the marginal net proceeds curve intersect at a point vertically below this. But in equilibrium the short-period marginal revenue is below the marginal cost. I liked to think that this construction was a fitting tribute to Chamberlin.

Essays 9 and 10 were written for this volume and had not previously appeared. Essay 10 ('Profiteering: an Ethical Study') contains a rational explanation of the notion of moral obligation, which I first expounded in an article in *Mind* ('Utilitarianism', revised, 1936). Its theory links economics to ethics, because a beneficial course of action becomes a moral obligation, only when there are 'increasing returns to scale'; i.e. when $x+1$ actions of a certain type in relation to a certain type of situation lead to more than an $(x+1)/x$ net increase in human welfare. Thus the theory of moral obligation and the theory of increasing returns to scale in imperfect competition are shown to be basically merely different applications of the same fundamental axiom—shall we call it of logic or of the principles of human reason?—as exemplified both in theory (logic) and in practice, namely in the principles that should govern the maximisation of human welfare (economics).

This volume contains also my early contributions to the theory of 'growth economics'. I call attention, in particular, to Essay 11, entitled 'The Expansion of Credit in an Advancing Community' (first published, August 1934).

It already seemed to me at that time that the controversy then raging between Keynes and von Hayek could not be resolved, to the intellectual satisfaction of its auditors, on the basis of the current values of the determinants of prices and income distribution that were operating at a given point of time. I deemed that we could form a valid judgement only by reference to the nature of the determinants of increase in an 'advancing community'.

About three years later Keynes's famous *General Theory of Employment, Interest and Money*, the proofs of which I had read and re-read, appeared. A few months later I attempted to summarise it at an international conference at Oxford in a lecture which is included in this volume (Essay 12). I draw attention to its concluding page, which explains that there was no theory of economic dynamics in Keynes. His creative contribution was a masterly construction of a system of ideas that constitutes what in later language we call macro-statics.

During that year I worked with great assiduity on incorporating a dynamic element in the Keynesian scheme. The book embodying this, entitled the *Trade Cycle*, appeared in the bookshops in the same year as the *General Theory*—publishing delays were then not so long as they became after the war. The essence of my book was a conflation of Keynes's 'multiplier' theory with what has since come to be called the 'acceleration principle'; as regards the latter I drew inspiration from J. M. Clark's *Strategic Factors in the Business Cycle*. But my *Trade Cycle* still contained no basic axiom relating to growth theory. I continued thinking furiously, and two years later excogitated such an axiom, which is formulated in Essay 13 of this volume. Essay 14, first published in this volume, was my rejoinder to a criticism of my growth formula made by Professor Sidney Alexander.

Some might hold that Essay 1 ('The Population Problem') would have been better suppressed in this reprint. It consists of a memorandum submitted to a Royal Commission on Population, to which I also gave oral evidence, in 1944, and recommends measures designed to encourage larger families.

In 1921 our birth rate fell below the level that would ensure the maintenance of the population. Unless it rose, there
would be a progressive decline, leading eventually to extinction. The death rate fell after that year, owing to improved
medicine etc., but, even so, there was bound to be a cumulative fall in our numbers. In making my calculations I used the
'net reproduction rate', a concept defined by Dr. Kuczynski.
The large decline was due to appear in a matter of decades,
not centuries.

In the year before I gave my evidence the birth rate had
a sudden rise. At the time this was attributed to the conscrip-
tion of women for war work; mothers of babies were exempted;
it was thought that many women preferred the chores connected with having an extra child to work in the forces. But it
has not fallen for most of the subsequent period below the
replacement level. Why?

During my period of gloom, I recall Oliver Strachey, a
wiser, although not a wittier, man than his more famous
brother, Lytton, telling me not to fuss about this. Nature
would find a cure. This was not detailed enough to satisfy my
mind. On subsequent reflexion, it has occurred to me that
there may be a U-shaped curve. The very poor are feckless.
When at a somewhat higher standard of living an extra child,
if decently cared for, entails reducing one's expenditure on
food, warmth or housing, the balance of advantage may seem,
to those who look ahead, to be against having an extra child.
But at a higher standard of living the charm of parenthood
may seem to outweigh the pleasure given by, say, a second
motor car. Thus in the 1921–43 period we may have been
around the bottom of the U-shaped curve. (In paragraph 14
of Essay 1 only the left-hand side of the U-shaped curve is
discussed.)

It was put to me at the time that it did not matter if the
British race died out, since others would keep the human race
alive on this planet. I had two counter-arguments.

1. I believed that what the British did today (perhaps now
we should say what the Americans do today), the rest of the
world would do tomorrow. Birth rates were falling in all
advanced countries. Less developed countries were likely in

due course to follow suit. There were discussions at that time about what species of animal was most likely to inherit the earth, when humans were extinct. It was not generally thought that it would be monkeys. I do not now recall which species was most favoured.

2. I was anxious that the British in particular should not die out; they were then first on the list for self-destruction by excessive birth-control. This may seem a deplorably patriotic, nationalistic, not to say, jingoist, point of view. I was, and still remain, a great believer in the existence and importance of a variety and inequality of stocks; in this matter I was much influenced by the thinking of the great R. A. Fisher. This had relevance not only for the British as a race, but also to the fact that during much of the nineteenth century those British whose ancestors had made outstanding contributions to the progress of the country were having smaller families than those who had not. At the time of my testimony this phenomenon had ceased; but it was evidence in favour of my view that what the top people do today, the rest will do later.

I believed that the British had been able, owing to their innate qualities, to make greater contributions to the progress of the human race around the world than had many other peoples; it was accordingly expedient, for the sake of mankind, that they should not eventually die out.

In the more recent period, when referring to this theme, I have been in the habit, in order to safeguard myself against the charge of unthinking egoism and nationalism, to name the Japanese, as, despite all their faults, the greatest nation in the world. I am afraid that this does me no good in the opinion of besotted egalitarians.

I have the idea that my evidence to the Royal Commission on Equal Pay for Equal Work (1945) (Essay 2) which favours unequal pay—even less popular now than it was then—still makes good sense.

Finally, I would like to thank John Wiley & Sons Inc. for their kind permission to reproduce Essay 16, 'Increasing Returns', from *Essays in Honor of E. H. Chamberlin*, first published in 1967.

*January* 1972

# PREFACE TO THE FIRST EDITION

THIS volume is a collection of essays, some reprinted, others new. Of old papers I have not included any that I do not judge still relevant to economic science in the phase that it has now reached. The subjects treated of are various and may appeal to different specialists; the excuse for bringing them together is that they all bear on central topics in which the general economist who is not a specialist in any of the fields has to interest himself.

The first essay is concerned with population. Population theory was an integral part of the older economics and should, my opinion, be reinstated in modern treatises. While this essay discusses the causes and cures of the danger of depopulation in wealthy countries, I should claim that its principles spring essentially from Malthus's thought upon this topic and are in accordance with it. I developed them in submitting a plea to the Royal Commission on Population, and, as I do not think that I can improve on my method of presentation on that occasion, I have reprinted the text as it was submitted. (The reader will find my practical proposal developed in detail in Vol. V of the Appendices to the Report of the Commission). I have also preserved the original form of my memorandum to the Royal Commission on Equal Pay; as well as being a contribution to the topic in question, this essay constitutes an illustration of the principles of wage determination; I was happy to be taking up a favourite subject of my former mentor, F. Y. Edgeworth.

The eight essays that follow relate to the theory of imperfect competition. This has created much stir in the world of economists during the last two decades. First came the exciting development of a new branch of theory; then there was a lull during which the new findings were provisionally accepted by many of the younger generation; recently there has been reconsideration and the possibility of rather acute controversy; those responsible for teaching economics have become somewhat puzzled about what they can purvey even as a first approximation to the truth. In this transitional phase, existing controversies cannot be dissociated from history of the doctrines in dispute. It would be a counsel of despair to recommend that a wholly fresh start should be made; if existing doctrines are to be revised, it is important to understand their origin; this may make clear at what point error has crept in and give a clue to the character of the revision required.

The third and fourth essays included in this volume were published by me before the appearance of the treatises by Mrs. Robinson and Professor Chamberlin, which had so much influence on the further development of the subject. I believe that it may be of value to readers to study this independent line of approach carefully. A new view of the issues, as they presented themselves to a theorist at that date, may well be illuminating. The articles in question are highly condensed, and if I attempted to rewrite this bit of history in new words, I should certainly add to the number which the reader had to peruse. I will not conceal, however, that the pride of authorship has been one motive for re-publication. It appears to me that the most important points in the doctrines subsequently developed are present in these two articles.

The sixth — very brief — essay offers a solution of the problem of duopoly. The economist attacks the problem of duopoly primarily with a view to elucidating the case of oligopoly, of which ever more is being heard. What the theory of imperfect competition essentially did was to apply the theory of monopoly to the whole field in which competition was not perfect. It has been repeatedly claimed that monopoly principles are not applicable to the case of oligopoly, and that thus the doctrines of imperfect competition do not cover the whole ground, but leave the theory of oligopoly in an unsettled state.

It was the purpose of the article — if it can be dignified by such a name — to propose that the technique of analysis applied in the case of imperfect competition, particularly the marginal revenue curve, was also applicable in the case of duopoly (and thereby oligopoly). The famous historic attempts to solve the problem of duopoly have essentially rested upon arbitrary assumptions about what the 'other' duopolist will do in reaction to a change of output by his competitor. In my solution there is no such arbitrary element ; it is merely assumed that the other duopolist will do what it is in his interest to do. This is a subject which requires for its further elaboration a greater mathematical *expertise* than I have. None the less it may be that what I have set out supplies the correct basic principle. According to it, there is a determinate stable equilibrium in the duopoly case, intermediate between that of perfect competition and that of monopoly.

The seventh article presents the recapitulation of the doctrines of imperfect competition which I wrote after I had studied the works of Mrs. Robinson and Professor Chamberlin. Those were days of exhilaration at the new findings. I now hold (see eighth article) that I accepted rather too much. I think that this article gives a fair summary of what came for a term of years to be the accepted doctrine. Professor F. H. Knight had it reprinted for use in his seminar at Chicago ; in doing so he dropped the third part of it, which relates the phenomenon of imperfect competition to trade-cycle theory. None the less I remain of opinion that the point made in this section has its importance and have accordingly not followed Professor Knight's example.

During the four years that followed the publication of the seventh article there occurred a series of interviews between Oxford economists and business men. These interviews have .given rise to discussion and misunderstanding. As one who took an active part in them, I venture to make a comment.

To elucidate their significance it is necessary to go back a little. During the century following Adam Smith, certain doctrines concerning competition held the field in political economy. They were stated in the King's English, which does not always allow the finest degree of precision. The last third of the nineteenth century witnessed a sharpening of definitions and postulates and a restatement of principles in mathematical language. This process removed ambiguities and vaguenesses and rendered everything clearer and more precise. There may, however, be value in an ambiguity. The doctrines of competition purported to relate to a real world in which the circumstances and procedures of competitors were various. There was the danger, not perhaps fully recognised, that in the very process of sharpening analytical concepts, the mathematical school might render them inapplicable to the real world, or to some part of it. The concepts might, while rendering possible a more precise analysis of what occurred in one sector, be inapplicable to another sector within the broad field of competition. The implication of the general theory of value in its mathematical guise, as applied to competition, was perfect competition. It may have been assumed that this was good enough, since what occurred in conditions of perfect competition might be taken to occur, subject to friction, in imperfect competition also.

What happened in the 'twenties was a growing sense that this was *not* good enough, that the divergence of the theoretical model of perfect competition from reality was too great to be tolerated any longer. The theory of competition may be called a deductive one; it proceeded from certain assumptions about behaviour; the later refined theory used the more precise assumptions designated as those of perfect competition. What the theory of imperfect competition, as developed in the 'thirties, did was to vary the assumptions, so as to bring them nearer reality in that part of the field in which competition was not perfect. The theory of imperfect competition, like that of perfect competition, was still essentially a deductive theory. But if it was based on assumptions that more closely reflected one part of reality, the propositions inferred would be likely to approximate more closely to what really happened in that part. It was hoped that the new assumptions were sufficiently realistic — no one claimed for them absolute precision — to provide a good working theory.

What the Oxford interviews suggested was that these

new assumptions, on which high hopes had been built, were still deplorably far removed from the reality. Precisely the same urge, which inspired the revolution that we may call the theory of imperfect competition, got to work to suggest that further qualification was needed. While this renewed urge has inspired various interesting lines of thought, it cannot be said that a second revolution has yet been successfully achieved. I hope that the eighth essay in this volume may carry the matter one stage forward.

I would submit that some of the criticisms directed against those who have written under the influence of these Oxford interviews have been misplaced. I do not think that anyone has claimed that the interviews were of such a character that one could base new *inductive* laws of economic science upon the evidence collected. Messrs. Hall and Hitch in their celebrated article certainly did not claim so much. Rather what the interviews did was to give a great shock to complacency. They certainly confirmed the view that the assumptions of perfect competition were quite inappropriate; but they also suggested that the assumptions of imperfect competition were in drastic need of revision. They set our minds working.

While it may be admitted that no clear-cut and abiding theory has yet emerged, there is a type of criticism brought against those influenced by the interviews at which I would protest most strongly. What is suggested is that the economists present at them were wrong in being shaken in their complacency, that the doctrines of imperfect competition as laid down in the 'thirties have a secure logical foundation, and that the interviews only disturbed the economists because the economists did not fully appreciate that the business men did not understand what they were doing, or did not know how to express themselves. This investigation has been spoken of as though the Oxford economists had done no more than ask a few busy men to fill in a *questionnaire* in their spare time. It has been suggested that a sample of about forty was too small; it was small; it was certainly too small for the formulation of an inductive law, but by no means too small to bring home the wide gulf between certain economic assumptions and the facts of business.

Each entrepreneur was interviewed separately, during the course of some three hours, by about ten economists. Pity the poor victim! The proceedings were strictly confidential, and every attempt was made to obtain an atmosphere of intimacy. The victim was entertained with all the hospitality, such as it was, available in the colleges of pre-war Oxford. Sir Hubert Henderson was in the chair; he already had much experience outside the academic world, and he often rendered valuable service in interpreting the language of certain strict academic theorists present to the entrepreneurs, and conversely. The economists at that time had two points upon which they wished to clear their minds, namely the effect of changes in interest rates on business behaviour, and the price policy of business men in response to varying marketing conditions. Every attempt was made to get mutual understanding about the issues involved. The economists were men of first-rate calibre, some of whom have subsequently established notable reputations. Many of the business men were of first-rate calibre also, and, despite difficulties of economic jargon, acquired a good understanding of what the economists were driving at. It has been suggested that a list of the questions addressed to the entrepreneurs should have been published along with the Hall-Hitch paper. The wording of the questions, which formed our agenda, was of small importance. We very soon got beyond the questions in our resolute attempt to penetrate deeply into the motives governing behaviour.

I must add one further point. It has been suggested that the responses of the entrepreneurs were influenced, or were interpreted, along lines that conformed with the economists' own tendencies of thought. The exact opposite is the case. Many of those present were at that time actually engaged in propounding in class-room or lecture-room the very doctrines about interest rates on the one hand and about imperfect competition on the other that the business men were up-setting. The economists' partiality, to the extent that they had one, was all on the side of getting the entrepreneurs to confirm the doctrines that were their stock-in-trade with pupils. If these were upset, what should they put in their place? Every effort was made to coax out of the entrepreneurs answers favourable to what were then established doctrines. If a contrary result emerged, this was not in conformity with, but against, the wishes of those conducting the interviews.

No one could claim that this enquiry was final. It is to be hoped that many more will be undertaken. Having regard to the limited objectives that the interviewers had in mind, I cannot imagine a more efficient method of conducting a field enquiry than that then employed, and I venture to say that it would have been a very stupid economist who, if present at those interviews, did not allow them to have a profound influence on his thinking. The qualms to which they gave rise in my own mind were expressed in an article which I wrote in Oxford Economic Papers, No. 2 (1939). I have not reprinted it here, as the thought contained in it is further developed in the three new essays which follow.

In the eighth essay I have, after a lapse of time, attempted a revision of some of the established doctrines of imperfect competition. Meanwhile Mr. P. W. S. Andrews has been conducting more extensive investigations in the field. I submitted this eighth essay to him and received a number of suggestions which have proved of great value. I cannot claim, however, that he is in complete agreement with all that I have written. In this connexion I should like to define a difference — with which he may not agree either — between his approach in his recent important work on these problems and mine. Basing himself for theory on the doctrines of Marshall, he has sought to formulate certain generalisations about business behaviour which are essentially derived from his wide observation of the facts. He has examined a large number of cases and detected certain uniformities. My procedure, by contrast, has remained deductive. Just as the original doctrines of imperfect competition were themselves reached by varying the assumptions from which the argument proceeded, so my conclusions have been reached by a further variation of the assumptions. I hope that the new assumptions are both more reasonable and more realistic than the old. But I have not gone beyond what can be deduced from the assumptions. There remains a gap between my deductive generalisations and Mr. Andrews's inductive generalisations. It should be the endeavour of theorists and empiricists alike to close the gap. Generalisations yielded by field observation can be improved by further observation; generalisations deduced from certain basic assumptions can be improved by a variation in those assumptions that brings them closer to reality. Thus the gap may eventually be closed, but it cannot be closed without effort. The theorist will continue to veto assumptions that seem in conflict with wider economic principles, such as the quest for gain. The empiricist on his side cannot allow the validity of generalisations that appear in conflict with observed behaviour. The subject is clearly still a live one.

The third section, which includes my summary of the quintessentials of Keynesian economics, develops the theme that it is needful, especially in connexion with full employment studies, to formulate a systematic theory of the laws of economic growth.

I have hoped that, after traversing a rather long stretch of strict economic theory, the reader may be cheered by a sally into political science which was provoked by Professor F. A. von Hayek.

I must express my indebtedness to Her Majesty's Stationery Office for leave to reprint my submissions to the two Royal Commissions and to the editors of the *Economic Journal*, the *Quarterly Journal of Economics*, *Economica* and *Econometrica* for leave to reprint the third, fourth, fifth, sixth, seventh, eleventh, twelfth, thirteenth and fifteenth papers.

*January* 1952

# I

# MAN-POWER

# THE POPULATION PROBLEM[1]

1. The proposal which I have the honour to submit here-with presupposes that the present situation is critical and gives ground for alarm. With this basic assumption it would be wanting in sense of proportion to recommend an antidote that would strike an ordinary man as of trivial importance. The decision to have or not to have more children is governed by strong emotional forces; it is not taken without heart-searching; we cannot hope to influence that decision in a great number of cases without making an adjustment in the prospects of parents which they will readily judge to be of appreciable significance. I am accordingly making a pro-posal which is more far-reaching than the measures recently adopted on the continent of Europe or than the flat rate of allowance of 8s. per week for each child after the first proposed by Sir William Beveridge. But it is not so far-reaching as to be inconsistent with the main features of our economic structure.

2. I submit no evidence in support of the 'basic assump-tion' that the position is serious, as the relevant figures will no doubt have been provided by experts in vital statistics. We should be most impressed by the persistence of the down-ward trend in this country during the sixty years before 1933, the magnitude of the decline in the gross reproduction rate from 2·3 to 0·9, and the spread of the habit of low reproduction outwards from the original source of 'infection', that is, from the higher income grades to the whole popula-tion and from France and England to most of the other countries. It should be observed that the gross reproduction rate of 2·3, estimated by Dr. Kuczynski for mid-Victorian England (1870-72), is not an abnormally high one, either by

[1] Memorandum submitted in 1944 to the Royal Commission on Population.

comparison with our own rates in earlier periods, in so far as these can be computed, or with rates in other countries in that period. It seems to me probable that a natural historian who observed the reproduction rate of a species fall to less than two-fifths of its normal level, would infer that some lethal factor had been introduced into its environment dooming it to fade out of existence. If a way is sought to bring the gravity of the situation home to the general public, the following calculation strikes me as effective. If the difference between the actual births in the period after 1933 and the births which would have occurred had the gross reproduction rate been at the mid-Victorian level (2·3) be regarded as a 'loss of life', the loss of life to the country owing to low reproduction was about as great as the loss which would have occurred had we been waging five wars, with fatal casualties in each as high as those in the war of 1914–18, simultaneously and without end.

3. Not much consolation can be drawn from the comparative stationariness in the gross and net reproduction rates in the decade after 1933, first because the gross rate was too low to secure survival even if mortality below the age of 45 could be eliminated entirely, and secondly because the average age of marriage was declining. The net reproduction rate is a valuable measure of what a population is doing to replace itself but not in every case a perfect one. If the average age of marriage falls there is a windfall once-over accrual of births, separate from and additional to any increase which may be due to younger marriages yielding larger families. Consequently, during a period of declining average age of marriage the recorded net reproduction rate requires correcting to obtain a 'true' net reproduction rate; and if during such a period the recorded net reproduction rate is stationary the true rate must be falling. Moreover in a society such as ours which is tending ever more to uniformity of social habits as between different income levels, one must have doubts whether the trend to lower reproduction has reached its limit so long as the lower income groups show a higher rate.

4. Nor can consolation be drawn from the very recent

improvement, since a small degree of avoidance of calling-up orders would be sufficient to account for it. It is indeed possible that some evidence may be forthcoming of a 'change of feeling' on the part of representative parents. Hopes may be built on this change proceeding further and producing a considerable revival after the inhibitory influences of the war are removed. It may be argued from this that we should wait a little longer and give the alleged new trend of feeling a spell of peace in which to assert itself, before adopting radical measures. I offer two arguments against further delay.

5. If we are to avoid great losses in numbers the rise in the net reproduction rate must come quickly. We have leeway to make up, since it has been below the survival level for some twenty years. The comparative stationariness that has been predicted for our population during the next thirty years, should reproduction remain at the same level and the downward trend in mortality be continued, masks a decline of about one-quarter in the under-45 section of the population which is due to occur on those hypotheses. Thus even if the net reproduction rate rose suddenly to unity at the end of thirty years a loss of many millions would occur thereafter. But it is not likely to rise suddenly to unity in a given year and so the subsequent losses would probably be greater still. If we are to avoid large losses, it must reach unity in much less than one generation from now, and it is hardly likely to do that unless the rise begins immediately. These propositions take no account of the loss of young manhood in the present war, which will seriously aggravate the situation. In these circumstances we cannot afford to allow ourselves a further period in which to wait and see.

6. Secondly, the proposal I put forward may be recommended by its inherent justice as well as its tendency to encourage reproduction. Consequently, even if we could be sure, as we certainly cannot be, that the alleged change of feeling would be sufficiently potent to secure survival, there would still be a case for adopting the plan. The fact of the matter is that parents as a class and mothers in particular have had less than justice in our economic arrangements.

5

Parents of larger families have been under greater economic pressure than other members of the community. This has always been unjust in itself, but justice often has to give way to expediency, and in this case the tendency of the race to reproduce itself too rapidly, especially after the decline in mortality in the late eighteenth century, had to be kept in check to prevent over-population. Now that the tendency no longer exists we may redress the balance without peril in favour of parenthood.

7. It may be worth stating at the outset that we cannot contemplate a return to the old level of gross reproduction. Malthus was quite right in supposing that it is impossible to combine the low mortality rates, which obtain in civilised conditions, with the birth-rate which would result from giving free rein to reproductive instincts. The geometric increase would soon lead to grotesque overcrowding. Birth control in its widest sense is a pre-condition of continued civilisation. Thus it would be wrong as well as fruitless to tilt against the modern idea of deliberately planning the size of the family. It is not required that normal parents should think in terms of a family of six or eight, but rather of four or five, although the more philoprogenitive parents may be encouraged to contribute more than their fair share to the next generation, subject to humane regard for the health of the mother.

8. In devising remedies to meet the serious situation I submit that two principles should be applied, namely, (i) they should be adequate in scale and (ii) they should be national in scope.

9. If we take a broad survey of history and pre-history, we find a great variety of social and economic arrangements, some of which were favourable, others unfavourable, to reproduction. It is very probable that there was a causal connexion between the type of social system in operation and the contemporary tendency to over- or under-population; Malthus's work failed to stimulate as much enquiry into these problems as their interest and importance deserve; there is an almost virgin field here for the anthropologist with a biological and mathematical training. Examples are

6

infanticide, and the system of serfdom, under which children were unable to escape from the hereditary plot of land, so that, it being impossible to enlarge the productive resources available to the family, there was a strong prudential motive to limit its size. In historic times it may well be that the Christian condemnation of infanticide was responsible for the increase of serfdom which followed it and provided an alternative check to the undue growth of numbers. On the other hand, systems have from time to time prevailed which were especially favourable to reproduction. Thus, where there was a strong clan nexus and flexible territorial arrangements, the more reproductive families would, by their superior power, be able to gain not merely elbow-room for their larger numbers but a larger quantity of land per head. It is against the background of these great variations in fundamental institutions affecting reproduction that one should think of the proper scale of remedy to meet the present situation.

10. It is most improbable that these various customs and institutions were consciously devised in order to stimulate or retard population growth. They probably came about by natural or social selection in reaction to a change in the environment favourable or unfavourable to population growth. Such changes might be climatic or bacteriological or due to new methods of cultivation, providing greater means of subsistence — or smaller means, when disturbing the ecological balance — or the change might be due to the mere lapse of time, as when a group having increased for a number of generations began for the first time to press upon the means of subsistence. In the new situation, if one community had a variant in its social system, favourable to larger or smaller numbers as the case required, it might survive and replace its neighbours by ordinary natural selection, or through its superior power and prestige causing its neighbours to copy the favourable variant. It is possible that human survival will once again be secured by one or other of these selective processes. But this is not a solution that we can view with satisfaction, if the more favourable arrangements originate elsewhere. Consequently the task

7

before us is a new one, namely, to bring about with conscious intent and by deliberate planning the kind of fundamental social adjustment that has probably hitherto in human history been brought about by a selective process. It may seem a formidable task, but is also, I submit, an inspiring one, and must fill us with a supreme sense of responsibility.

11. The idea that it would not be satisfactory to wait for other peoples to give the lead in reviving births does not rest only on a narrow nationalist prejudice. Not that we should altogether despise such prejudice — the events of 1940 have demonstrated the strength and revived the prestige of nationalism in this country, in the sense of a determination to remain masters in our own house. But there is an argument to meet even those who refuse to be impressed with the importance of the mere maintenance of British stock and independence. New institutions favourable to reproduction may well come to birth not in isolation but as part of a wider ideology. For example, it is by no means proved that the Nazi ideology is favourable to reproduction in the long run. But if it is favourable, and if free countries do not of their own volition adapt their social system to the need for higher reproduction, then, despite its defeat in this war, Nazi ideology, or something similar, will triumph in the end. It would be a sad story if our mighty efforts in war were rendered of no avail by the mere failure to reproduce our kind. The free democratic system relies largely on the power of reason and discussion to secure necessary reforms. This population question is the acid test of its power. Unless the free societies which seek to solve their problems by reason are able to maintain their stock, they will in due course be effaced or dominated by others. This might mean another dark interlude in human history.

12. The incentive to larger families should be national in scope. We need a revival among all British men and women whatever their party, creed or walk in life. Our plans should be of universal application, and neutral as between conflicting views about the ideal economic organisation of society. Thus we should seek a redistribution of national income favourable to the parents of larger families and the

plan should be put into effect whether or not another redistribution as between rich and poor is proceeding at the same time. The issues are quite distinct in idea and should be kept distinct in practice. Sir William Beveridge's plan for an allowance of 8s. a week for each child in excess of one is excellent in itself, but is not a solution of our problem. It will not appeal to the ordinary man as adequate in scale when assessed against the background of ideas set out in paras. 9-11. And since it was conceived in accordance with his terms of reference as a protection against 'want', it is unlikely to solve the problems of those who would not in its absence experience want; thus its operative effect would be sectional, not national, in scope.

13. I do not propose to enter into the very deep question of the causes of the fall in the birth-rate, save to make two points, one negative and one positive, which are immediately relevant to my proposal.

14. It is often urged that parents have been caused to reduce the size of their families by the *facts* of insufficient livelihood, social insecurity and the fear of war. This is not a plausible explanation. Whether we compare birth-rates in different countries, different periods or different income strata, it does not appear that a hard lot in life is inimical to reproduction. Rather the other way. This is a very important point. If one accepted the hard-luck story, one might build one's hopes for a revival in births on the general improvement in living standards, employment prospects and international security which we are determined to achieve when this war is over. But if an easier and more secure lot in life is not in itself favourable to reproduction, then we must resolutely discard the hope that an improvement in general conditions will encourage births and we must seek other means. This conclusion is not inconsistent with the view that the *ideas* of insufficient livelihood and insecurity are coming to have a more important influence on parents. The fact of the matter seems to be that as man's actual condition improves, his idea of what is due to him and necessary to his existence rises more rapidly; his ambition always tends to outstrip his achievement. It is a paradox,

but well borne out in everyday experience, that the better-off people become the more they complain of not having enough money. In regard to the fear of war, it should be observed that this was not very widespread in Great Britain, either before 1914 or between 1919 and 1933, the periods of great decline. It is no good bewailing the tendency of man's requirements ever to outstrip his means of satisfying them. We are not likely to succeed in extirpating this trait in human nature, nor should we wish to do so, for it is the motive power of progress. If our people ever became content with their lot, that would be a sure symptom of imminent decadence.

15. At this point notice must be taken of a widespread fallacy. It is often argued that if being better off does not induce people to have more children, family endowment will not do so. The fallacy is crude but prevalent. It is perfectly consistent to hold that an improvement in the average *absolute* standard of living will not encourage births, and at the same time to argue that an improvement in the *relative* condition of parents of larger families will do so. If it is seen that the parents of larger families are more prosperous and more secure than the less reproductive members of the community, that will be an inducement to people to achieve that privileged status.

16. There is one change in social conditions to which we may safely — in so far as any statement in this field is safe — ascribe the wide diffusion of a low reproduction rate, namely, the public provision of 'social security'. Among the mass of people in the past children have been the principal or sole means of insurance against want. For instance, if there were six children, two might fail to make good in life, another two might be stony-hearted and indifferent to their parents, but it would be very bad luck if two out of the six were not found with means and affection sufficient to keep their parents out of the workhouse. The parents of but two children would be in a much more precarious position. As one cause of want after another, industrial accident, old age, sickness, unemployment, have come under the care of the public, the need to insure oneself by having children has faded out. Not only were parents of large families in fact

better placed to face the vicissitudes of life, but were also
seen to be, and thus became objects of envy to their neighbours.  Now so much is the situation changed that they have
become objects of pity and even sometimes, it is to be feared,
of contempt, for being simpletons.

17. The argument that 'social security' is a cause of
infertility is not designed to cast any slur upon social security.
On the contrary, the case for that reform is unshakable and
it would be a slur on any nation, which had achieved the
general standard of living of our own, if it did not provide in
full measure for the needy.  After all, insurance by having
children was a rough and ready method which left those
who could not have large families in an exposed position.
We have reached a level of well-being at which we must
regard such a method as intolerable.  But the point is that if
one introduces a very far-reaching change (like social
security) in the balance of forces which maintain society in
being, one must be on the look-out for the necessity of com-
pensating changes.  The physiologist well knows what a
delicate balance of forces is the human organism; the
ecologist understands the intimate interconnexion of animal
life, plant life, methods of cultivation and the water-table
and that a disturbance in the balance may have most far-
reaching consequences; it would be foolish to suppose that
the balance of forces in the social organism is any less
delicate, but unhappily sociology has not yet found its feet as
a scientific study.  Still, we may venture as far as the
elementary proposition that if the primary self-regarding
motive for having children is removed, there is danger to
survival if a substitute is not found.

18. In touching on the causes of the fall in reproduction,
I have confined myself to two points, one negative and one
positive, which seem to bear directly on the plan which I
have to submit.  The general question of the causation is a
vast subject and to enter on it would prolong this introduction
beyond reasonable limits.  But while I have not referred to
numerous other causal factors, it must not be supposed that
I have not had them in mind nor given them weight in
considering remedies.

19. The question is sometimes raised whether we should put more emphasis on a spiritual remedy or a material remedy for the present state of affairs. Those who stress the spiritual side sometimes argue that without a prior change of heart the material remedy will be of no avail and therefore should not be pursued or at least should be postponed until we see the effect of a spiritual change. I do not share this conclusion for the following reasons. In the first place the intrinsic desire for children must be so deeply rooted in the constitution of our species and has played such an important role through countless vicissitudes, that it must surely be regarded as an abiding element. Some hold that the fall in reproduction is due to the growth of selfishness and the decline of parental love. On biological principles it is most unlikely that there has been a loss of strength in the funda-mental parental instincts in the last two generations. Self-righteous persons in every age have railed against the growth of selfishness in their own; but their testimony is unreliable and taken in the aggregate self-contradictory. The fall in reproduction may be accounted for by the great changes in the environment which have occurred, and there is no need to resort to the improbable hypothesis of a change in human nature. But if it is needlessly cynical to suppose a decline in parental love, it is unscientifically optimistic to imagine that it can be whipped up above its normal level by spiritual exhortation. Parental love is a force of great but not infinite potency. If excessive material obstacles are put in its way it may be overcome. What we need, to secure survival, is that parental love and more self-regarding motives should work together in harmony to encourage parenthood, as they have done in the past. It is wrong to put too much strain on the altruistic elements in human nature; society should be so arranged that self-regarding motives play some part in getting fulfilment of the two basic tasks of doing an honest job of work for society and providing the next generation. The better that is arranged, the more can the fund of altruism be released for works of supereroga-tion, kindness to the needy and suffering, the pursuit of new ideas and new adventures, and all the other good works on

which we depend for the progressive amelioration and refinement of the human race.

20. Secondly, even if a spiritual *aufklärung* were capable of having a marked effect on reproduction, it would not be within the power of the public authority to bring it about. Official propaganda would be of little use: indeed it is probable that most British citizens would greatly resent any official exhortation on these very personal matters. It is true that a man of genius, a Dickens or a Mr. H. G. Wells, may have a profound influence on the way in which people regard their own private affairs and their attitude to life. But we do not know if there are such men of genius among the coming generation and it is most unlikely that, if there are, they would be willing to employ that genius for a given purpose on an official suggestion.

21. Thirdly, I suggest that far the most effective method open to the state to bring about a spiritual change is by applying a material remedy. The average citizen will not be impressed by propaganda, but he will be impressed by action. If a Royal Commission recommended and a British Parliament enacted a far-reaching measure to provide a basis for family life, that would be an event likely to strike the imagination. It would lead to heart-searching and intimate discussion. Once serious thought is provoked, we may rely on the conscience and reason of each individual to secure some revision of our scale of values. Whatever his religious convictions or moral code, the case for handing on the torch is so strong that he will recognise it, if he has any principles at all. I submit that the natural order of events is as follows. Public discussion, such as is now taking place, is necessary to get sufficient public opinion behind a Parliamentary measure; but this discussion is likely to have little influence on private conduct. The primary purpose of the measure must be to provide a material remedy, but if the measure provokes thought at a deeper level it may have some influence on the individual's notion of his duty. Whether this spiritual by-product will be important or not, it is difficult to judge. I submit that it is the only way in which the state could bring about a spiritual change, and, if this is

so, it means that the need for a change of heart reinforces the case for early Parliamentary action on the material plane.

22. I am only submitting one main economic remedy. Action on a number of subsidiary lines — *e.g.* housing, household appliances, domestic help, town-planning — is also desirable and I shall make brief reference to them later. But I do not think that all these measures added together would be either adequate in scale or likely to produce the moral impression referred to in the last paragraph. At the centre of the array of measures we need a straightforward provision of family endowment.

23. I propose an endowment to be paid to all out of public funds, to consist of a flat rate for every child after the first. I do not intend to argue in favour of this, assuming that it is already widely accepted. Sir William Beveridge, having regard to what is necessary to stave off want, proposed 8s. a week for each child after the first. In considering the population problem we are more concerned with giving an adequate status to motherhood and securing that the mother's condition is not too much less eligible than that of the unmarried woman worker. From this point of view I should prefer 10s. as a minimum. On such a scale a mother with three or four children in addition to the first, and her husband contributing his fair share to the household expenses, might not be far below the unmarried worker in her standard of living. But in the scales set out in my 'submission' I have assumed 8s., not 10s., so as to secure my results without imposing a greater strain on public funds than that proposed by Sir William Beveridge.

24. Compulsory insurance payments should be charged on all incomes in excess of £250 p.a. at the rate of 1s. per £ of income with a maximum contribution of £50 p.a.[1] I propose that the endowment payable in respect of children should be in proportion to contributions in such wise that a man of average life and with an average number of children

[1] [The figures in this essay are based on the general price level as it was in 1944. For current reference, all figures should be scaled upwards to allow for the general rise in price and income levels which has occurred since. The proposed levy of 1s. in the £, however, being a ratio, need not be changed. 1952 and 1972.]

in excess of 1 (reckoning the second as a half: cf. next sentence) would receive an amount precisely equal to what he paid in contributions (the details are explained in the 'submission', see pages 36-41, below). I propose that a full rate of endowment be paid in respect of every child after the second and a half rate be paid for the second. I propose that

TABLE

ENDOWMENTS PAYABLE PER CHILD FOR EVERY CHILD AFTER THE SECOND; HALF RATES ALSO PAYABLE FOR THE SECOND CHILD

(For certain selected Income Situations)

(For Parents who pay Insurance Contributions of 1s. per £ of Income)

| Annual Income of Father* | | Benefit in Each of the First Seven Years of the Child's Life (0-7) | Benefit in Each of the Next Six Years of the Child's Life (7-13) | Benefit in Each of the Next Five Years of the Child's Life (13-18) |
|---|---|---|---|---|
| | | £ | £ | £ |
| At whatever age of father* child is born | 1. 1000 constant | 67 | 134 | 201 |
| | 2. 800 ,, | 56 | 112 | 168 |
| | 3. 600 ,, | 46 | 92 | 138 |
| | 4. 400 ,, | 35 | 70 | 105 |
| | 5. 300 ,, | 30 | 60 | 90 |
| Assuming child is born when father* is 29½ years old | 6. 300 in 22nd year rising by 100 at 3-yearly intervals to 1000 after 21 years | 39 rising to 46 | 92 rising to 106 | 159 rising to 174 |
| | 7. 300 in 22nd year rising by 80 at 3-yearly intervals to 860 after 21 years | 37 rising to 43 | 86 rising to 98 | 147 rising to 156 |
| | 8. 300 in 22nd year rising by 50 at 3-yearly intervals to 650 after 21 years | 34 rising to 37 | 74 rising to 82 | 123 rising to 126 |

* Or mother, if *either* her unearned income in the year before the child's birth *or* her earned plus unearned income in the last year before marriage is higher than the income of the father in the year before the child's birth.

this endowment should be supplementary to the flat rate of allowances proposed in the last paragraph.

25. Is this adequate in scale? When we consider the great variations of economic system revealed by the anthropologist and the economic historian and the catastrophic nature of the recent fall in reproduction, we may think ourselves lucky if we can secure survival by such a modest

impost as 1s. in the £. The case rests on the adjoined table which shows what endowments could be provided. I think they would strike the average man as a reasonable assistance to parenthood and as sufficient to influence the decision of parents doubtful of their financial ability to add to their family. The matter could only be tested by experience. If the endowment proved insufficient, the scale of contributions and endowments could be raised within the framework of the scheme.

26. I submit that only by compulsory insurance is it possible to have an acceptable plan that is *national in scope*. The purpose of the plan is to reduce the disparity between the living conditions of larger families and those of smaller families (including childless persons). Since incomes are unequal, a flat rate of endowment which might go some way to reducing the disparity of those with incomes below, say, £250 p.a. would do much less to reduce disparities among those substantially above £250 p.a. No flat rate can have an appreciable effect that is national in scope. Endowments must be proportional to income. But Parliament is unlikely to be willing to vote such proportional endowments out of public funds. The future incidence of the burden would depend on the varying public policy in regard to taxation and it could be represented that such Parliamentary endowment might in certain circumstances involve a transfer from the poor to the rich. It is most important that a national scheme to encourage larger families should be neutral as between different income grades, professions, trades, etc.; it should be equally effective whether we proceed far on the road to greater equality of incomes or not; it should not raise party or class conflicts. Under my scheme what the class of people with incomes of £400 a year get, over and above the flat rate available for all, is paid by the class of people with £400 p.a.; similarly in the case of those with £500 p.a., £600 p.a., etc. Each income grade is self-financing. There is no question of one grade financing another, no interference with the income structure as it is at present or as it may be subsequently re-shaped. It neither aids nor hinders any re-shaping of the structure that may be desired.

27. I propose that no one should pay a contribution in excess of £50 and that endowments to parents with more than £1000 a year should not exceed those to parents with £1000 a year. £1000 is of course an arbitrary figure and some other figure may be preferred. There are two arguments in favour of this proposal. (i) While for a wide range of incomes the amount of money which parents feel it incumbent on them to spend on their children rises (for reasons stated in para. 34 below) roughly in proportion to the income of the parents, this rise does not proceed without limit. Very rich people are not likely to spend as large a fraction of their income on their children as those in the moderate range. I submit for consideration that the endowment shown in the Table for a man with £1000 a year would be sufficient to constitute a reasonable offset to the expenses incurred in respect of children by richer people, that, if money was the consideration holding richer parents back from adding to their family, the endowment proposed would suffice to remove that deterrent, and that, consequently, the limit of £1000 may be accepted without infringing the principle that the scheme must be *national in scope*.

28. (ii) While there is no question, under my insurance proposals, of the public financing the endowment of richer parents and each income group finances its own endowment, those keenly wedded to the egalitarian principle might object even to taking that indirect official cognisance of the existence of larger incomes which a compulsory insurance scheme enforcing proportionate family endowment might be deemed to imply. By fixing the limit of £1000 such a scruple may be overcome. Remembering that the endowment project is an urgent one, which must bear fruit in the next thirty years, if the population is to be saved, we have to consider the social structure that is likely to prevail in that period. As I understand it, the British Labour Party would not wish to narrow the range of incomes more closely than from £250 p.a. to £1000 p.a. in the immediate future. It is doubtful if even Communists are intolerant of such a range. Consequently, taking a hypothesis most favourable to the wishes of egalitarians, that a Parliament was elected after the

war prepared to take immediate action to secure a radical redistribution of incomes, narrowing the range of incomes to £250-£1000 p.a., my proposal would still be necessary if the endowment scheme was to be national in scope.

29. The question has been canvassed whether endowment could be provided by extending the existing system of income tax reliefs in respect of children. I have examined this carefully and regretfully conclude that an adequate endowment could not be provided by this method. The main point is that there is no escape from the dilemma that *either* the amount yielded by the relief will be quite inadequate in scale, as at present, *or* only rich parents will get any benefit at all in respect of the later children. As one enlarges the amount of relief per child, one raises the level of income at which there is any relief in respect of the third, fourth and fifth etc. children. This result would be true even with income tax as it is at present. In making calculations one should, however, assume some amelioration. For example, one might take (pessimistically) the standard rate at 7s. 6d., £160 personal allowance for a married man, £165 at half rate and an earned income allowance of one-fifth. An allowance per child of £100 instead of the present £50 would only provide £37 : 10s. a year — an inadequate amount; it would be necessary to have more than £575 a year to get any relief at all for the fourth child and to have £906 : 5s. a year to get the full relief of £37 : 10s. To make the allowance more adequate one might increase the relief per child to £200; but then a man would have to have more than £950 p.a. to get any relief for the fourth child and he would have to have £1406 : 5s. a year to get the full relief. He would have to have £1656 : 5s. a year to get the full relief for a fifth child. Not a very democratic system ! The fact of the matter is, that to make a substantial reduction of the present disparity it is necessary that the endowment for parents with a family of four or five children should be more than they are likely, unless rich, to pay in income tax; consequently, Parliament would not only have to relieve a man of all his income tax but to vote positive sums in payment to him ; and this, for reasons already stated, it is not likely to be willing to

do on a proportional scale to persons with middling incomes.

30. The same cause that makes the income tax relief method an unsuitable one for dealing with this problem makes it especially eligible for the Insurance method. The burden of a large dependent family is heavy, but it only lasts for a comparatively small period in a man's whole earning life. Consequently the premiums may be spread and the endowment concentrated; this enables the latter to be generous by comparison with the former; it is in relation to such a pattern of events that insurance has always had greatest success.

31. There is one feature of this proposal, however, which is uncharacteristic of insurance. A man would have to continue to pay contributions after ceasing to have any expectation of drawing benefits from the scheme. This is one reason why the insurance should be compulsory. A voluntary organisation would find collection excessively difficult in those circumstances. My proposal is that a man should be liable to pay contributions until his sixty-sixth birthday. This extension of the liability beyond the normal age of reproduction is necessary to get a good spread, it is equitable and it is also necessary to avoid discouraging early marriage. If an endowment fund had to be accumulated in advance of fatherly responsibilities, young men would have to contribute not one but many shillings in the pound at a time when their incomes were still slender. And in order to get a good endowment they would have to postpone father-hood; this would be inimical to an increase in reproduction. Another reason for compulsion is to get the necessary spread of numbers contributing. A man should certainly be free from all pressure to become a father if he does not wish to (see also para. 51, below); but he should not be free to opt out of making his contribution to the costs of raising the next generation.

32. After these preliminary remarks I should have preferred to present my scheme and let it speak for itself. I am conscious, however, of a class of objections that may be raised and ought to be forestalled. They turn on the idea that a proportionate endowment might offend the egalitarian

sentiment of the present age. I hope that not much weight will be attached to this. I have subjected myself to cross-examination in many audiences containing all types and classes of people and this type of objection was seldom raised in the body of the hall. It seems to come from a minority whose interest in these questions is doctrinaire rather than practical.

33. The objections to be met may be classified as follows :

(i) Parents with larger incomes ought not to spend more on their children ; their problem should be met on the lines of enabling them to dispense with such expenditure.

(ii) If, none the less, these parents refuse to have more children unless they can afford to give them extra amenities, we should neglect this class altogether and rely exclusively on those with modest means, since their numbers are sufficient to secure the survival of the race.

(iii) Proportionate endowment is inconsistent with the idea of equal opportunity, involves perpetuating the inequality of the social structure and is therefore inadmissible.

34. Too much stress is often laid on the cost of schooling. This is a vast subject on which I do not propose to enter. But I submit that *quite apart from this cost* the expense of children is within a certain range proportional to income. One has only to examine how a man with £500 or £1000 a year spends his additional money compared with a man with £250 per annum. A few of the obvious items are size of house, location of house, domestic help, a car, holidays, recreations, books, pictures and other cultural amenities. Under each and every head there is a corresponding item for the children. The two-seater must be replaced by the family car, the small house by a larger house. Of course a man may seek a larger house in a cheaper neighbourhood, but this would mean introducing that very disparity between his own circumstances and those of a man with the same pay doing exactly the same professional service for the community that we wish to avoid. What is not possible is to arrange for the man to enjoy the same amenities as his colleague himself while spending no more than one of lower income on his

children — not possible at least on lines which British citizens would tolerate. Of course it would be possible to regard the home as a mere breeding ground and hand the children over to state institutions which would do the rest, treating all children as equal. Such a solution is entirely unacceptable. So long as parents are allowed to have unequal incomes (within a certain range) they will want, and it is right that they should want, to share the resulting amenities with their children. The idea that the father should have one standard of living for himself and a much lower one for his children (so as to secure equal opportunity for all) is atrocious. It would not be endorsed by any section of the British public, whatever its aspirations for a new social order. That order must be achieved by some other method than the gross callousness and selfishness of parents and a break-up of the united life of family homes. It is not possible to solve the problem on the lines of dispensing parents with larger incomes from the need to spend proportionately more money on their children.

35. The critic might grant that we cannot and ought not to prevent better-to-do parents from sharing their amenities with their children, but argue that, this being so, we must acquiesce in their having smaller families, leaving it to the group with £250 p.a., or less, which is in a numerical majority, to increase their families and secure race survival. There are three weighty arguments, each alone strong enough to rule this solution out of court. (i) It will lead to race decline if our better stocks are relatively infertile (argument from stock). (ii) It will lead to a general lowering of standards and of efficiency if the parents who are best equipped in experience, knowledge and culture are relatively infertile (argument from environment). (iii) If members of the community doing relatively more responsible work — scientists, statesmen, administrators, doctors, technicians, business managers, foremen, teachers, etc. — do not decide to have larger families, the other members of the community will not do so either (argument from social example). I will expand each of these in turn briefly.

36. The argument from stock is supposed to be contro-

versial. Not that there is any reasonable doubt that valuable qualities are hereditary or that the various families which compose the nation possess these qualities in unequal measure. Where the doubt comes in is as to whether the families who at present enjoy a relatively favoured position do in fact embody the best qualities, some arguing that they owe their position to feudal pillage or capitalist exploitation in the past. This is an extreme view. Not many British people are so Marxist in outlook as to deny virtue to the middle class families who in the nineteenth century — to go back no further — have made such immense contributions in science, industry, commerce and statesmanship and have left us the permanent possession of their poetry and novels. Not many would argue that their anti-social qualities, which no doubt they had, outweighed their contribution to progress which has made possible the higher standards of living that all now enjoy. Not many would think it a good thing that the progeny of these people should fade out altogether. But it is not necessary to our purpose to engage in this controversy. We must think of the future. Our society is becoming more fluid and democratic and we are planning to accelerate this tendency. The idea of equal opportunity is that the individuals who, whatever their birth, have ability and valuable social qualities, should be able to rise and occupy positions of responsibility, not only those at the very top, but all down the scale. That is the plan for the future; what happened in the past is irrelevant. Then it becomes of vital importance that the people in such positions should not be sterilised. It is planned in each generation to comb out of all classes and sections of the nation the best endowed individuals and give them work commensurate with their capacities. If in each generation these same individuals are sterilised, it is obvious that very soon all that is best in the nation will be lost. The national sponge will be squeezed dry of all ability and the precious fluid thrown down the sink. In fine, the more flexible our society, the better we realise the ideal of equal opportunity, the broader we make our educational ladders, the more important it is to have proportional family endowment. This is the argument from stock; so far from implying any favour to privilege and status, it only obtains its maximum strength in a fully democratic system. Family endowment is a corollary of equal opportunity and if we neglect it we may expect a rapid decadence in the innate qualities of our race.

37. The argument from environment is more popular but not always well based. It strikes the ordinary man as hard on the next generation that the more comfortable home should be comparatively empty while children abound in homes where means are scanty. This is a natural humane view, attaching importance to the amenities which the more affluent homes provide. It has an element of truth, although it is doubtful if these amenities contribute much in the long run to the good citizen. There is a much more important aspect. It is the question of education, not in the sense of schooling, but of education in the home. Civilisation consists in an accumulation of wisdom, knowledge and culture. We wish to diffuse this as widely as possible. But it is inevitable that the actual people who are plying the arts and sciences or occupying responsible positions, involving experience and skill in human relations, should be in a special sense the repositories of our accumulated wisdom, knowledge and culture. This is quite independent of the economic system and would be as true under communism as under free enterprise. These people are not and cannot be schoolmasters. The main channel by which the accumulation can be handed down is education in the home. Otherwise it will be lost and we shall deteriorate. The accumulation is not a corpus of doctrine which can be written down or imparted in a class-room; its continued life depends on the sustenance provided by the actual experience of the people who are playing their various parts, exalted or comparatively humble, in the community. It is imparted by parents to children not in instruction but by hints and examples thrown out in the ordinary course of family life over a term of years. This home education is valuable not only for the doctrines and maxims imparted but also as a preparation for schooling. It is a natural and healthy instinct for children to hate their lessons; but if they do so

they will fail, even if they pass certain examinations, to get full value from them. Home education prepares them to be receptive; it is often only when the school lesson gets linked up in the mind of the pupil with some line of thought which has been started in his home and is therefore connected with his *amour-propre* that his interest is engaged and his real education begun. By exception, no doubt, a boy of genius may owe nothing to his home. For a greater number the background of home culture is a valuable fertiliser. The conclusion is that, if our standards are to be maintained, those who by reason of their actual vocation in life are in a special sense the repositories of current wisdom and culture should contribute at least their fair share of children to the next generation.

38. Finally, I submit that the proposed solution (leaving it to the lower income groups to do the main part of the breeding) just will not work. The habit of the small family has spread from the more affluent groups to the main body of the population by social example. We are not likely to get a revival by the reverse process. I do not know if the manual workers, who undertake heavy drudgery for the community, would regard it as a compliment to be asked also to take on the main part of having and rearing the next generation. There is something fantastical in the idea. It must be remembered that our whole social structure is graded from top to bottom not only by income — those differences could in principle be ironed out — but also by the responsibility and intrinsic importance and social prestige of the jobs undertaken by the various members. The example of those one grade higher in responsibility or prestige, whether they be objects of respect, admiration or malicious envy, is bound to carry weight. They are the relatively successful people, they have more freedom of action and they are presumed to know what is what. If they for the most part think a very small family the right and proper thing, this will impress the minds of those less fortunate. This is a matter in which women have some say; and they are notoriously influenced by fashion. This is no reflection upon them; they have their own part to play in guarding

the fortunes of the family and their secret wisdom makes them wary of taking action which will bring upon the family some measure of social contempt. There was a time when it appeared that the main mass of people might resist the example of the small family; they have not done so. It is one thing to resist a new habit which violates inherited standards; it is quite another to embark on a new line of action, contrary to the direction of social example. I conclude that family allowances which have no effect on the size of the families of parents with incomes over £250 p.a. will have little effect on the size of families at all.

39. Forced to admit that better-to-do parents will not and ought not to be asked to have one standard for themselves and a lower one for their children, that with the present financial arrangements these will confine themselves to small families, that the sterilisation of higher income groups will lead to decadence in a fluid society and that if these groups maintain the habit of small families, we are not likely to get a revival elsewhere, the critic might still entrench himself in the position that proportionate endowment was inadmissible, because it perpetuated the existing inequalities. He would argue that this principle is clear while the alleged consequences are only conjectural. I submit that this implies much too narrow a view of equality of opportunity, which would not be endorsed by the majority. There is widespread discontent with the system by which certain families can maintain a favoured position generation after generation whether they contribute anything valuable to the community or not. This does not mean that we have to go to the opposite extreme and line all children up on a touch line so that they can start the race from the same place. This is altogether too atomistic a view of the social process; it is doctrinaire and would not be widely supported. The fact is that it takes more than one generation to equip a man for the more responsible positions. A man of exceptional genius, the occasional freak of nature, may, it is true, make the whole way himself. The experience and wisdom that are necessary for many positions are more than can be acquired by most people, able and talented though they be,

in a single lifetime. This is a matter of the commonest experience. How many there are, who have done valuable work, with the sense that they could have done much more, if only they had had a better start, not in the form of more algebra at school, but more wisdom and guidance. This difficulty of crowding enough lessons into one lifetime cannot be overcome by altering our social system, because one cannot make the social system simpler. On the contrary, it becomes ever more complicated and is likely to continue to do so. We cannot provide citizens capable of coping with it, if we seek to expunge the wisdom acquired by one generation from the consciousness of the next. We cannot afford to have our society run by half-baked people. There must be some continuity of experience. Therefore the atomistic idea of making all children start life with identical advantages is unpractical. There must be equal opportunity; but interpretation of this principle must not be narrowed down to the life of a single generation.

40. There is another point of view from which such an atomistic arrangement may be seen to be undesirable. Socially it is in the interest of society that the best use should be made of the talents and capacities of all her members. To this end the individual must co-operate. Full realisation of a man's gifts cannot be achieved without some sacrifice of comfort and the common pleasures of life, even of the claims of friendship and domesticity. These counter-claims are healthy and will always make a strong appeal to the majority, including men of ability. Against them society has to offer the inducements of prestige, power and monetary reward. Hitherto we have had an inducement to exertion, which in the case of the normal individual is probably stronger than any of these, the desire to give one's children a good start in life. If it ever happened that under the influence of a doctrinaire interpretation of equal opportunity we removed this inducement, only the selfish inducements would remain. Only vulgar careerists would be candidates for positions of responsibility. This would not only be displeasing in itself, but would involve evil social consequences. The purely egoistic man is not likely to discharge

his duties in the best social interest. Then would indeed be realised that régime of ruthless self-seeking which extreme Marxists have unkindly attributed to the bourgeois civilisations of the past. There is truth in the wisdom of Confucius that only a good father can make a good statesman. The dictum applies, of course, not only to the great positions of state, but to the small entrepreneur, the foreman, in fact, to all the minor positions of responsibility. We must apply the dictum of equal opportunity so as not to prevent a man from creating by his exertions a favourable setting for his family in the next generation. What is required by the dictum is that the favoured position should not continue for more than two or three generations save in return for good services rendered. From this point of view it might be desirable to consider reducing death duties on money passing for the first time, while applying progressive rates of tax, on the lines of the well-known proposals of Rignano, rising perhaps to 100 per cent, on money passing for the second, third and fourth times.

41. By great confusion of thought, it is sometimes argued that family endowment would weaken what may be called the dynastic motive for exertion. This might be true in circumstances in which birth control (in the widest sense of that expression) was altogether impossible; the number of children being an unalterable datum in a man's situation, he would be driven to work to provide them with necessities and any external assistance would enable him to relax. But if the size of the family can be adjusted at will, this argument does not apply. Family endowment does not in any way interfere with the system by which the more a man betters his position the more he can give his children. Paras. 34-41 of this essay have been composed to rebut the objections set out in para. 33.

42. Before concluding it, I wish to make a few observations on the position of women, which must obviously be carefully considered in any problem connected with population; I wish to refer to two matters in particular, namely, (i) domestic help and (ii) the status of women who rise high on the educational ladder.

43. The relative rise in the price of domestic help compared with other purchasable goods and services may be one of the causes — I have not attempted to explore the broad field of causation in this essay — of the decline in births. This relative rise is the natural consequence of the increased productivity of labour in the general field. In that field wages rise roughly in proportion to the increase in output per head, but the price the consumer has to pay does not rise because the higher wage is offset by the reduced quantity of labour that is required per unit of output. Wages for domestic help also rise in proportion to the general increase in labour productivity owing to the competition of the wages offered in other occupations: but in the case of domestic help there is no offsetting factor corresponding to the increased output per unit of labour employed. Naturally as all or most other purchasable conveniences become relatively cheaper consumers tend to direct their expenditure to them. Fifty years ago few would have thought of having a carriage who did not have four or five domestic servants; now many who have no full-time domestic servant run a car. This means a relative decline in the amenities of the home; and the decline in the birth-rate is a by-product.

44. Domestic help must not only be thought of in relation to the well-to-do. It should be available to mothers of all income grades. No woman should be expected to keep the house decent and at the same time look after four or five children. That is a corollary of our higher standard of living (due to the higher productivity of labour) and the wider diffusion of education. In the case of parents with more than £250 it is a public interest they should spend as much as possible of this on domestic help; the more that is so spent, the more the home becomes the centre of gravity in life. All means should be explored for securing that good value is received for money so spent.

45. Of primary importance is the status of domestic service. If the status is bad, employers have to pay not only in proportion to the labour involved in the task but something extra as an inducement to enter an unfashionable

occupation.   Domestic service ought to rank above factory work, shop assistance, service in restaurants or typewriting. How can this revolution of ideas be achieved?   Public recognition might be given to the status involved, for instance, by diplomas in domestic science available for all who do certain courses before leaving school.   There might be a financial inducement, *e.g.* by the granting of additional public pension rights (not available in respect of the employments referred to above) per year spent in domestic service. Even more important probably is a regulation and clarification of the duties involved.   It is the suspicion that behind the four walls of a house the servant may be ordered about in an arbitrary way, be humiliated, partake in unsavoury scenes and live in squalid conditions that lowers her prestige in the eyes of her acquaintances.   From many points of view it might seem a pity to introduce Trade Union rules into an occupation where relations between employer and employed are so personal.   On balance, it would, however, probably be an advantage to do so.   It is certainly an occupation in which the bad employer is prominent.   Bad conditions in a number of cases lower the status of the whole occupation. The badness may more often be due not to malice or oppressiveness but to lack of experience in handling and lack of clarity as to mutual rights and duties.   Inherently the occupation has attractions.   The work is diversified and skilled, and by comparison with similarly or better paid occupations, interesting.   It should be possible to eliminate the frictions which make the occupation unpopular and the employer ill-satisfied with the results of his outlay, by giving the service a status which would ensure mutual respect and by defining duties with some precision.   As in the case of the domestic industries, it is difficult for a Trade Union to grow naturally, and it may be desirable to start with a Trade Board which would encourage the foundation of a Union and then be wound up or not as the circumstances suggested.

46. There has for some time been a tendency towards the system of sleeping out.  But from the point of view of employers getting the best value for money, this is not good.  Owing to

the spread of overheads the employer can provide lodging, board, light, heat, etc., at a smaller cash cost than would be required to bring the wages of the employee up to a level to provide all these things for herself. Here again a code of standard rules might revive the popularity of a sleeping-in job. Thus, for instance, a latch-key should be accorded as a matter of course and no instructions to be in by such and such a time should be allowed. Subject to the efficient discharge of recognised duties the employer should feel no more entitled to supervise the private life of the domestic servant than would a manager in charge of factory workers. The servant should have the right to receive one or two guests (without interrogation by the mistress) outside the standard working hours. She should be emancipated from the caprices of her mistress, whether due to misguided benevolence or an interfering temperament. To many these points may seem obvious; but the prestige of the occupation is injured by the less enlightened employers.

47. Finally, the possibility should be considered of a subsidy from public funds. Some years ago this idea might have seemed fantastical; in the interval there have been deep heart-searchings, old values have been discredited and people are ready for new ideas. In quite another sphere of thought, the idea of using subsidies to maintain certain industries or to provide additional employment is no longer taboo. Once it is recognised that there are few women and will soon, with rising standards, be no women willing to look after three or four children and do all the housework without help, domestic service becomes the most vital occupation there is, since without it survival is impossible. To some the maintenance of the fertility of our soil seems a proper charge upon the taxpayer; but by comparison with the maintenance of a stock of live human beings, the agricultural objective is clearly of trivial importance. Domestic help may without exaggeration be regarded as the industry which produces the nation itself. Again, from quite another point of view, this occupation is particularly worthy of support in any plan to provide full employment; employment is given and the consumer enjoys the benefit without

the necessity of any additional import of raw materials,[1] and the whole of the money provided by the public goes into the pocket of the employee without any profit rake-off. The subsidy should be available in the case of an employer with more than two dependent children towards the wages of one full-time employee, or, alternatively towards those of a number of part-time employees. It might be objected that the family endowment should be sufficient to cover this charge, the parents being free to lay the money out according to their own estimate of needs. There is force in this objection, and I submit that we should generally eschew all plans for paying part of the endowment in kind as leading to a servile state. Only if subsidies are to be provided anyhow out of public funds for the purpose of raising the quantity of

[1] [The judicious reader will perceive that this point is of cardinal import-ance in relation to our post-war economic troubles. I am convinced that since the war much too much stress has been laid on 'Production' in the narrow sense of manufactured output, and that the boosting of this particular form of occupation, so far from tending to cure, has aggravated our difficulties; particularly obnoxious has been the encouragement of women to leave their homes for factory work. I am gratified to find this early reference to the point. Despite the contrary trend of general opinion, I have from time to time reiterated it. In *Are these Hardships Necessary?* (1947) I wrote: 'There is a tendency to say, whenever the man-power shortage is discussed, "take it away from distribution". This notion should be accepted with caution.' In reviewing the first report of O.E.E.C. on European recovery, I wrote, 'Pro-duction in this group of countries is to be raised by approximately 30 per cent above its pre-war level. This project is indeed heroic. . . . But there is another deeper question than whether it is over-optimistic, namely the question of whether it is at all sensible . . . this project of production entails a higher level of imports than would otherwise be necessary, and by consequence an intensification of the balance of trade problem. . . . The product of industry available for home consumption will rise by 30 per cent. But gross incomes will only rise by 20 per cent. This means that consumers are expected to devote a substantially larger proportion of their incomes to the products of industry. . . . The enormous stress that has been laid in all discussions of European Recovery for expanding industrial production seems exaggerated.' (*Sound-ings*, March 1949.) 'Rather deep thinking is required on the question of production. . . . It was long since exposed as a fallacy that labour which makes something is "productive", while the labour of such people as actors who provide recreation or other services is "unproductive" . . . consumers who find satisfaction in services rather than material goods are being positively helpful to an economy in the special position of Britain; it is better that their purchasing power should be "mopped up" in paying those who provide them with direct service rather than in paying people to make them tangible goods, for the latter require imported materials and factory equipment' (*Financial Times*, 27 May 1952). 1952.]

employment, then domestic service should be first on the priority list. As a means of attracting labour into the domestic service market, a public subsidy might have some advantage over the use by individuals of their endowments to attract such labour, because the public recognition, implicit in such a subsidy, that this occupation is of essential national importance might help to raise its status.

48. Domestic help should be regarded as complementary, not alternative, to the provision of modern labour-saving devices in all homes. Modern gadgets are essential not only to assist the housewife herself, but also to raise the status of domestic help. A home must be mechanised like the factory, if the occupation is to be regarded as a clean and attractive one. Again we may bring in an argument from another sphere of thought to reinforce this conclusion. A central economic problem is to find sufficient investment opportunity to utilise British savings at their high current level and thus avert unemployment. An increase of consumers' durable goods financed by the instalment purchase system may be an important contribution. This is a perfectly logical and natural development of our existing system; hitherto savings have been largely used to provide producers' capital goods, but when they become redundant for this purpose, what more reasonable than that the money which one lot of people are setting aside for life insurance, company reserves, etc., should be used by others to buy durable consumers' goods in advance of their ability to pay for them? The system is perfectly sound provided that the aggregate amount of outstanding indebtedness on instalment purchase account grows at a moderate and steady rate. The convergence of two arguments, drawn respectively from the two most important domestic national problems, the population problem and the employment problem, upon the desirability of increasing labour-saving devices in the home, surely provides a reason for the state to take some interest in the matter. Unlike many spheres in which 'planning' is recommended, the objectives — rearrangement of the social system in a sense favourable to reproduction and a balance between the aggregate supply and demand of savings — are

beyond the powers of private initiative to achieve. I suggest three lines along which the state might give assistance: (i) arrangement for the provision of credit for instalment purchase at rates within a narrow margin of the gilt-edged rate of interest, (ii) a system for the regular reduction of instalment payments during periods when the purchaser qualified, by reason of inability to earn, for social security benefits, and (iii) arrangement for the supply of 'utility' gadgets at prices equal to cost plus profit, thereby breaking price-rings or prices held at an enhanced level by the exploitation of patents.

49. Many women now seek a college education, often with a view to pursuing occupations in life for which this education qualifies them. While it must be recognised that there is a minority of women temperamentally unfitted for family life many of whom are highly qualified to do most valuable work as spinsters, it would be most undesirable if the majority of women who go to college were deflected from the tasks of motherhood. To some extent already they comprise the most gifted women in the nation and will come to do so more, as the educational ladder is broadened. The arguments from stock and environment (paras. 36 and 37) alike require that these women should in due course become mothers. Already on average they have to make a sacrifice in their standard of living to do so. The position will be worse if the system of 'equal pay' is more widely adopted. Although this system may displace some women from their occupations, for others, presumably the more gifted, the sacrifice entailed by renouncing their profession in favour of motherhood will be still greater. It is to be feared that the scheme which I have the honour to submit would not completely redress the balance. As a further easement I suggest that in organised professions, opportunities should be given to women to return later in life. For instance, a young woman, having begun a career as a teacher, might get married after four or five years. Then after she had spent some twenty years on family duties, it should be open to her to return, say in the late forties, with suitable increments of pay and status. This project might wean away some who

love their professional work and are reluctant to leave it, and at the same time might improve the lives of older women, who are apt to feel that, with their children already adolescent, the world has no more use for them. Although they would lack the experience of what we hope would be a minority who remained in the profession, they would have gained another kind of experience perhaps not less valuable. Refresher courses could be provided. It should be assured that these women during the course of the period they devote to their own children have sufficient leisure to carry on the education begun at college.

50. This brings us to an important dilemma. On the one hand it is essential that the majority of gifted women should go through a period in which they devote themselves to bringing up their families. On the other, it is now established, with justice, that the educational ladder is to be open to women. But education is only begun at college; it is continued through life. In the case of the man, his own work in science, the arts or a position of responsibility involving intricate social relations is often itself educative and it is organised in a way which allows him some leisure for further reading and study. But it must be confessed that the woman who devotes herself from morning till night to housework and children may fail to continue the process of education altogether. In that case her spell at college may have been a mere waste of time, absorbing part of our severely limited supply of teaching capacity for no good purpose either for the woman herself or the community. With our ambitious plans for extending education we cannot afford such a waste of teaching resources. Consequently it should be clearly recognised that the lives of the majority of women, who have shown themselves worthy of a college education but afterwards devote themselves, as we wish they should, to motherhood, ought to have sufficient leisure for them to continue to improve their minds. This brings us back to the problem of domestic help. No woman, who has had the benefit of a higher education, should feel it her duty to devote the whole day to household work. On the contrary it is a prior duty to continue to cultivate her mind, and so

justify the expenditure of precious national resources on her higher education. This self-regarding insistence on her own culture will be of value to the community if she returns to a profession; part-time work (*e.g.* three or four mornings or afternoons a week) should also be made available in the organised professions like teaching. But there is a still more important way in which this extended culture may bear fruit. In para. 37, stress was laid on the vital importance of home education if national standards are not to deteriorate; the mother can play a valuable part in this, if she keeps her mind active by continuing the education begun at college. Thus her own college education which launched her on the journey to higher things may find its chief outward effect in enabling her to give the minds of her children that fertilisation without which they are likely to derive little advantage from their own schooling. This is another illustration of the continuity through generations of the social process and the falsity of the atomistic theory that each generation can start from scratch.

51. Reference was made in para. 49 to the minority of women whose true vocation in life may be altogether outside family duties. There are men also, who are temperamentally unfitted for family life. These kinds of people, both men and women, are often especially gifted and of exceptional value to the community. It is important that they should not be harried by the movement of public opinion in favour of family responsibilities. Let each do according to his capacities. If those who do love children were relieved from pressure and enabled to have as many as they would ideally wish, it is probable that the population could be maintained without forcing into service those to whom it is temperamentally uncongenial. Our community will only prosper if the fullest toleration is shown to the diversity of types. The solution of our problem is to make parenthood less burdensome, not to dragoon unwilling citizens into parenthood. If the insurance scheme is adequate a man (or woman) will have done his duty to society when he pays his contribution; the fund will enable child lovers to do their part in grateful willingness.

52. I venture to surmise that the attitude of public opinion to proposals for family endowment is as follows :
 (i) The public is still in some doubt whether the alleged population crisis is real or a scare raised by statistical faddists.
 (ii) It is likely to be convinced by an announcement by a Royal Commission that the danger is real.
(iii) When so convinced, it will certainly desire a remedy that is adequate in scale and national in scope.
(iv) The average man is not likely to regard 1s. in the £ as a disproportionately large contribution; on the contrary he would probably regard a smaller sum as indicating unwillingness to face up to the problem. I propose that this insurance scheme should be supplementary to the flat rate of 8s. for every child after the first, as proposed by Sir William Beveridge.

## SUBMISSION

1. There should be a compulsory insurance contribution of one shilling in the pound on all incomes in excess of £250 p.a.

2. The maximum contribution should be £50 p.a., which would be due on an income of £1000 p.a. All persons with incomes in excess of £1000 p.a. should be treated as though their income were £1000 p.a.

3. In the case of persons with incomes in excess of £250, the first £250 of their income should not be exempted from contribution. If such exemption were allowed, it would not be possible to provide adequate endowment for incomes much below £1000. But to prevent individuals suffering loss on increments of income immediately above £250, the contribution should be tapered from, say, one farthing in the pound on £251, one halfpenny in the pound on £252, etc., to one shilling in the pound on £298.

4. The contribution should be payable by all income receivers between their twenty-first and sixty-sixth birthdays.

5. For the purpose of establishing the contribution, the income of husband and wife should be aggregated, but during the period from the end of the first year of marriage to the end of the twenty-first the earned income of the wife should be treated

separately if it exceeds £250 p.a. The aggregation is necessary in equity since the endowment will be scaled, for reasons stated in para. 14 below, to the income of the richer party only and not to the joint income.[1] The exception is desirable so as to exact contributions from women who choose to remain in full-time paid occupations after marriage during the period of potential motherhood.[2] In such cases joint contributions up to £100 p.a. would be payable (where each partner earned £1000 or more), but endowments would never rise higher than in proportion to a contribution of £50.

6. In a scheme which I published in 1943 I proposed to exempt women completely from the contribution, on the ground that, since women generally receive lower pay in consideration of their lack of family responsibilities, it would be unfair to make their incomes contribute to family endowment. If public opinion crystallised against the idea of 'equal pay for equal work' it would be proper to exempt women. But the opposite seems more likely. If women receive equal pay for equal work they must certainly make their contribution to endowment. It may be thought that there is likely to be strong resistance to 'equal pay' in industry; but, as the scheme relates particularly to middling incomes (of which, in the case of women, teaching is a very important constituent) and low incomes are exempt from contribution, the inclusion or exclusion of women should be decided by reference to what is likely to happen in the middling sphere.

7. To the endowment financed from the contributions there should be added a flat rate of 8s. per week [3] per child, for every child after the first, paid out of the Exchequer. Where the parental income did not exceed £250, this Exchequer payment would constitute the whole endowment.

8. The principle which governs the scale of endowment is that the contributor who has an average number of children in excess of one (reckoning the second child as a half) receives back in

[1] *I.e.* aggregation is *more* equitable than separate levies on the two incomes. It cannot be claimed to be entirely equitable. [In an amended submission, not here reprinted, I removed this anomaly and brought in the contributions of both parents. 1952.]

[2] An exception to the rule might be allowed in the case of women marrying after a certain age.

[3] As explained in para. 23 of the essay, I should prefer a somewhat larger sum; but in this submission I confine it to 8s. in order to show what considerable endowment can be obtained by the Insurance method without further burdens on the Exchequer.

endowment sums in total equal to 8s. a week for every child in excess of one plus what he has contributed or is expected to contribute should he live to enjoy an average period of income receipt (in accordance with the Life Tables) up to his sixty-sixth birthday. Thus, apart from the flat rate of allowance available to all, each income group receives back precisely what it pays in and there is no question of one income group subventing another. The incidence of the 8s. a week depends on the general system of taxation in force from time to time.

9. The 'full' rate of endowment, as shown in the Table (page 15, above), should be paid for every child born to a woman after her second, and a half rate should be paid in respect of the second child.

10. When the total endowment payable per child has been computed, it should be divided into 34 parts (called 'endowment units'), of which one each should be paid annually during the first seven years of the child's life, two each annually during the next six years and three each annually during the next five. This corresponds to the rising need and power of the child, to share in the consumption of goods and services on which the family income is expended (see para. 34 of essay). Also the relatively high figure receivable during the adolescent period may serve as a greater psychological inducement to parents to have an additional child than the same sum of money more evenly spread over the years.

11. The endowment payable in respect of each income level should be published, so as to have its proper effect. As some of the assumptions on which the scales are calculated are necessarily subject to verification, there would have to be a periodic revision. But parents would be entitled during the eighteen years of the beneficiary period to the full scales in force at the time of the birth of the child.

12. To secure the greatest possible advertisement effect, endowment arising from the Exchequer contribution of 8s. a week or £20 : 16s. a year should be aggregated with that provided by the insurance fund in the published scales. If endowment is provided in bits and pieces parents will be slow to appreciate the total benefit available.

13. Owing to the plan for making the benefits rise with the child's advancing years and for giving only a half rate for the second child, persons with incomes less than £500 a year would actually receive under the scheme less than £20 : 16s. a year in respect of the second child during its first seven years. This

would be undesirable; no one should receive less than £20 : 16s. in respect of the second child; by a small adjustment the full amount of £20 : 16s. should be paid for the second child during its first seven years and a corresponding amount deducted from payments in its next six years.

14. The scale of endowment should be governed by the income of the richer parent. If the joint income was taken there would be a strong inducement to the wife to postpone motherhood in the hope of accumulating a larger endowment. This would be undesirable; it is important to encourage early motherhood. On the other hand, we should not go to the opposite extreme and scale the endowment to the income of the father in every case. It is only just that a gifted woman, who wished to cast her lot in life with a bad earner, should be able to secure an endowment related to the income position she had been able to build up for herself.

15. In order to compute the appropriate scale of benefit, it is necessary to assess the father's probable length of life up to his sixty-sixth birthday. This is a comparatively simple matter. The Life Tables published in 1931 show the male expectation of life on the twenty-first birthday, assuming that everyone is deemed to die on his sixty-sixth, as 39·43 years. Since then there has been a notable reduction in mortality, and it is safe to take the expectation of life as defined as 40 years.

16. A more difficult matter is the assessment of what a man is likely to contribute per annum after the period when the endowment begins to be paid. I suggest that it should be assumed that his income as assessed in the last preceding year continues until his sixty-first birthday (viz. till the end of 40 years after his 21st). Some incomes will in fact fall while others rise. It would not be considered fair that a man should pay 1s. in the £ on all increments of income accruing after the receipts of the last instalment of endowment he was likely to enjoy. Nor would it probably be necessary since average income has an upward tendency with advancing years. It would probably be sufficient, in order to offset declines in income after the endowment had been paid, to require a man to pay contributions on any subsequent increments of income up to but not exceeding, say, 20 per cent of the income accruing at the end of the endowment period. The end of the endowment period may be defined as the date on which a child reaches its eighteenth birthday, provided that there are no younger children then in existence.

39

17. The amount of endowment payable to the individual parent should be reassessed annually, having regard to his last recorded income level. As it will be assumed that this level will be maintained subsequently until the sixty-first birthday, an increment would make a substantial difference to the amount of endowment due. Where a man has a very variable income, it could be arranged, at his option, that the endowment should be related to the average income in the last preceding five years rather than to the income of the last year.

18. This annual reassessment is very important. A man may still be earning a very modest income at the time of contemplating marriage or after the birth of his second child, but may have a reasonable expectation of advancement during the next fifteen years, whether by regular increments of salary or by normal progress in his profession. The greater part of the endowment comes at a fairly late stage, namely, in the second decade of the lives of the third and subsequent children. The amount of the endowment then accruing is strongly affected, as may be seen by comparing lines 5 and 6 of the Table, by advances of income which accrue in middle age. If a man has a reasonable expectation of such advances he should be able to rely on corresponding increases to endowment and to know from published tables what these will be when he takes stock of his position at the time of deciding on marriage or on having additional children.

19. It should also be explained in the published tables that a man who has three children gets more than all his contributions back (in addition to the state subvention) and that a man who has four children can double his money (also in addition to the state subvention). If it were generally known what handsome results can be obtained by an insurance scheme, there would surely be a wide demand for it.

20. It may be worth observing that in published tables the gross amount of endowment payable should be stated and not that amount less the contribution due from the father. There is some danger that an official responsible for drawing up the tables might, out of an incorrect idea of accuracy, state the net amount. Such a method of drawing the tables would not only reduce the psychological inducement to parenthood, but would be in substance untruthful. The true benefit accruing to parents when they have, say, a third child, is their income if they have that child less what their income would be if they did not have it. As they have to pay the same contribution whether they have it

or not, the 'true benefit' in respect of this child is the gross endowment payable, not the endowment less the current contribution. Furthermore, this gross amount should be paid in full at regular intervals; the contribution should not be set off against it but should be collected separately, perhaps at the same time as income tax.

21. The scales in the Table are computed on the assumption that the net reproduction rate has risen, under the stimulus of the scheme, to 1. If it did not so rise, the scales, which should be revised every five years in the light of the experienced net reproduction rates, could be increased and a further stimulus to reproduction could thus be provided. *Per contra*, if the net reproduction rate rose above 1, the scales, and thereby the stimulus, would have to be reduced (subject to the protection of vested interests, as stated in para. 11 above). Thus the scheme contains within itself a self-righting mechanism, by which, when the stimulus is inadequate, it is increased, and conversely. It must be recognised, however, that even so the scheme may fail to produce the required result; in that case the contribution of 1s. in the £ might have to be increased.

22. I have worked out the scheme in some detail. No doubt any scheme actually proposed would differ from my scheme in various particulars. None the less it seemed worth while to work through the details in order to demonstrate that a scheme of this kind would in fact yield endowments of the handsome order of magnitude that I claim.

# EQUAL PAY FOR MEN AND WOMEN [1]

## TERMS OF REFERENCE

A NUMBER of individuals eminent in economic studies were
invited to submit written statements on the subject defined by the
Commission's terms of reference, and in particular on the implications of the claim of equal pay for equal work. In addition, the
witnesses were invited to express their views on the following
three special points:

1. It has usually been argued that the failure of industrial
   employers in normal times to substitute women's for men's
   labour in cases in which, at the prevailing relative rates of
   wages, it would apparently pay them to do so, is due to conventions and pressures of various kinds. It has, however, also
   been suggested that it is due to a limitation in the number of
   women available for industrial employment, coupled with a
   superiority of bargaining power on the part of employers,
   which prevents the women from obtaining the higher wages
   which, if competition were perfectly free, they would in these
   conditions be able to secure. Which of these two explanations
   (if either) do you favour?

2. If you incline towards the former, would you kindly comment
   on the following passage from a memorandum which is before
   the Commission? 'Now on the one hand the raising of the
   women's wage will lessen the inducement to employers to
   ignore or override these conventions and pressures; "the
   most powerful lever for increasing the opportunities of women
   is taken away if they are not allowed to do the work cheaper".
   On the other hand the reassurance that they will not be undercut may induce the male employees to relax the conventions and
   pressures in circumstances in which they would otherwise have
   maintained them. It seems impossible to say *a priori* which
   of these two influences will predominate in any particular case.'

[1] Memorandum submitted to Royal Commission on Equal Pay, 1945.

3. Would you be good enough to make plain the bearing of any general analysis which you submit on the particular case of the public educational services, assuming as the basis of your argument: (i) that the salaries of women teachers are broadly speaking 80 per cent of those of men teachers; (ii) that the standards of training and work demanded from the two sexes are the same; (iii) that it is regarded as a matter of public policy to preserve something like the pre-war balance of numbers, viz. approximately 1 man and 2 women, in the profession? You will, of course, recognise that, in asking you to make these assumptions, the Commission are not to be understood to be themselves expressing any view whatsoever on matters of educational policy, which would not be within their province. It is, however, essential to their proper comprehension of the argument that it should rest on some agreed hypothesis.

1. I am asked to define my terms before proceeding to answer the three specific questions that have been put to me.

2. When I use the expression 'Equal Pay for Equal Work' or, more briefly, 'Equal Pay', I shall mean equal time or piece rates in a specified billet or for a specified task. In a matter which is of so much interest to the general public one would naturally wish to make one's use of words conform to that of the man in the street. And I have the impression that this is what he usually does mean when he employs the phrase.

3. I have a second reason for this choice. Equal pay is commonly regarded as a clear principle which might be adopted, I suppose, in the first instance by the Government for its employees and subsequently by other great employers and in collective bargaining, and which is substantially different from the principle which at present governs rates of pay for men and women. I can think of no principle that is clear and simple in itself and clearly different from the present principle save that defined in para. 2 above.

4. A rival definition of Equal Pay for Equal Work would be equal pay for equal result. It is true that the man in the street, having hastily assented to the definition already stated, will often wish to modify it on second thoughts,

43

saying, 'Oh, well, what I really mean is payment by result; if a woman in a given time does not produce so much, she should be paid less in proportion. That is what I mean by Equal Pay.'

5. One then goes over the difficulties with which the Commission is no doubt familiar. Even in the case of piece rates, where the two definitions seem to come to the same thing, equal piece rates may mean paying the woman more per unit of result, if the average woman produces a smaller number of pieces per day, for then each of her pieces will cost more in overheads; similarly if there is more absenteeism among women; similarly if there are differences of quality in the work, and the average woman has had less time and therefore less experience in her job than the average man. But the greatest part of manual work has to be paid by time rates. In this case it is often impossible to measure output precisely, or, where it is possible, it may only be done in factories with exceptionally scientific methods of costing. In the case of brain work, output usually has to be measured by quality, not quantity, and the difficulty of doing this has only to be stated to be understood. The man in the street may still feel that these difficulties should be overcome. I ought perhaps to have said man or woman in the street; I am thinking particularly of the 'fair-minded man' who considers Equal Pay a desirable reform.

6. One may carry the argument a stage further. What reason has he to suppose that the present spread between rates does not reflect — roughly, indeed, but in this matter we can clearly only reach an approximation — the comparative efficiencies of men and women? And driving the matter home, one may ask, is it really credible that employers up and down the country will employ men and women side by side, at the expense of their pockets, when all the time they are getting more out of the women per pound expended on them than out of the men? Of course, if the employers are mainly men, they may, out of stupid male prejudice and conceit, underestimate the value of the work that the women are doing for them. In that case is the demand for equal pay no more than an appeal to men to be

more fair-minded in assessing the work of women? The man in the street will not be satisfied with this, feeling that unequal pay is in some sense an established national institution — capable of disestablishment — and not merely the resultant of the prejudices of individual employers. But he will probably retire from the argument at this stage, blessing Providence for having provided a Royal Commission to grapple with these intricacies, and leaving the definition of Equal Pay in abeyance.

7. The first question addressed to me seems to imply the view that 'the failure of industrial employers . . . to substitute women's for men's labour in cases in which, at the prevailing relative wages, it would pay them to do so', is a common phenomenon of widespread and not merely exceptional occurrence. And I am invited to choose between two explanations. I do not know whether the Commission has yet amassed its information on this subject or if the implication is merely a preliminary hypothesis put forward for discussion. I should have supposed that it was relatively uncommon for men and women to be employed side by side in industry on identical jobs, at which they were equally efficient, at different rates. Where something rather similar to this happens in certain higher grades of employment (administration, teaching) I should have suggested an explanation (see para. 13, below) different from either of those given in the question. Furthermore, I judge that it is the widespread presence of a differential, which, so to speak, simulates unequal pay for equal output, but is quite different from the phenomenon described in the question, that accounts for the perplexities of the man in the street. I should like, therefore, before proceeding to the task of answering the specific questions, to describe the nature of this differential.

8. I shall use the term 'category' of billets or jobs. I say that two jobs are in the same 'category' if they require the same amount of general education, specialised training, apprenticeship and experience for their efficient execution. But the specific nature, as distinct from the amount, of the training, etc., need not be the same. Thus a certain grade of administrative billet and a certain grade of school teaching

billet might be in the same category. In the long run, subject, of course, to frictions and irregularities, persons of similar aptitude may expect to get similar pay in billets of the same category.

9. Men and women clearly have different aptitudes. One seldom hears of men being employed as nursery maids or women as furniture removers. In each category there will probably be jobs for which men have superior aptitude and jobs for which women have superior aptitude. The differential between the rates for men and the rates for women in each category will tend to depend on the relation between the supply of men and of women in the category and the numbers of jobs in the category for which men and women respectively have superior aptitude.

10. In a certain category we might, for instance, find the rate for women 20 per cent below the rate for men. This should mean that there were enough women in this category for women to be employed in all jobs in it for which they had superior aptitude, and that these women having been placed, there were enough women over to fill all the jobs in which their aptitude on average, although below that of men, was not reckoned to be as much as 20 per cent below it. Men, on the other hand, would be employed in jobs where their aptitude was reckoned to be more than 20 per cent above that of women. Where the aptitude of women was 20 per cent below that of men, men and women would be employed indifferently. But, as results can seldom be measured with precision, there might be a fairly wide range of jobs in which men and women were employed indifferently.

11. If this were the state of affairs prevailing there would be a limited number of jobs in which men and women worked side by side. In these the differential between rates would have a rough correspondence to the differential between efficiencies, and the man in the street would have no complaint. But in the majority of jobs in which women were employed men would not be employed at all, so that there would be no direct criterion by which to compare the pay of each sex with its output. But if we compared

jobs in which men were employed with jobs in the same category in which women were employed, comparing jobs, that is, which require the same amount of education, training, apprenticeship and experience, we should find rates for women running 20 per cent below rates for men, in spite of the fact that if one tried to employ men in the jobs earmarked for women they would not be able to produce 20 per cent more than women and in many cases, perhaps the majority of cases, would not be able to produce as much as women. If in the category as a whole rates for women are running 20 per cent below rates for men, they will be paid 20 per cent less even in jobs for which they have superior aptitude and this may well be the majority of all jobs in which women are employed. It is this, I believe, that strikes the man in the street as unfair and gives impetus to the demand for reform. There are women employed in jobs which no one claims they do not do as well as or better than men, who have been through all the grind that men who are employed on similar jobs have been through, earning substantially less than these men. Is this right or fair? Yet this is the characteristic situation, not merely in isolated cases, not merely in one category, but in most categories throughout the economic system.

12. This situation is brought about by the 'ineluctable laws of supply and demand'. There is no need to refer to pressures or conventions to account for it. But the man in the street may feel that, even if this explanation is correct, the consequential state of affairs is not satisfactory. Does not this involve the conception now obsolete that human beings should be treated as commodities, fetching what they may in a market which has no regard for human considerations? Is it not fair that a woman, who goes through the same training, etc., as a man and takes up a job which admittedly a man would do no better or perhaps not as well, should get as good pay as the man who holds some other job requiring the same amount of training?

13. There is a class of cases, which may be quite a large one, which makes this anomaly seem all the more flagrant. I refer to certain jobs of higher grade, such as administration

or teaching. It may be held with good reason that in an organisation or school it is desirable to have a certain sprinkling of men. Take the case of a school. It may be that men and women are regarded as equally efficient in this kind of teaching, but that it is desirable to have a certain minimum number of men on the staff, so that a male point of view may be represented. This does not in itself imply a factor favourable to men since it might also be desired to have a certain minimum number of women on the staff so as to secure that a feminine influence was also present. As far as the demand for services in this school went, there would be an exact parallelism between the demand for men and that for women. We suppose them to be considered equally efficient and that a certain minimum number of each is required. Yet if this grade of teaching belongs to a category in which male rates are running above female rates, the male masters will be paid more than the women. This seems flagrantly unfair. The reason is, of course, that we suppose that in this category there are other rival jobs in engineering, law, accountancy, salesmanship, etc., in which the male aptitude is greater, which makes the demand/supply relation more favourable to men in the category as a whole. It is this phenomenon, I am sure, that strikes the attention of the man in the street.

14. And there is a further phenomenon to reinforce the impression. Rates are not adjusted like the prices of stocks and shares so as to keep the demand and supply in balance from day to day. The whole idea of rates of pay tending to be equal for persons of similar aptitude in one category relates to a long-run tendency. It may well happen that although from a long-run point of view the differential between men and women is correct, in particular localities and in particular occupations there may be a relative shortage of women. Men might then be brought in and paid rates appropriate to men in the category as a whole and so above those for women, even although in this particular occupation there was no question of men having superior aptitude. We should then have the phenomenon of men and women being employed side by side at jobs for which

they were equally good in an organisation where there was no requirement that there should be a minimum number of men, and yet the men would be paid at a higher rate. This would be an exceptional rather than a normal occurrence, but it might none the less occur quite frequently and attract attention.

15. There are two ways in which this situation could be reformed in the direction of greater equality between men and women. (i) Women's rates could be raised in all occupations in which they are not in direct competition with men, namely, in occupations in which their aptitude is greater than that of men, and kept down in other occupations. This would involve *unequal* pay as between women of equal aptitude in the same category. There are serious objections to this solution which I can conveniently consider in answering the third question addressed to me. (ii) Women's rates could be raised to equality with those of men throughout each category. This would involve displacing women from all the jobs where they are at present employed in which their aptitude is reckoned to be less than but not as much as $x$ per cent less ($x$ per cent being the existing differential) than that of men, and a proportion of women from jobs in which their aptitude is judged to be equal to that of men. I feel confident that this would involve a very considerable displacement of women from occupations.

16. I can now return to the question of definition. As the demand for equal pay is not usually accompanied by the corollary that among women of the same aptitude and category there should be unequal pay as between those in competition and those not in competition with men, I think it is the second rather than the first proposal referred to in para. 15 that is favoured. And as between equal pay in the same billet (para. 2 above) and equal pay for the same result (para. 4 above) I think we are now in a position to see that it is the former which is demanded, for the following reasons.

17. Let us suppose that there are factors unfavourable to women, over and above those of the supply and demand situation, of the kind referred to in the first question addressed

to me. Let us suppose that in a certain category the supply
and demand situation would lead to rates for women being
20 per cent below those for men, but that on average in that
category rates for women were 30 per cent below those for
men. This would mean that women would be employed
only where their aptitude was not less than 20 per cent
below men, but that to overcome prejudices and conventions
it was necessary to charge 30 per cent below men to induce
employers to take them in all these cases. Thus, in the cases
where men and women were working side by side pay would
not be in proportion to result, women only getting 70 per
cent although they were producing 80 per cent in comparison
with men. The principle of equal pay for equal result
would be satisfied by a reform requiring their rates to be
written up to 80 per cent in these occupations and throughout the category, together with measures to overcome the
prejudice against employing them where it was profitable
to do so. I do not think that such a reform would meet the
objection of the man in the street. It would meet him so far
as the cases where men worked side by side with women were
concerned (save those referred to in paras. 13 and 14 which
are many), if he accepted equal pay for equal result ; for the
20 per cent discount on women would reflect their inferior
output. But when we move away from the frontier where
they work side by side we should still have the phenomenon
of women of given training, etc., in jobs where their aptitude
was indisputably as great as or greater than that of men
earning 20 per cent less than the men of the same amount of
training, etc. This phenomenon would still be very widespread. And in cases like school teaching, where men may
have no greater aptitude but a minimum number of men is
required on the staff, we should still have higher rates for
men. It is precisely this phenomenon that gives rise to the
sense of unfairness. Therefore I think that equal pay for
equal work is taken to mean that men and women with the
same training, etc., should be paid the same by time or by
piece if they are employed in the same billets.

18. I have a further reason for this interpretation to
which I would invite careful attention. 'Equal Pay' is

regarded as a clean-cut reform, which could be introduced by the Government as regards its employees, by semi-public bodies, by large responsible employers amenable to the influence of public opinion, and, finally, as a principle in collective bargaining between associations of employers and trade unions. But equal pay for equal result does not provide a clear cut criterion for rates, but is *in essence* — and not only owing to difficulties of measurement — ambiguous ; and it is a reform which could not be introduced by the kind of process described. I must deal with each of these points in turn.

19. Payment according to result has to be determined by reference to the occupations in a given category where men and women are working side by side. It does not apply to jobs in a given category where only men or only women (subject, of course, as always, to occasional exceptions), are employed. In these cases there is no meaning in saying that payment is proportional to result. If one looked at jobs in the category where men have a decidedly superior aptitude, one would say that in this category men should be paid at higher rates ; but if one looked at jobs in the same category where women have a decidedly superior aptitude one would say exactly the opposite. But men and women cannot both be paid higher than the other. Thus, in jobs where only one sex is habitually employed the idea of payment by result is not applicable. The relative rates of pay must therefore be determined by relative output in the jobs where they are employed side by side.

20. But this is ambiguous, because the criterion entirely depends on what the jobs are in which they are employed side by side. If one adds to the formula, equal pay for equal result, the proposition that where men have superior aptitude men should be employed and where women have superior aptitude women should be employed, then, if the principle is applied in practice, men and women will be employed side by side where they have roughly equal aptitude. On this condition equal pay for equal result comes to precisely the same thing as equal pay in the same billet. But if it is desired to absorb more women into employment and employ

them where their aptitude is anything down to 80 per cent of that of men, then they will be working side by side, not in occupations where their aptitude is equal, but where the aptitude of women is 20 per cent below that of men. Rates for women will be 20 per cent below those for men in this category, not only in jobs where they work side by side, but in all jobs in the category even where the aptitude of women is greater. This arrangement fulfils the criterion of equal pay for equal result as well as the other. And there are an indefinitely large number of such arrangements which would all fulfil the criterion. Thus the criterion is essentially ambiguous. It does not say what the rates ought to be, unless one also specifies how many women in this category one wants to keep in employment. Thus one could not fix, for example, rates for teachers, until one had decided how many women of the same category one wanted to retain in *other* jobs of this category (*e.g.* business administration).

21. But supposing that one accepted this difficulty and were willing to specify what amount of female employment one desired, one still could not secure equal pay for equal result by the method proposed. One might lay down that one only wished women to be employed where their aptitude was superior or equal; or, alternatively, that one only wished them employed where their true aptitude was reckoned as not below 90 per cent of that of men. Then one would presumably fix women's rates at 100 per cent of those of men, or at 90 per cent of those of men, according to the alternative chosen. But this would not secure the desired reform.

22. Let me approach this point by asking: are women now as a general rule paid equally with men in proportion to their output where they are working side by side? If they are, then no reform is required. Measures to raise the pay of women would not be substituting equal pay for equal result in place of some other arrangement, but would merely alter the frontier where men and women are employed side by side on the same jobs and drive a certain number of women out of paid occupations, leaving those still employed with higher remuneration. Or suppose the

answer is that women are not paid equally in proportion
to output at present, but that owing to circumstances
referred to in the first question addressed to me their pay
is uneconomically depressed. Suppose, for instance, that
whereas in fact, where they are normally employed side
by side with men (save in the cases referred to in paras. 13
and 14), their output is 80 per cent, their pay is only 70 per
cent. We suppose that the 10 per cent margin is needed to
overcome certain other factors working against women. To
raise the pay to 100 per cent would leave those factors, if not
as they are, at least nearly as they are — see my answer to the
second question put to me. Consequently we should still,
despite the reform, have unequal pay in relation to result for
men and women working side by side. What would happen
would be that employers, finding themselves compelled to
pay equal rates, would only employ women in cases where
their aptitude was judged to be 10 per cent above that of
men. In that case women would still not be getting equal
pay for equal result, since they would be getting equal rates
where their output was 10 per cent higher. In fine, if it is
true that women are not now paid equally in proportion
to their output and it is desired that they should be, this
object cannot be achieved by raising rates for women by
Government decision, collective bargaining, etc., but only
by a campaign of education and propaganda designed to
overcome the forces which make individual employers
unwilling to employ women unless they can produce substantially more than in proportion to their pay.

23. For these two reasons, set out in para. 17 and in
paras. 18-22 respectively, I regard the demand for equal pay
as primarily a demand for the same pay for men and women
employed in the same billets. This would entail that men
and women working side by side on the same job would
receive the same pay. (Where it is possible to pay by the
piece, it would not necessarily involve equal daily earnings,
but if women on average produced less pieces an employer
would only employ them if he reckoned his consequential loss
on overheads and by absenteeism not appreciable, or if the
women had greater aptitude on the side of quality, though

inferior on the side of quantity). By this principle of equal pay for the same billet, and by this principle only, could we secure that men and women of the same category, viz. having had the same amount of education, training, etc. etc., would be paid at the same rates, each in their own specific jobs, viz. where only men or only women were normally employed. It would also secure equal pay in such jobs as school teaching where a minimum number of one or other sex was required (para. 13). Only by this principle could we secure that women, who have gone through the same grind (in training, experience, etc.) as men in the same category, should secure as good pay in jobs for which they, the women, have by agreement as good aptitude as the men, as the men are getting in jobs in the same category, for which they, the men, have aptitude. I am sure that this requirement is basic to the demand by the man in the street for a fair deal for women, which he expresses by the formula of equal pay.

24. I think there is also a requirement, which is important although secondary, for equal pay for equal result. This cannot be achieved by fixing rates for women at any particular level, but only by a campaign of education and propaganda to persuade employers to employ women in cases wherever their aptitude is superior.

25. If equal pay in the sense of equal pay in the same billet entails higher rates for women in the various categories than those required to make demand equal to supply, a displacement of women from paid occupations will have to be accepted if the reform is to be adopted.

## Question 1

26. I must now turn to the specific questions. Two alternative explanations are offered why industrial employers do not substitute female for male labour where it would apparently pay them to do so. I think that the digression has been worth while, because it suggests other causes for rate differentials which are often regarded as unfair — and from one point of view justly so. If I give my own impression as to the comparative importance of

the two explanations, it must not be inferred that in my own person I should have wished to submit either of them as the principal causes of rate differentials. The Commission will have far better means than I for knowing whether men and women were employed side by side over a wide field of occupations at rates not proportional to output and in cases not covered by my explanations stated in paras. 13 and 14 above.

27. The first cause suggested requires no elucidation. If there are 'pressures and conventions' preventing the employment of women, this would clearly account for employers retaining men although it would pay them to take women in substitution.

28. The second cause alleged is also valid, although it may seem surprising, since a shortage of women might naturally be regarded as a force tending to raise women's rates rather than one tending to hold them down. It operates owing to the imperfection of the labour market. I think one ought to state at least two conditions as being necessary to a perfect market. (i) There must be a large number of buyers and sellers, so that a variation in the demand by one buyer does not appreciably affect the total demand in the market, or, by consequence, the price ruling there. To this we must add a second, (ii) that there must be some organisation in the market so that the whole demand is in some sort of touch with the whole supply. If each buyer has his own 'channels of trade' he may have to bid up his price in order to attract supply even although his own demand is quite small by comparison with the aggregate. Ideally a market should have a group of jobbers who mark up the price to a level which will in their judgment equate supply to demand.

29. We may suppose the case of a typical employer who has 400 billets which he fills with women at 50s. a week, and another 200 billets for which women would be equally good which he has to fill with men at 65s. He is under no pressure not to employ women, but they are just not there. In fairness to this explanation we need not suppose that there are never any women available. He may feel that he cannot

make the substitution — for reasons of accommodation, etc. — unless he can reckon on getting these extra 200 women regularly over a fairly long period in future. In conditions of a perfect market he — and other similarly placed employers — would notify the jobbers that they could take extra women. Aware of this extra demand the jobbers would independently mark up the price of female labour in this category. This would affect all employers. As the rate went up certain other employers would release women who were employed on jobs where their aptitude was decidedly inferior to that of men. Either sufficient women would be released at 55s. or 60s. to fill all the 200 billets for this employer and for other employers similarly placed, in which case men would no longer be employed in these billets at all, or the female rates would rise to 65s. and there would be equality of pay as between the men and women employed side by side. Both solutions put an end to inequality, the former by displacing men from this class of billets altogether, the latter by equalising the rates of men and women in them.

30. But in the absence of jobbers this chain of events may not occur. With the shortage of women, women's rates are not marked up automatically. The typical employer in the situation described in the last paragraph might argue as follows. 'I now employ 400 women at 50s. and 200 men at 65s.; total wage bill £1650 a week; if I have to offer 60s. to the women in order to attract another 200 to my employment, I shall have to pay all my women 60s. and my total wage bill will be 600 × 60s. or £1800 a week; in fact, I should be worse off.' Similarly placed employers may argue in the same way, with the consequence that they acquiesce in employing men at a higher rate although the women, if only they were there, could do the job as well. If the employers combine in an Association to bargain with the women, the same motive will lead them to resist the price of women's labour being marked up against themselves, even although many of them are short of women. If there were jobbers, the price would be marked up against them whether they liked it or not; alternatively

if the women had a strong enough Union they could secure 60s., or whatever the equilibrium price might be in the circumstances, without any loss of employment.

31. Now while this reasoning is quite sound as a piece of economic theory, and while this kind of situation may in the past have held rates for women below their equilibrium level and have caused employers to employ men and women side by side at unequal rates, it must be remembered that this depends on the assumption that there is a persistent and widespread shortage of women. Otherwise the employers would tend to employ the women in substitution. I am assuming that there is no 'pressure' to prevent their doing so, since the 'pressure' explanation is an alternative and separate one and has no special connexion with the phenomenon of 'imperfect competition' and bargaining inferiority. If we consider the situation in the decade before the war it does not appear that there was a widespread and persistent shortage of women's labour; and consequently I do not believe that this cause is responsible for the level of women's rates that we find on the outbreak of the war.

32. Consequently, if the phenomenon mentioned in the question was widespread and important and could not be accounted for by the explanations given in my paras. 13 and 14, *I give preference to 'pressures and conventions' as the more probable cause.*

33. The Commission no doubt has it in mind that much depends on this. In so far as a depression of women's rates was due to inferior bargaining power conjoined with a shortage of female labour, rates could be raised without jeopardising the employment of women. But if the depression was due to 'pressures and conventions', a rise of rates would cause a displacement of female labour, except in so far as the rise of rates itself tended to reduce the 'pressures and conventions' in proportion. This brings me to Question 2.

## Question 2

34. 'On the one hand the raising of the women's wage will lessen the inducement to employers to ignore or override

these conventions and pressures.' 'On the other hand the reassurance that they will not be undercut may induce the male employees to relax the conventions and pressures in circumstances in which they would otherwise have maintained them.' 'It seems impossible to say *a priori* which of these two influences will predominate in any particular case.' *I cannot agree with the concluding sentence.*

35. Let us take the case most favourable to this contention, namely, that the dislike by male employees of being undercut is the *only* kind of convention and pressure tending to depress women's rates below the level at which they would otherwise be. Let us suppose that in the category in question the supply/demand rate for women (as defined in paras. 8-10) is 90 per cent of that for men, but that 'conventions and pressures' reduce the actual rate for women to 80 per cent. In the jobs in the category in which men and women work side by side the aptitude of women is then 10 per cent below that of men, but it takes a further premium of 10 per cent in the pocket of the employer to induce him to meet and overcome the trouble he makes for himself with his men by employing women, and thus the women's rate is set at 80 per cent.

36. Now clearly if rates are raised above 90 per cent, the employment of women will be reduced even if no 'convention and pressure' at all remains. If rates are raised to 100 per cent in this category, women will be swept out of all jobs in which their aptitude is reckoned as lying between 90 per cent and 100 per cent of that of men, and the removal of 'conventions and pressures' will not help them. Or suppose that rates are raised to 90 per cent or some point below it. One has to make some assumption about the rate at which the resistance of the male employees is relaxed as women's rates are brought nearer their own. From the psychological point of view it seems likely that a great part of the resistance will remain until equality is achieved. But to help the argument under criticism we may suppose that the strength of resistance falls in proportion as the margin is reduced. At 90 per cent there would then be half the resistance that there formerly was; but the employer

has no financial inducement to employ the women at 90 per cent since this reflects their aptitude; therefore he will not employ them if there is any resistance at all at 90 per cent; therefore he will not employ them at 90 per cent. Or suppose the rate is set at 85 per cent; resistance is then reduced by a quarter; but the premium which the employer gains by employing women is reduced by a half; therefore if the premium was previously just sufficient to induce him to overcome the resistance, he will not employ them at 85 per cent. Similar reasoning may be used to show that he will not employ them at any rate above 80 per cent. Consequently, if a rise to 90 per cent is imposed, the frontier of competition between men and women will be shifted and women will be displaced from a large number of jobs. If at 90 per cent the strength of male resistance is reduced to a half, women will presumably still be employed where their aptitude is reckoned at 95 per cent, but they will be displaced from all jobs where their capacity is reckoned to be between 90 per cent and 95 per cent.

37. It might be argued on the other side that if 90 per cent is the supply/demand rate, men will not feel that they are being undercut if women are employed at that rate. But that is not so. The economic function of a 90 per cent rate is to secure that women shall not be displaced from certain jobs although their aptitude is inferior. But that is precisely what the male employees resent. They do not acquiesce in the existing supply situation. They feel that many of these women should be taken off the labour market altogether and go and mind a home.

38. Or, again, it might be argued that this criticism would not hold if the supply/demand rate was itself 100 per cent. It may be 100 per cent in certain categories. But I do not think that this can be so in the great majority of categories. Taken in conjunction with assumption at the outset of para. 35, on which the arguments of paras. 36 and 37 depend, it would lead to the absurd conclusion that the *only* reason why women's rates run below those for men over so wide a field is that men dislike being undercut!

39. The assumption, however, of para. 35 is far too

favourable to the proposition criticised. The dislike of being undercut is not the only cause of 'pressure' against women. The male employees dislike women taking their jobs; the undercutting may inflame that dislike, but is not the sole cause of it. And the matter goes deeper. So far, the resistance has been represented as due to self-interest, and that is no doubt very important. But the sentiment against women may also spring from a sense of justice in the minds not only of male employees but of employers also, a sense that women *ought* not to be taking jobs which men with their family responsibilities could do as well or better. And alongside these causes are others such as mere male prejudice leading to undervaluation of the efficiency of women, or a belief that they are more difficult employees temperamentally and may cause managerial friction. Some of these adverse factors may be reduced by education or propaganda. The effect of this would be to reduce the amount of female labour displaced by a given rise of wages, not to make a rise of pay as likely *a priori* to lead to an increase as to a decrease in the employment of women !

40. It must be remembered that even if it were possible to remove 'conventions and pressures' completely, it would still only be possible to raise women's rates to the supply/ demand level — not to an equal level — without causing a displacement of women from employment.

## Question 3

41. In answering questions 1 and 2, I have assumed that a proposal to make rates more equal would take effect throughout a given category, that if rates for women were raised in a particular type of job, they would be raised simultaneously (or after a time lag) in all other jobs requiring roughly the same amount (though not necessarily the same kind) of general education, specialised training, apprenticeship and experience. What was said about the displacement of women from occupations depends for its general validity on that assumption.

42. It would, of course, be possible to raise rates for women in particular occupations where they were not near

the margin of competition with men, *provided that the rise could be confined to those occupations*, without setting up a tendency for women to be replaced by men. This would entail having unequal rates of pay as between women in different jobs in the same category. The objection to this policy — apart from the inherent difficulty of pursuing it in the long run — is that it would attract women to the better paid occupations without there being any increase in demand for them and would thus tend to create pools of unemployed women seeking employment.

43. In the case of the public educational service, I suppose that this phenomenon would not arise, or not in any marked degree. If women failed after some efforts to get their feet on the first rung of the ladder, they would relinquish their ambitions to be schoolmistresses and dispose of their lives otherwise.

44. Consequently, it appears that rates of pay for women in the public educational services could be raised without prejudicing the employment of women, always provided that it did not provoke a rise in other occupations of the same category where women are closer to competition with men. But I do not think that this proviso is tenable. The example of the school teachers' pay would cause women to press for rises in sister occupations, and employers might be disposed to grant them in order to keep a due proportion of higher quality women in the supply of women coming to them. If the rise was thus generalised there would be a tendency for women to be displaced from some occupations, as already explained.

45. It has been suggested that the rise in schoolmistresses' rates might have an adverse effect on the supply of schoolmasters. I cannot offer any submission on this point as I am not clear about the grounds of the contention. I suppose a man might argue that, teachers' pay being governed by budgetary considerations, there might be greater obstacles to future advances of salary in harmony with the general progress of society and with advances in salaries for other jobs of the same category, if the women had to be carried upwards simultaneously at full male rates. There may be

something in this contention, but it does not seem a very weighty one.[1]

46. Some considerations I am submitting outside the scope of the three specific questions have great bearing on the question of general policy regarding school teachers' pay.

47. In addition to three specific questions I have a general invitation to state my views on the subject defined by the Commission's terms of reference. These include consideration of the social implications of the claim for equal pay.

48. So far I have been considering mainly economic causes and effects — the working of supply and demand, of imperfect competition and the economic effects of certain conventions and pressures. But there are also social causes for unequal pay. I have in mind two causes in particular, namely:

(i) To secure that the proportion of the national income flowing into the hands of parents is not unduly restricted; and

(ii) To secure that motherhood as a vocation is not too unattractive financially compared with work in the professions, industry or trade.

49. I have stated these two causes in a way to suggest that we are in the presence of laws that have a very different manner of working from that of economic laws. The Commission would not wish me to expatiate upon the different types of law in sociology. I will only say this. Economic laws usually express the effects of the fully conscious efforts of classes of individuals to take advantage of the opportunities for exchanging their labour or their goods. In the laws I have cited on the contrary, certain things happen because they serve important ends in society, but they do not necessarily happen in consequence of any individuals consciously acting to achieve those ends. Though no one has deliberately planned it so, I have no doubt that the two social purposes stated in para. 48 are the true reasons why

[1] [In oral evidence before the Commission I allowed greater weight to this contention, having in the interval been persuaded in that sense by Sir Hubert Henderson. 1952.]

the pay of 'occupied' women has for long been inferior to that of men.

50. It may be objected that as I have already given economic reasons, which by economic theory must be sufficient to account for the phenomenon, it is not legitimate to bring in further reasons, it is not legitimate to explain the same thing twice over. In the language of science the occurrence would then be 'over-determined'. The matter is not quite so simple. One may perhaps express it that the economic system which has the consequences described has been maintained in being precisely because it has not failed to achieve — or not failed too dismally to achieve — certain social purposes. If during the last two centuries the forces of supply and demand and of imperfect competition had resulted in wages for women being two or three times as high as those for men, I have no doubt that the economic system would have been altered deliberately, or by a succession of subconscious motives, so as to yield a different result. When, with the progress in our general standards, conditions in the sweated trades came to seem intolerable, we had deliberate legislation to alter the effects of supply and demand and imperfect competition; or, again, a manorial system may give place to an individualist system or an individualist system, suddenly or by cumulative small changes, to a communist one.

51. In the case under consideration, however, the social causation has not been completely impersonal, because the 'conventions and pressures', to which reference has been made, do represent in part a conscious effort to secure, in the face of economic motives pulling the other way, the position of the 'breadwinner'. Resistance to the infiltration of women may be based on a proper sense of social priorities; 'women should not be given jobs when there are fathers with family responsibilities in need of them'. The 'conventions and pressures' should not therefore be condemned out of hand. Indeed it is for consideration whether they should not be encouraged and reinforced.

52. It is often objected that this cannot be the true reason behind the 'pressures and conventions', because if

it were, the bachelors would also be docked. I am strongly
in favour of the proposal to dock bachelors (see para. 67);
but as a criticism of a diagnosis of past and present facts this
objection shows complete misunderstanding of the working
of these laws. Where the social purpose is achieved without
conscious planning we cannot expect nice adjustments. An
economic system is evolved which achieves many good things
but fails in others; it fails incidentally to give enough to the
majority of women, who are mothers. Competition yields a
certain discrepancy between male and female pay; the
social purpose working in its rough-and-ready way seizes
upon this discrepancy and tries to exaggerate it — for the
benefit of parents. Competition does not produce a margin
between the pay of childless men and fathers so that the
social purpose has nothing to get to work on. The economic
system yields it, so to speak, a smooth surface with no handle.

53. It is important to recognise that unequal pay does
redound mainly to the advantage of parents (social purpose
(i) of para. 48). It redounds also to the advantage of
childless men, but this class is comparatively small. The
proposal to raise the rates of women to equality with those of
men is the same as a proposal to reduce the incomes of
parents. Public opinion probably does not fully appreciate
this. Because it thinks in terms of women getting more
money and no one else getting less it imagines to itself a
benefit accruing without countervailing loss. But of course
there must be countervailing loss. There is nothing in the
proposal tending to increase the total flow of goods and services to the nation, the 'national cake' as it is sometimes
called. (The proposal for equal pay is of course totally
distinct from the proposal to raise the rates of women in
underpaid trades where the improvement in pay might
be balanced by a proportional improvement in health and
productivity.) Consequently if women get more,[1] the 'real'
income of parents will be reduced, whether through higher

[1] It might be objected that women will not get more since some will be
displaced; but this loss of income to women as a class will be offset by a
reduction of output, and by a reduction in the size of the 'national cake'.
Higher pay to those remaining in will reduce the size of that part of the 'national
cake' which is left over for parents and bachelors.

prices or higher taxes or both. To give the public a fair
chance of forming a judgment, the question ought to be put
not in the form — is it desirable to increase the pay of
women? — but — is it desirable to transfer part of the
income of married folk (together with part of that of the
small class of bachelors) to 'occupied' women?

54. In any social evaluation the highest priority must
always be accorded to reproduction and parenthood. All
other social purposes depend on the existence of people.
If there are no people to enjoy them, material goods, tradi-
tions, knowledge, liberties are all worthless. In many
periods this truism might not have been worth stating, when
reproduction was sufficient and showed no signs of faltering.
But the birth-rate has for a number of years been at a level
which, unless it is raised, will soon bring about a rapid decline
in our numbers leading to eventual extinction. This fact is
not in doubt and a Royal Commission is now deliberating on
what is to be done about it. It is absolutely essential therefore
that before any proposal is recommended for such a radical
change as equal pay to women, its effects upon the status and
well-being of parents should be most carefully weighed.

55. It has been suggested that equal pay might be good
for the birth-rate by displacing a large number of women
from their paid occupations. My answers to the specific
questions have tended to confirm the view that a considerable
number of women would be displaced. This argument has
a certain plausibility, but it leaves me a little uneasy. It may
be well to divide the subject into two parts : (i) the marriage
market, and (ii) what happens thereafter.

56. Now while it is no doubt true that there are some
women of high capacity and earning power who are less
attractive to men than the average woman, and there are
other women incapable of doing a hand's turn who are
highly attractive, yet in the broad run of women, leaving
out extreme types, there is probably a rough correlation
between the gifts making for success in employment and
the gifts which make a woman desirable as a wife. Appearance, general competence, good sense and tact have their
power in both fields. Though it may seem a paradox to say

it in this wicked world, yet it is probably true in the broad average, when all allowance has been made for exceptions and anomalies and injustices, that the virtues are recognised by the employer and the suitor. With higher pay for the woman and no increase in the earning power of a prospective husband, employment becomes relatively more attractive to the woman. There are likely to be a number of high-quality women therefore, who at the old rates were on the margin of doubt whether to give up their careers, for whom the better prospects in their careers will just tip the scales. No high-quality women who said 'No' to a suitor before the scaling up are likely to say 'Yes' after it; but some who would have said 'Yes' before it may say 'No' after it. The tendency will be for a larger number of high-quality women to remain fixed in their occupations instead of marrying. At the other end of the scale there will be a larger number of rejects from industry available for marriage. The number of potential husbands is the same as before; the number of women prepared to say 'Yes' will be greater; but out of all women the selection prepared to say 'Yes' will have declined in quality. Some men rejected by women who were just induced by the better prospects to say 'No' may not in consequence marry at all. Others who, had women not been displaced, would have been unable to persuade any woman, may now find a partner among the rejects from industry. There will clearly be some tendency for the average quality of the married couples to decline; whether there will be an increase in quantity it seems difficult to decide *a priori*.

57. The number of women who are deflected by their careers from motherhood after having married is probably not large. Of those who are, the great majority may be assumed to be very devoted to their careers and presumably competent in them. It seems likely therefore that out of the group of women, who were ejected from their occupations by reason of the higher pay, there would not be many married women who had hitherto been kept from motherhood solely by the desire to remain 'occupied'. To the extent that such women were ejected, there would be an increase in parenthood.

58. It seems doubtful therefore whether the ranks of mothers would be increased by anything like the number of those displaced from earning; I do not think it can be assumed that the increase in mothers would be large. On the other hand the tendency for there to be some decline in the average quality of mothers seems indubitable. This is very important in itself.

59. I submit that it may also have an important indirect effect on the number as well as the quality of children. The point is perhaps a subtle one, but I should like to place some emphasis upon it in submitting it for the consideration of the Commission. From the numerical point of view more is to be gained by increasing the average size of families than by increasing the number of mothers. To achieve the former object we need a great reversal of existing valuations; we need to revive the status, dignity and prestige of motherhood as an occupation. At present motherhood has come to be regarded as one of this world's experiences which it is as well to sip in passing, rather than as the grand and principal object of a woman's life; hence the prevailing family of one or two children. In order to get a widespread revaluation and change in point of view, it is necessary in the first instance that a number of high-quality women (in all walks of life) who are admired and respected, should adopt it. We want more women of the type who take their work in life seriously, and believe that what is worth doing is worth doing thoroughly, to adopt motherhood rather than a paid occupation as their vocation. If such women have larger families, they will be an example to others. Therefore anything tending to reduce the average quality of mothers may well have an adverse effect not only on the quality but also on the quantity of the next generation. In fine, the principle of equal pay would tend to increase the material attractiveness and indeed the status — the psychological point is an important one — of paid occupations for women without doing anything to help motherhood, at a time when it is supremely important to move in the opposite direction.

60. It has been suggested that 'equal pay' would tend to increase the supply of domestic servants. This, if true,

would be very valuable from the population point of view. The argument is that the women thrown out of industry would flood into the domestic service market and that wages there so far from rising in sympathy with those in industry would fall by reason of the surplus supply. This view must not be accepted too readily. In the first place it must be remembered that although 'equal pay' would reduce the number of jobs in industry, it would increase the relative attractiveness of industrial (and commercial) employment, if there were no corresponding rise in pay for domestic help. It is possible that a typical woman on losing her job would prefer to remain registered as an applicant for industrial employment rather than lapse into less well-paid domestic service. It must be remembered that unemployment rotates among a much larger number than those unemployed at any one time. It is possible that the actuarial prospect of gain by women in industry would not be reduced by equal pay; thus if a rise of wages from 80 per cent to 100 per cent of those of men caused one-fifth of the women to be displaced, the chance of being employed for forty weeks at the new rate might be deemed as good as that of being employed for fifty weeks at the old — nay better, because there would be ten weeks in which to rest and recuperate. Actually, the women displaced, being those of worst quality, would not have such a good chance as this; but people seldom rate their own capacities as below the average. Secondly, even in the domestic service market there may be some element of imperfect competition and convention; the example of the rise of pay in industry and commerce might induce women to stand out for higher pay in domestic service — it would be a question of retaining some part of the war-time gains — whether by tacit mutual understanding or by the formation of a trade union, and to accept the resulting unemployment as worth while. Finally, it may be questioned whether, even if despite these arguments, the supply of domestic servants were improved, these scourings of industry would really be valuable assets for the housewife. Domestic service would be even more than at present the Cinderella of female occupations. Is this the right way to try to rebuild home life and relieve the harassed mother? I do not wish to be dogmatic upon the subject, but I put these points for consideration by the Commission before they endorse the view that equal pay in industry and commerce would encourage family life by improving the supply of domestic help.

61. In a paper which I recently submitted to the Royal Commission on Population [Essay 1], I suggested that the problem should be tackled in exactly the opposite way, namely, by up-grading domestic service so that it might rank in prestige as an occupation above factory work, shop assistance or typewriting. I suggested that this should not be attempted by means of raising domestic servants' pay, since this would defeat its own objects. Whatever system of family allowances may be adopted, mothers of moderate income would not be able to afford it. Rather I suggested that it should be attempted along the lines of regulating conditions of employment, especially in the case of servants sleeping in, of raising the prestige of the domestic arts by national training schemes, the provision of diplomas and certificates, by the granting of differential pension rights at public expense, etc. The whole object would be to increase the quality of domestic help available to mothers without increasing its cost.

62. In the foregoing paragraphs I have been concerned to marshal some arguments against the proposal for equal pay. I have done so with some reluctance, since I am one of those who hold that women have had a very raw deal in recent historic times and that much is still due to be done to raise the lot of women in life by comparison with that of men. I am bound therefore to have an initial predisposition in favour of 'equal pay'; it is a case where the argument of the head speaks against that of the heart. But the matter cannot be left there. If it were decided to say *non possumus* to this proposal that has been bruited abroad and makes so wide an appeal on grounds of equity, I suggest that something ought to be proposed in its place — not merely to placate public opinion, not merely to appease the women and their champions, but in equity and for the good of society.

63. I suggest that this can only be done if the Commission

on Equal Pay will allow itself to take a broader view, and survey the whole question of earnings and needs in relation to family conditions. If it did so, I feel that public opinion would follow it and that the demand for equal pay would be merged into wider proposals.

64. A Royal Commission on Population is now sitting and will no doubt consider the question of family allowances. At its request I have submitted a comprehensive proposal worked out in some detail and at length. It embodies a scheme for national compulsory insurance to a fund from which family allowances would be paid. It is of the essence of the scheme that each income and salary grade should be self-financing so that there would be no question of the poor subventing the rich or conversely; contributions and allowances would be in proportion to incomes; this is necessary because we want to secure not only that the factory worker shall have a financial compensation for renouncing her paid job in favour of motherhood but also that, say, a school teacher shall have a compensation which is in adequate proportion to what she gives up.

65. In this submission I did not deal with the special problems of the Equal Pay controversy. I felt sure that, had I done so, the Royal Commission on Population would have argued that as a Royal Commission on Equal Pay was in existence, it could not concern itself with those special problems. However, there is a danger of a vicious circle. I do not know if it is permitted to Royal Commissions to communicate with one another, or to set up a joint sub-committee. The plain fact of the matter is, that apart from the statistical and medical investigations of the Royal Commission on Population, and apart from detail, the main subject on which the two Royal Commissions are deliberating is one and the same.

66. I should like to put before the Royal Commission on Equal Pay two alternative proposals. These are different from my proposal to the Royal Commission on Population and I shall only set them out with extreme brevity. The first should be adopted, if it desired to avoid (i) a considerable displacement of women from paid occupations,

and (ii) a diversion of high-quality women into paid occupations and away from motherhood.

### Scheme A

67. (i) I propose that employers should continue to pay for men and women at present rates. There would thus be no disturbance to the existing distribution of jobs as between men and women. Fathers and women should receive what the employers pay out. But childless men should only receive pay at the female rates, the difference between what the employers pay out and what the childless men receive going into an Insurance Fund. This fund should be used to make disbursements to fathers with more than two children. From the calculations made in the elaborate scheme which I submitted to the Royal Commission on Population I am able to state that it would be possible to pay to a father of three the whole of his previous contributions to the fund with interest and a similar sum for each subsequent child, the money for these further children coming from the contributions that have never been drawn out owing to their contributors not having had more than two children. (This allows for a very large rise of the birth-rate above its present level, namely, to the replacement level). Thus a childless man would be paid at women's rates; when he had his first child, he would be stepped up to the full male rate. If he had more than two children he would draw handsome endowments from the Insurance Fund which would be spread over their period of dependence.

(ii) In occupations in which women were not usually employed, a deduction would none the less have to be made from the pay of childless men. Some conventional deduction such as 20 per cent or 25 per cent, based on the prevalent discount for women's work in other occupations, would be applied in the case of all childless male earnings throughout the country and would have statutory sanction.

(iii) Where a mother herself had to work to support children by reason of the death or physical incapacity of the father she should be entitled to receive the full male rate, the difference between that and the female rate being made up to her out of the Insurance Fund.

68. Scheme A seems to remove the unfairness of the present system which consists essentially in the payment of higher rates to childless men. Higher rates would continue to be paid for men, but the premium of male over female rates would not be paid out to them unless they had children. Premiums paid by employers in respect of bachelors or married men without children would be paid into a Fund, but the men would not subsequently recover this money unless they were sufficiently philoprogenitive to have at least three children. Men with more than three would gain at the expense of those with less than three. The advantages of this scheme are that it would not disturb the existing distribution of jobs as between men and women and would not tend to attract able women into paid occupations.

### Scheme B

69. This would introduce Equal Pay for men and women. The employer would pay out at the same rates for each sex. But a statutory deduction of 25 per cent (or 20 per cent) would be made from the pay of childless men and from that of women, save in the case of mothers where the father was dead or physically incapable (cf. para. 67 (iii) above), and be paid into an Insurance Fund. Money would be paid from this fund to fathers and mothers of more than two children on the same principles as in Scheme A. The advantages of Scheme B are that it pays more explicit lip service to the idea of Equal Pay and that it provides greater endowment for children. One disadvantage is that it offers an inducement to women to postpone marriage and motherhood, and this might have a depressing effect on the birth-rate.

70. I regard Scheme A as preferable.

71. May I be allowed to sum up in favour of such a scheme (Scheme A) :

(i) There is a widespread sense that it is unjust that women who go through the same training as men and have no less aptitude or greater aptitude in certain jobs than men, should receive less pay than men, merely because the balance of supply and demand decrees that it should be so; it is felt that in this human question of pay we should not be entirely at the mercy of supply and demand. On the other hand it must be recognised that the general adoption of equal pay might lead to a widespread displacement of women from their paid occupations, a great dislocation in the labour market, tiresome readjustments in office or factory routines, special difficulties for a government bent on securing 'full employment' and might on balance do women, whom it is intended to benefit, more harm than good.

(ii) It cannot be gainsaid that equal pay might divert high-quality women from motherhood to careers at a time when it is supremely important to do the utmost on behalf of motherhood, which even more, nay far more, than paid women's work, has been unjustly treated in our system of rewards for service rendered to society. At the same time no immediately practicable scheme for the endowment of motherhood is likely to be great enough in scale fully to redress the balance in favour of motherhood.

(iii) The economic system should be our servant, not our master. If we do not like the effect of the balance of supply and demand on women's rates we need not acquiesce in it; but nor need we go over and blindly follow an alternative hard-and-fast rule that the occupant of a given billet should receive the same pay, whether man or woman. There is no reason why we should not use the economic system, if we can, to secure that rewards are apportioned to family need.

(iv) As between women with no family responsibilities and fathers there should be no sense of injustice at the latter receiving more money. They have their children to look after. If the balance of supply and demand goes some way to bringing this about, that should be regarded as a happy coincidence, a blessed harmony, rather than an evil. And if there are certain conventions and prejudices which reinforce these effects of supply and demand, these should not be condemned out of hand; they may be consciously or unconsciously supported by the social purpose of getting enough money into the hands of those who have to bring up the next generation.

(v) The real injustice is between women and childless men.

(vi) There is also serious injustice as between the parents of small families and those of larger families.

(vii) Let us therefore adopt a proposal which remedies both the injustice referred to in (v) and the injustice referred to in (vi). Let us deduct from the pay received by childless men an amount which reduces it to the level of women's pay and pay the difference into a Fund. Let all fathers continue to get the higher rates. And let the parents of more than two children get a further endowment paid out of the money previously deducted from their pay when they were still childless, and subvented also by the deductions from the pay of other childless men who do not subsequently have any children or not more than two.

(viii) Where women for any reason have to earn money to support children, their rates should be raised to the male level, not at the cost of their employers since this would tend to drive them out of occupation, but out of the Fund made up by deductions from childless men.

(ix) In this way we could get an equitable adjustment not only as between men and women, but also at the same time as between childless persons and parents and as between parents of smaller and parents of larger families, without interfering with the present scales of payment by employers to men and women, and therefore without causing any displacement of women from occupations or disturbance in the labour market.

# II

# COMPETITION

# NOTES ON SUPPLY[1]

THE following notes do not profess to give a comprehensive survey of the problems of supply. Attention is concentrated on a few isolated points. The intricate questions connected with external and internal economies which have recently received important treatment by Professor Pigou (*Economic Journal*, June 1928) and by Mr. Shove (*Economic Journal*, March 1930) are not dealt with. This paper is propaedeutic rather than supplementary to those studies.

I

In this section it is proposed to consider cost conditions in individual sources of the supply of a commodity, and for this purpose to make certain simplifying assumptions, namely, (1) that the cost of production is in each source a function of the output of the source only, and (2) that the industry can obtain its factors of production at a constant price.

1. *The Short Period*

A source of supply may be conceived as an aggregation of productive factors within which a dichotomy of costs into prime and supplementary can suitably be made. Sources are demarcated from one another by reference to the limits within which the two classes of factors are co-operating. A structure of fixed equipment or organisation gives the unity which the notion of 'a source' of supply requires. Such a source need not be a business firm. Within any business firm the dichotomy is possible, and a firm may therefore be regarded as a source. But sources may be divided into sub-sources, manufacturing plants for instance, within which the dichotomy

[1] Reprinted from the *Economic Journal*, June 1930.

may be reintroduced, and the following analysis applies to sources, sub-sources, subdivisions of these, etc.

Various suppositions may in abstract theory be made with regard to the behaviour of costs as the output of a source increases.[1] The only supposition which is likely to be true in fact is that, if there is a fixed amount of equipment or supplementary cost, prime costs per unit of output fall in the early ranges of output, but begin to rise after production has reached a certain level. Supplementary costs are taken to be constant in the short period over the range of produc-

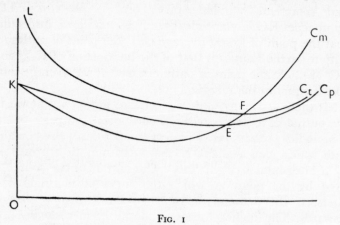

Fig. 1

tion considered; and costs which vary with the output are regarded as prime; this is justified by the definition of a source. If fixed equipment is required at all, it should clearly be assumed that beyond a certain point increments of factors applied to that equipment will get a diminishing output per unit.

In the adjoining figure the curve $KC_m$ represents the marginal prime cost per unit of output. The marginal prime cost of $x$ units is conceived as the total prime cost of producing $x$ units less the total prime cost of producing $(x - 1)$ units. The curve of $KC_p$ represents average prime

[1] It is assumed throughout that by $x$ units of output from a source is meant $x$ units of output, per unit of time, at a given point of time, T. To suppose an 'increase' or 'decrease' of output is to suppose $x$ larger or smaller at T.

costs. If P is any point on $KC_m$ and a perpendicular PM be dropped to the horizontal axis, then $KC_p$ is the locus of a point Q on PM or PM produced, such that KPMO = the rectangle OQ. It appears from direct inspection that the point of lowest average prime cost is the point at which the curves intersect (E), that is, the point at which average prime and marginal prime cost are equal.

The curve $LC_t$ represents average total cost per unit and is the locus of a point R vertically above Q such that if RS be drawn perpendicular to the vertical axis, $RQ \times RS$ is constant and represents supplementary costs. The curve $LC_t$ approaches $KC_p$ asymptotically. It appears from inspection that the point of lowest average cost (the point of optimum output for the source) is that of the intersection of $KC_m$ and $LC_t$ (F). At the point of optimum output the average total cost is equal to the marginal cost.

If there are many sources of supply, so that variations in the output of a single source do not affect the price of the commodity (conditions of perfect competition), the demand with which such a source is confronted may be represented by a horizontal straight line. The output of the source is fixed by the point at which the curve of marginal cost intersects the demand curve when the former is sloping upwards. The higher the demand the greater the supply. The output of the source consequently obeys the law of increasing supply price.

If the demand curve cuts the marginal cost curve of a source at a point between the minimum marginal cost and E (or lies below all the cost curves), prime costs are not covered and the source can only continue to produce on the expectation of an improvement in demand; it is convenient to call this condition absence of short-period equilibrium. If the demand curve cuts the marginal cost curve between E and F, there is short-period equilibrium, production will continue, but supplementary costs will not be covered. If the demand curve cuts the marginal cost curve at a point to the right of F there is a surplus yield.

The expression 'supplementary costs' is ambiguous. A given market price must be paid for liquid factors; otherwise they will not be forthcoming. But the fixed factors are *ex hypothesi* already acquired and immobilised. They are no longer able to demand their market prices; they can only receive what can be obtained by the most satisfactory working of them. The reward of the fixed factors is Marshall's quasi-rent. If the demand curve cuts the marginal cost curve at P and the perpendicular to the horizontal axis PM (or PM produced) cuts $KC_p$ at Q, quasi-rent is represented by $PQ \times OM$. This is positive if P lies above Q and negative if Q lies above P.[1] There is then no predetermined supplementary cost, the price payable to the fixed factors being in the short run passively determined by the relation of the demand price to prime costs.

The consequence of this is that the concept of supplementary costs represented by the curve $LC_t$ seems to be meaningless. To overcome this difficulty, it is convenient to suppose that the fixed factors should receive a 'normal' profit or return. In the equation $RQ \times RS = K$, which determines the locus of R (the curve $LC_t$), K (the supplementary cost) is taken as the sum which gives a normal return to the fixed resources. If the demand curve intersects the marginal cost curve to the right of F, the fixed factors are getting an excess reward, if at F a normal reward, if between F and E a subnormal reward, and if to the left of E a negative reward.[2]

Different sources may be expected to differ in efficiency; some may earn excess profits while others are earning subnormal profits; in the short period they may all be earning excess profits; or they may all continue to earn sub-normal profits, until the quantity of output is curtailed by equipment wearing out and not being replaced. A survey of sources taken at any one point of time is likely to show various rates

[1] If $a$, $b$ and $c$ units of the liquid factors, A, B and C are employed, if $f(a,b,c)$ is the output which they can obtain when used in conjunction with the fixed plant and $p$ the price per unit of output, then quasi-rent $= p\{f(a,b,c) - af_a - bf_b - cf_c\}$. $f_a$ is the rate of output of factor A at the margin with $b$ and $c$ constant, $pf_a$ the rate of reward of factor A and $apf_a$ the total reward of factor A. Similarly with $f_b$ and $f_c$.

[2] PQ is the actual rate of quasi-rent per unit of output, RQ the rate per unit of output which would give normal profit. Normal profits are actually earned, therefore, if output is represented by the point of intersection of the locus of P and that of R (F).

of profits according to the efficiency of the sources and also various rates of working. A source which is making subnormal profits must be working below the optimum capacity. (Output is represented by a point to the left of F.) One which is making excess profits must be working above its optimum capacity. The point of optimum capacity is always a point at which marginal costs are rising. It is also the point of normal profits. The point representing actual output must be one at which marginal costs are constant or rising. If it can be shown of any source of production that this last proposition is not true, it may be inferred that the condition of perfect competition is not fulfilled. The apparently frequent occurrence, in fact, of sources working 'under capacity' in the sense that average prime costs (including those of transport and marketing) could be reduced by an expansion of output of the source, is evidence that conditions of quasi-monopoly are much more widespread than used to be supposed. Cost conditions in a monopolistic or quasi-monopolistic source are briefly discussed in Section II.

The short-period supply schedule is a list of the quantities contributed at a point of time, T, per unit of time, in response to various possible prices at that point of time, the fixed equipment being incapable of increase or diminution. Short-period equilibrium in the industry is attained if no source is working at a loss, that is, if quasi-rent is nowhere negative. The supply schedule of each source shows increasing supply prices and, if external economics are absent, so does the supply schedule of the whole industry.

## 2. *The Long Period*

With the short period may be contrasted the long period. In discussion the length of the long period is too often left indefinite or taken as infinite. It is useful to have regard to something intermediate between a single point and infinity, say, to a finite interval of time, $s$. Short-period supplementary costs may be divided into those which are prime and those which are supplementary relatively to $s$. Fixed equipment may be repaired, replaced or extended. Part of the fixed equipment, whether building and machinery, or a core of organisation and good-will, may be expected to survive the period *s*. If *s* is infinite, all organisation becomes obsolete, good-will is forgotten and railway embankments become level with the surrounding countryside. That section of the fixed equipment material or immaterial which survives *s* intact is called supplementary or fixed relatively to *s*. That which is subject to replacement or reconstruction within *s* is supplementary relatively to a short period but prime relatively to the long. Long-period supplementary equipment may be increased but not diminished in any source during the long period. It may be diminished in the industry as a whole by sources going out of action.

In the long period, long-period prime factors must receive a normal reward, their market price, or they will not be forthcoming. The reward payable to them per unit is equal to their marginal product. If a source is in long-period equilibrium the marginal products of the long-period prime factors must be equal to their market prices; also these factors must show decreasing returns.[1]

If a shrinkage of demand supervenes upon the equilibrium, the marginal product of the long-period prime factors falls below their price. They will consequently not be renewed in the long period. The curtailment in the use of these factors in connexion with a given amount of long-period equipment will raise their marginal product to equality with their price. As a result of this shrinkage in short-period fixed equipment, when a second long-period equilibrium is achieved, the short-period prime cost of production will be greater throughout the range of production.[2]

---

[1] If *x* units of short-period prime factors (X), *y* units of long-period prime factors (Y) and *z* units of long-period fixed factors (Z) are used, output$=f(x,y,z)$. If Z is constant throughout we may say, output$=f(x,y)$. $f'(x,y)$ (*x*, constant) and $f'(x,y)$ (*y* constant) are both positive. $f''(x,y)$ (*y* constant) is always negative in short or long equilibrium in conditions of perfect competition, for otherwise the employment of *x* would at once be increased. $f''(x,y)$ (*x* constant) is negative in long-period equilibrium, for otherwise the use of *y* would tend to increase.

[2] $f'(x,y)$ (*x* constant) is positive for all values of *x*. Consequently, $f'(x,y)$ (*y* constant), which is the reciprocal of the short-period marginal prime cost of production, is smaller the smaller is *y*. But *y* has *ex hypothesi* been reduced between the two equilibria.

The long-period effect of the fall in demand will be to raise the short-period supply schedules of all sources affected in this way.

The fall in demand may be expected to reduce quasi-rents in some sources below zero and to eliminate those sources. This mitigates the decline in demand for the products of the other sources. The diminution of sources will tend to be greater the smaller is the proportion of long period supplementary to prime costs. The greater the elimination of sources the less will be the rise of the short-period supply schedules in the residual sources. This gives the basis of an important classification of industries, namely, by reference to the extent of the rise of the whole short-period supply schedule in response to a fall in demand. We are still within the domain of the law of increasing costs; the kind of response analysed here might be called the *law of decreasing cost conditions*. All industries obey this law for the range of production below an initial long-period equilibrium, except those industries none of whose fixed equipment survives the period *s*. The curve of decreasing cost conditions is less elastic the greater the permanent equipment.

This law does not hold generally for the range of production above an initial point of equilibrium. This asymmetry is due to the fact that the long-period fixed equipment of sources may be increased but not decreased. If the quasi-rent accruing to this permanent equipment is below normal in a source, that source is not putting its permanent equipment to its optimum use, and a rise in demand will cause more short-period fixed equipment to be used in conjunction with the already existing permanent equipment, and the short-period supply schedule for that source will fall in response. If the sources in which these quasi-rents are initially below normal preponderate in the industry, the whole industry will probably be subject to *decreasing cost conditions* for a certain range of production in excess of the initial quantity. But if permanent fixed equipment is already being put to its optimum or to an excessive use at the initial point in most sources, the law does not hold.

To sum up, where the law of decreasing cost conditions

holds, the following propositions are all true of a long period. (1) An increase in demand would reduce the short-period prime cost of production and consequently the supply schedule of the industry. (2) An increase in demand would also reduce the average cost of production if all kinds of overhead charges are included. (3) Notwithstanding this an increase in demand would raise the price of the product, and consequently the industry is subject to the 'law of increasing costs' as commonly understood. Confusion has arisen through failure to observe that these propositions are mutually consistent. The possibility of this complex state of affairs is due to the fact that certain elements of supplementary cost, especially the immaterial elements of organisation and goodwill, are often not destroyed within what may reasonably be regarded as a long period. Long-period equilibrium is consequently compatible with there being too many sources, that is, too many centres with a core of permanent equipment, and every one or many of these centres working below their optimum capacity.

## II

We shall now consider the case where the source of supply is not small in proportion to the whole industry. When that is so, the source is confronted with a falling demand curve. When there is one source, the demand with which it is confronted is that of the whole market. Where the curve showing the demand for its output is not horizontal, the output of a source is not determined by the point of intersection of the demand curve and the marginal cost curve. The demand curve of the market shows the price per unit at which suppliers can find buyers for $x$ units for all values of $x$. From this curve may be deduced another (Fig. 2), which I propose to call the increment of aggregate demand curve,[1] and which shows the aggregate price that suppliers can obtain for $x$ units of output less the aggregate price that they can obtain for $(x - 1)$ units for all values of $x$. If P is any point on the demand curve DD′, and PM a

[1] [This is the famous 'marginal revenue curve' of later literature.]

perpendicular to the horizontal axis, then the increment of aggregate demand curve (DD″) is the locus of a point p on PM such that DpMO = the rect. OP. The output of a monopolistic source is determined by the point at which the marginal cost curve cuts the increment of aggregate demand curve.

Marshall laid down that the entrepreneur 'endeavours to employ each agent up to that margin at which its net product would no longer exceed the price he would have to pay for it'.[1] This is true alike of the monopolist and the competitive entrepreneur if the 'net product' is valued in the right way.

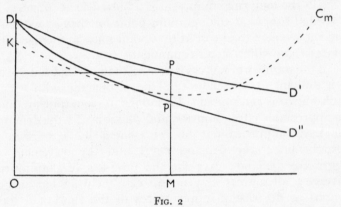

FIG. 2

Where the sources are many, value of the net product can be given its face meaning, viz. the price of the $x$th unit, when $x$ units are produced. In other cases the value of the net product must be taken to be the difference between the price of $x$ units when $x$ are produced, and the price of $(x-1)$. units when $(x-1)$ are produced. Where there are many sources, both interpretations yield the same result. Consequently the second interpretation has general application. The increment of aggregate demand curve shows the total price of $x$ units less the total price of $(x-1)$ units for all values of $x$. When the sources are many and the demand for the products of a source is shown by a horizontal line, the demand curve and the increment of aggregate

[1] Marshall, *Principles of Economics*, 8th ed., p. 406.

demand curve for the product of that source are coincident.

In the short period a monopolistic source may obey the law of decreasing supply price. In Fig. 2, $KC_m$ intersects $DD''$ only at a point where marginal costs are falling. In this case the monopolistic source is suffering from excessive capacity. If the demand is steady and the fixed equipment of the monopolistic source is adjusted to that demand, it will *probably* obey the law of increasing costs in the short period, since marginal costs increase in the neighbourhood of optimum output (see Fig. 1). In the long period a monopolistic source may well show decreasing supply prices, since in the long run equipment is adjusted so as to produce a normal supply at the optimum point for that equipment, and the average total cost at that point may be smaller with a large than with a small equipment.

If the number of sources is greater than one but not great, it is difficult to determine the kind of demand with which each source is confronted. Variations in its output produce an appreciable effect on price, and consequently the demand for that output cannot be represented by a horizontal straight line; the demand curve and the increment of aggregate demand curve for the products of that source diverge; all sources may in this case yield an increase of output at decreasing supply prices in the short and long periods.

### III

In recent discussions the old distinction between agricultural industry as subject to decreasing returns and manufacturing industry as subject to increasing returns has been lost sight of. Was it without foundation? Let us now withdraw an assumption made at the outset, that an industry can obtain its factors at a constant supply price, and suppose that an industry uses an appreciable fraction of the factors of production available. The value of this supposition depends on the definition of 'an industry'. Specific industries may be lumped together and a generic industry, like agriculture, may be considered as a unit. The larger the scope of an industry the more reasonable is it to suppose that the prices of the factors which it uses are influenced by variations in its demand for them. Different industries mix the factors of production in different proportions. Let us call the proportion in which the factors of production A, B, C . . . are mixed in use at the margin in national industry as a whole $a : b : c : \ldots$ This proportion should be a weighted average of the proportions proper to each industry at the margin of each. Any particular industry which uses the factors in the proportion $a : b : c \ldots$ at its own margin can draw to itself increasing supplies of the factors at a constant price. If the total supply of the factors is fixed, an increase of output by such an industry does not alter the relative scarcity of the factors. But if an industry using the factors in the proportion $a + x : b : c : \ldots$ expands, it can only get increasing quantities of A at an enhanced price in terms of B, C . . . But since, *ex hypothesi*, it uses more than an average amount of A, it can only get an increase in the sample of factors required for a unit increase of its output at an enhanced price. No doubt by the law of substitution $x$ will be reduced in consequence of the expansion of this industry ; but not to zero. An increase in the supply price of the factors required will raise the marginal cost curves of all sources ; consequently the supply price of the product will on this account alone rise in response to the rise of demand for it.

Under this head it follows that every industry which uses an appreciable fraction of the factors of production, unless it be an industry using them at the margin in the proportions of $a : b : c : \ldots$, obeys the law of increasing supply price. The curve of increasing supply price will be less elastic, the greater the industry in proportion to the whole of national industry and the greater $\frac{x}{a}$.

This analysis seems to clear up the problem of the old classical distinction between agriculture and the manufacturing industries. If A is land, and $a + x : b : c : \ldots$ the proportion in which the factors are mixed at the margin in agriculture as a whole, $\frac{x}{a}$ is clearly large. Agriculture as a whole is thus markedly subject to increasing supply price.

But the law of returns in agriculture is only a particular instance of the general principle.

Stress has often been laid on the inelasticity of the supply of the factor land. If it could be shown that the supply of land is less elastic than that of labour and the other factors, we should have an additional reason for expecting increasing supply prices to prevail in agriculture (as a whole). But it is by no means clear that the supply of land is less elastic. If the more familiar concept of the demand schedule be used, the demand of landowners for income in exchange for land has, if non-agricultural uses of land be ruled out, unitary elasticity. The amount of land spent in obtaining this income is constant, viz. the national supply of land. Little is known of the corresponding demand schedule of labour for a livelihood. It is not unreasonable to suppose it to have less than unitary elasticity. We no longer expect the population to expand in response to higher wages; and as wages rise the working day is reduced. In terms of supply this means that, while as rent rises the total supply of land remains constant, as wages rise the total supply of labour may fall. It is·probable, therefore, that the analysis of the text provides a better justification for the classical treatment of agriculture than any reference to the inelasticity of supply of land.

# THE LAW OF DECREASING COSTS[1]

In a former article I made an attempt to analyse the conditions of equilibrium in the long and short periods with reference to marginal prime, average prime and supplementary costs. Two classes of case were considered, first that of pure competition, and secondly that in which 'the source of supply is not small in relation to the whole industry'. It was maintained that in the second case the volume of output is determined by the intersection of the marginal prime cost curve and a curve derived from the demand curve which I called the increment of aggregate demand curve, and that the law of decreasing costs might then prevail in the long and short periods.

The increment of aggregate demand curve becomes relevant and the possibility of decreasing costs arises if and when a firm is confronted with a demand for its product of less than infinite elasticity. The definition 'where the source of supply is not small in relation to the whole industry' is too narrow to cover all firms confronted with a demand of this kind. Mr. Sraffa has, in a well-known article,[2] laid stress on the case when small individual firms are held in equilibrium by being subject to increasing marketing expenses. Where the product is not completely standardised or the market not organised, the individual producer may, although quite small, have increasing difficulty in marketing increments of produce.

I propose to examine in what follows the relation between the kind of conditions which Mr. Sraffa has envisaged and the law of decreasing costs. The first paragraph is concerned with the compatibility of competitive equilibrium with

---

[1] *Economic Journal*, December 1931.　　[2] *Economic Journal*, December 1926.

short-period decreasing costs,[1] the second is concerned with the compatibility of competitive equilibrium and short-period decreasing costs with profit, the third with the compatibility of competitive equilibrium with long-period decreasing costs,[2] and the fourth with the possibility that short- and long-period decreasing costs may be the normal condition of certain industries.

I

A firm whose product is not standardised or whose market is not organised may meet the difficulty of marketing increments of produce in two ways: by lowering the price, or by increasing marketing expenses. In so far as the conditions of the market allow a difference of price for the product of different sources, and the former method is adopted, the analysis of the equilibrium of the firm in this case may be assimilated to that provided in my previous essay, section II, 'where the source of supply is not small in proportion to the whole industry' (see page 84).

It is important also, however, to consider the status of marketing expenses. Mr. Sraffa holds that it is possible and 'formally correct' to include marketing expenses in the cost of production, but gives grounds for holding such a method of approach unsatisfactory and misleading  But so long as we use the concepts of supply and demand schedules in analysing the market complex, it is difficult to avoid putting these costs on the supply side.

For the purpose in hand we may confine our attention to marginal competitive marketing costs, *i.e.* those costs of marketing which are necessary to ward off the competitor at the frontier of a sphere of influence. It is assumed that any attempt to push out into the competitor's territory is attended with rising marketing costs per unit of sales, and that a surrender of territory to him would allow a reduction in them.

[1] 'Short-period decreasing costs' is defined as the condition in which a rise in demand for a short period brings about a fall in the marginal cost of production.

[2] See the definition of 'short-period decreasing costs', but substitute the word 'long' for 'short'.

## The Law of Decreasing Costs

Marginal competitive marketing costs can thus be represented as a function of the output of the individual firm. But it appears that they do not depend on this only. For let a rise in demand supervene on equilibrium, causing an increase of output : if the rise is evenly diffused over the whole market, firms should be able to maintain their frontiers without increase of marketing effort. A higher competitive marketing cost is the price of trespass into the neighbour's territory. If no trespass in either direction occurs, no rise in this cost per unit at the margin should occur. But all will be producing more in the new equilibrium.

It seems to follow from this that the marginal competitive marketing cost is a function not only of the quantity of output, but also of the state of demand. But if this is so, a complete reconstruction of the notion of a supply schedule becomes necessary. In the usual analysis supply and demand schedules are regarded as independent of one another. On the new view every demand schedule has its own appropriate supply schedule. To determine equilibrium after a change in the former, the latter also must be changed. The customary graphical representation of supply is no longer possible. Any given supply schedule of the old type is only valid while the demand remains constant. To draw a single supply schedule to be valid for all states of demand, it is necessary to use three dimensions. Cost becomes a function of two independent variables, quantity of output and state of demand.[1] Thus the traditional analysis breaks down.

This at once seems to throw light on the vexed question of how a condition of decreasing costs may be compatible with competitive equilibrium. In equilibrium the state of demand may be taken to be constant and the cost of production becomes a function of one variable, viz. quantity of output. It is thus a sufficient condition of equilibrium that costs should rise for increasing quantities of output. The expressions decreasing and increasing costs are, however, usually taken to refer to the response in supply price to

[1] If a change in the state of demand may be complex, *i.e.* involve elasticity as well as intensity, four (or more) dimensions are necessary for a representation of supply.

changes in demand. So long as the supply schedule was conceived as independent of the demand schedule, the effect of a change in the latter could be read off from a curve showing cost as a function of output; if that had an upward gradient between its points of intersection with the old and new demand curves, prices were expected to rise. But if to determine the new equilibrium a new supply schedule has to be drawn, derived from a cost curve, a component part of which is marginal marketing cost (now reduced throughout the relevant range), it cannot be determined *a priori* from the upward slope of the old curve whether the point of intersection of the two new curves will be above or below the old point. If the new price is below the old one, then in the accepted sense of the term the firm is subject to decreasing costs, and, if we may suppose the firm to be an equilibrium one in Professor Pigou's sense,[1] the whole industry is subject to decreasing costs. Thus competitive equilibrium is compatible with decreasing costs in the ordinary sense of that expression.

If it be supposed that in a firm costs other than competitive marketing costs are falling at the old equilibrium, but that the rise in the latter more than offsets the fall in the former, so that the total cost schedule (old type) is a rising one, it can be shown that the firm is subject to decreasing costs. For suppose an increase in demand evenly diffused among the various particular spheres of influence: an increase of market can then be secured for each firm without trespass on its neighbour's sphere, and therefore without increase of marginal competitive marketing cost per unit. But if the marginal marketing cost is the same as in the old equilibrium, and the residual marginal costs are lower owing to the larger output, combined marginal costs will be lower in the new equilibrium than in the old. Thus a firm which has costs other than competitive marketing costs falling, but is held in equilibrium by total costs, considered as a function of output only, rising, is subject to the law of decreasing costs.

[1] Pigou, *Economics of Welfare*, ed. 1929, p. 788.

## II

The second difficulty in supposing a competitive equilibrium to be compatible with the condition of short-period decreasing costs arises from the fact that if marginal costs are falling, the marginal prime cost will probably be less than the average prime cost,[1] and if the price is equal to the marginal cost, total prime costs will not be covered.

This difficulty is resolved when it is remembered that while competitive marketing costs must be excluded in determining whether an industry is subject to decreasing costs, in equilibrium the price must cover the marginal competitive marketing costs. The aggregated marginal cost curve (old type) is supposed to be rising in equilibrium. Marginal marketing costs will stand above the average marketing costs, and the difference should more than make up for the fact that marginal productive costs [2] are below average productive costs; in this case combined marginal prime costs, to which the price is equated, will stand above combined average prime costs.

A complete account of the matter is not quite so simple. Where the market is not thoroughly unified even a small individual firm may, as Mr. Sraffa observes, be confronted with a demand curve of less than infinite elasticity. The curve of the demand for the products from an individual source of supply is not in these circumstances a wholly unambiguous concept. Starting from a given equilibrium, if an individual firm desires to expand sales, it may adopt both the device of lowering prices and of increasing marketing costs; the converse applies to contraction inside a given point. How, then, should we plot out the demand curve with which the individual is confronted? It seems to be the best plan to assume that in departing from a given equilibrium the individual will follow the path of maximum receipts, will cut down prices by that amount and increase selling expenses by that amount which will in the aggregate

[1] See above, p. 78.
[2] The expression 'productive costs' is here used as equivalent to all prime costs less competitive marketing costs.

involve him in least loss of net receipts; or will raise prices by that amount and cut down selling expenses by that amount which will bring the greatest net gain. Then we may plot that section of the demand curve which lies on either side of equilibrium on the assumption that he would combine price regulation and selling expense in the way most advantageous to himself.

To illustrate how a falling particular demand curve affects the relation of costs to price, we may suppose that the whole manipulation of the market at the disposal of the individual firm consists of price regulation, and that the selling expenses are null. In such a case the marginal cost curve would be composed solely of productive costs. Even so, falling marginal costs are compatible with profit. For the point of equilibrium is determined by the point of intersection of the marginal cost curve, and the increment of aggregate demand curve.[1] A halt is called to production at the point at which the net increment of cost rises above the net increment of receipts due to it. But if the demand curve is falling, the increment of net receipts due to an extra unit is less than the price per unit. If $y_1$ is the price per unit and $\eta$ the elasticity of demand at the point of equilibrium, the increment of receipts falls short of the price by $\frac{y_1}{\eta}$.[2] If the elasticity is equal to or less than one, there are no net receipts. It must be remembered that the particular demand curve with which the individual is confronted has a far greater elasticity than that of the market, since the products of competitors are available as substitutes; indeed, it approaches infinity as the organisation of the market approaches perfection.

The statement that the marginal cost of production is, in equilibrium, equal to the price, less the price divided by the elasticity of demand, has universal applicability. Pure

---

[1] See above, pp. 84-6.

[2] The increment of aggregate receipts is $\frac{d(xy)}{dx}$.

$$\frac{d(xy)}{dx} = y + \frac{x\,dy}{dx} = y - \frac{y}{\eta}.$$

competition with a perfectly organised market is the special case in which elasticity is infinite, and the marginal cost of production is therefore equal to the price.

Since the price exceeds the marginal cost of production by $\frac{y_1}{\eta}$, there is a possibility of profit. Receipts will exceed total prime costs if the gradient of the particular demand curve is greater than that of the average prime cost curve.[1] If $z_1$ is the average prime cost at equilibrium and K represents overhead cost plus a normal return to capital invested, profits in equilibrium will be super-normal or subnormal according as $x(y_1 - z_1)$ exceeds or falls short of K.

The diagram on page 96 illustrates a position of equilibrium with normal profit and falling costs where marketing expenses are null. $KC_m$, $KC_p$ and $LC_t$ [2] represent marginal prime, total prime and total costs respectively. DD' is the demand curve and DD" the increment of aggregate demand curve.[3] Q is the point of intersection of $KC_m$ and DD". A perpendicular, QM, to the horizontal axis cuts DD' and $KC_p$ at P and R. QM represents marginal cost and PM price. QR represents the excess of average over marginal prime cost, and PR the excess of price over average prime cost. If $LC_t$, the total costs curve happens, as in the diagram, to intersect DD' at P, normal profits are earned.

The intention of the foregoing analysis has been to demonstrate the possibility of the law of decreasing costs

---

[1] In equilibrium the marginal prime cost is equal to the increment of aggregate demand. If $y_1$ is the equilibrium price and $z_1$ the average prime cost in equilibrium, $\frac{d(xy_1)}{dx} = \frac{d(xz_1)}{dx}$, *i.e.* $y_1 + \frac{xdy_1}{dx} = z_1 + \frac{xdz_1}{dx}$. Then $y_1 > z_1$, if $-\frac{dy_1}{dx} > -\frac{dz_1}{dx}$, *i.e.* if the gradient of the particular demand curve is greater than that of the average prime cost curve.

From the further condition of equilibrium that the increment of aggregate demand curve falls below the marginal prime cost curve, *i.e.* that $-\frac{d^2(xy_1)}{dx^2} > -\frac{d^2(xz_1)}{dx^2}$, it can be deduced that $-\frac{dy_1}{dx}$ will be greater than $-\frac{dz_1}{dx}$, and therefore that $y_1$ will be greater than $z_1$, if $-\frac{d^2y_1}{dx^2} \not< -\frac{d^2z_1}{dx^2}$. Thus in the simple case of linear supply and demand functions, $y_1$ must exceed $z_1$.

[2] *Economic Journal*, June 1930.      [3] *Ibid.*

co-existing with competitive equilibrium. To do this it had to be assumed either that there were competitive marketing costs, or that the market failed to be completely unified, so that a falling demand for the products of an individual firm was possible, or both. In the first case it was necessary to abandon the orthodox notion that the supply price can be appropriately regarded as a function of one variable, viz. quantity of output of the source, or, even as, in the manner of Professor Pigou, a function of two variables, viz. the

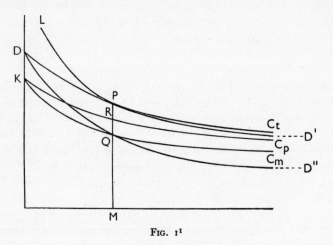

FIG. I[1]

quantity of output of the source and that of the whole industry. It must be regarded as also dependent on the state of demand.

With either or both of these assumptions, the two main difficulties in the way of supposing equilibrium to be compatible with decreasing costs are overcome, viz. the difficulty that the equilibrium firm would be tempted to expand output, and the difficulty that the equilibrium firm would be making a loss.

----

[1] [The figure in my original article was erroneous, since it made DD′ intersect $LC_t$ (cf. text). Although the principle of tangency is shown in reference to the relation between long-period and short-period costs in Fig. 2, I appear to have overlooked that the mathematics clearly requires that the total cost and demand curves should also be tangential. 1952.]

III

The next question to be considered is how far this equilibrium can be regarded as a long-period one. It should be noted, however, that orthodox theory does not even provide for a short-period equilibrium with decreasing costs. That is clearly a matter of importance for the analysis of the trade cycle. [Compare pages 132-8 below.]

If a source is subject to decreasing costs, it must be producing at what is, from the productive point of view, less than the optimum rate. Is this consistent with long-period equilibrium? Will it not be in the interest of sources in this condition to amalgamate, and so to raise the output of some to a point of increasing costs, while putting others out of commission?

It was put forward above that sources subject to decreasing costs may be held in equilibrium by increasing competitive marketing expenses. These should be understood to include all costs involved in invading a competitor's territory, and therefore to include the costs of transport. These costs form a part of the class of costs which rise per unit with an increase of output if the demand is constant, but depend on the intensity of demand in a given area. If the expansion of a source, *a*, is checked by the rising costs of transporting into *b*'s area, an amalgamation by which *a* received *b*'s good-will would not reduce these costs, or, consequently make any expansion of *a*, *ceteris paribus*, profitable. If the population or the market is sufficiently sparsely spread, it may be cheaper from every point of view to have a larger number of sources than would be desirable if transport charges could be neglected, to have, that is, sources producing at less than their optimum rate. Concentration might bring economies on the productive side; but these would only be net economies if and when the market became denser. Thus an industry may be in long-period equilibrium with productive costs falling, whenever the rise in transporting costs attendant on greater concentration would alone suffice to make gross marginal costs rise as a result of the concentration.    Such an industry may be in long-period equilibrium and subject to the law of decreasing costs.

The rise in competitive marketing costs may be due to the more intensive salesmanship required and not to higher transport charges.  If it could be assumed that all firms were willing to lose their individual identity in the interest of long-period profit, then the equilibrium maintained by rising competitive salesmanship costs could not be regarded as a long-period one.  Individualism should probably be treated as an influence of lasting importance.  It might be assumed, for the sake of argument, that errors of tenacious individualism are at all times and in all countries likely to be offset by a frivolous inclination to rush into injudicious amalgamations.  Such an assumption would constitute a pedantic refusal to take relevant factors into account, a parody of the proper use of the concept, economic man.  Mr. Shove has made a further elaboration of this point unnecessary.[1]  The period of the equilibrium maintained by the presence of these kinds of costs is a sufficiently long one.

## IV

It remains to consider how far a condition of decreasing costs can be normal to certain industries.  Must we content ourselves with saying that any industry may get into the condition of decreasing costs for short or long periods, but that such a condition does not arise out of the nature of any special class of industries ?  Must we abandon the expression 'increasing returns industries' ?

This topic must be divided into two parts.  (1) Costs are rising in response to short-period increases in demand, but falling in response to long-period increases, if the plant of the equilibrium firm is being used up to capacity, but is constructed on less than the optimum scale.  (2) Costs are falling in response to short-period increases in demand, if the plant of the equilibrium firm is not being used up to full capacity.

[1] *Economic Journal*, March 1930.

## The Law of Decreasing Costs

(1) Is there any general characteristic of an industry which is likely to lead to the result that the equilibrium firm has its plant constructed on less than the optimum scale? The presence of transport charges of appreciable importance or individualism or both must be assumed. By presence of individualism is meant that the pertinacious desire of firms to retain their individual identity prevails over the tendency to rush into injudicious amalgamations. The general characteristic may be stated simply : it is that, if technical improvements of a kind that involve a larger optimum source of supply are occurring, the rate of expansion of the optimum source of supply exceeds the rate of increase of the demand. Roughly, then, we may think of industries in which technical inventions make the optimum size of the source of supply increase rapidly as likely to be increasing returns industries. The decrease in cost will occur in this case in response to long-period, *i.e.* sustained, rises in demand.

(2) Are there any industries in which decreasing costs in response to short-period rises in demand can be considered as normal? *Prima facie* the condition in which the plant of the equilibrium firm was working under capacity would seem to be peculiar to certain phases of the conjuncture. Who, it might be asked, would construct a plant, the optimum capacity of which was in excess of the prospective normal demand? The objector to decreasing costs can be met even on this ground. If the prospective normal demand of the equilibrium firm is such that it will not absorb the optimum output of the optimum plant, it is probable that the firm will construct a plant, the optimum output of which will exceed the prospective normal output. In this case the plant, when producing for the normal demand, will show decreasing costs. If a firm is considering the desirability of reconstruction and the proper scale of operations, the question which it asks is, not — What is the plant the optimum output of which the normal demand will absorb? but — What is the plant with which the normal demand can be met most cheaply? If an increase of scale provides substantial economies, such an increase may be desirable, even if full advantage of the economies cannot be taken.

99

The truth of this can be very simply illustrated diagrammatically (Fig. 2). The cost of production may be represented by a family of parabolas, each of which shows the cost of any output from a plant of given size. The lowest point of the parabola shows the cost of the optimum output from its plant. The minimum point is supposed lower the larger the size of plant, and the locus of these points a curve falling smoothly for increasing values of $x$, the output. It is required to find the proper size of plant for any given prospective normal demand, $x_1$. This is the plant the

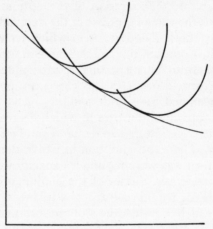

FIG. 2

parabola of which has of all the parabolas the lowest value for $x_1$; $x_1$ units can be produced most cheaply from a plant of such a size. Plot a curve (see Fig. 2) the ordinate of which is equal to the lowest of the ordinates of all the parabolas for each value of $x$. Such a curve (the envelope) may be called the long-period productive cost curve, for it shows the cost of producing the normally required output $x_1$, if that is properly foreseen. If, as we suppose, the equilibrium firm has its plant constructed on less than the optimum scale, the long-period productive cost curve is falling in the neighbourhood of equilibrium. The long-period productive cost curve must never intersect any parabola of the family, for if it did, it would for some value of $x$ stand above the lowest value of one of the family. It follows that the long-period productive cost curve is for every value of $x$ tangential to the parabola of the appropriate plant. But the long-period productive cost curve has a downward gradient. The parabola of the appropriate plant has, therefore, also a downward gradient at the point of normal output. This means that when the demand for the output of a firm is precisely that which the firm had in mind in constructing its plant, the parabola showing the costs of that plant has a downward gradient for that output, and the plant is being worked at less than its optimum capacity. Consequently in normal times the output of this firm may be subject to decreasing costs in response to a short-period rise in demand,[1] and the rate at which costs decrease in the neighbourhood of normal is precisely equal to the rate at which costs decrease in response to a long-period rise in demand.

The conclusions of this article may be briefly summarised.

1. If competitive marketing costs are present, or if the equilibrium source is confronted with a falling demand schedule, competitive equilibrium is *consistent* with decreasing costs in the short period. To give a correct representation of the effect of competitive marketing costs, the orthodox supply schedule is inadequate. Supply price must be considered as a function of the state of demand as well as of output. If marginal costs other than competitive marketing costs are falling at equilibrium, the firm is subject to the law of decreasing costs in the short period.

2. Profit is *consistent* with this equilibrium.

3. Competitive equilibrium is *consistent* with decreasing costs in the long period also, if appreciable transport costs are involved, or if a spirit of individualism is prevalent among entrepreneurs.

4. Competitive equilibrium with decreasing costs in the short and long periods may be regarded as *normal* to industries, the rate of expansion in the optimum plant of which exceeds the rate of increase in demand.

[1] It is not possible to say that the output *is* subject to decreasing costs in response to a short-period rise in demand, since the parabola is a total costs curve and rising marginal are consistent with falling total costs.

There has been no reference to the question of external economies.

The considerations brought forward seem sufficient to establish the legitimacy of the conception of increasing returns industries.

# A FURTHER NOTE ON DECREASING COSTS

INTERESTING additions to the theory of decreasing costs have been made in recent numbers of the *Economic Journal* by Mrs. Robinson [1] and Mr. Shove; [2] complete precision in this field is almost within our grasp; certain obscurities, however, remain to be cleared up. In particular Mr. Shove's criticism [3] of Mrs. Robinson has brought to light some difficulties connected with her conception of a normal rate of profit.

She defines a normal rate as that which neither attracts new nor drives out old competitors. [4] In the case of imperfect competition, however, it appears that this definition does not specify a particular rate, but only a range of rates.

If there were a unique rate such that any rate in excess of it attracted new competitors and any rate below it caused defection, we should surely be in the sphere of perfect competition. As Mr. Shove observes, Mrs. Robinson's treatment suggests free entry into the trade, and free entry is 'difficult to reconcile with the notion of an imperfect market'. Mrs. Robinson really does no more than define limits within which any rate may be considered as normal.

Nevertheless, in order to use an apparatus of cost curves effectively and to give any meaning to the expression, decreasing costs, it is necessary to specify a single rate of profit. It is this rate which has to be used in determining the supplementary cost due to a given capital installation.

---

[1] *Economic Journal*, December 1932.
[2] *Ibid.* March 1933.   [3] *Loc. cit.* p. 119.
[4] 'If profits are more than normal, new firms will tend to enter the industry. . . . If profits are less than normal, firms will tend to leave the industry.' — Robinson, *loc. cit.* p. 546.

Within the range of possible equilibrium rates which Mrs. Robinson's definition yields, one particular rate stands out with a marked claim to be considered *the* normal rate. This is the rate just sufficient to induce *the firm itself* to embark on additional fixed capital expenditure. It is likely to be lower than the rate required to attract new firms into the business and higher than the rate at which firms tend to fall out. In a period long enough to allow a firm to adjust its fixed equipment to the prospective demand, the rate of return to the marginal installation of fixed equipment tends to be equal to what the firm considers adequate. This rate of profit should be regarded as the supply price of fixed equipment for the firm, and should be used in computing its supplementary costs schedule.

It remains to consider how this definition of normal profit in imperfect competition affects the theory of equilibrium. In a short-period equilibrium, it will be remembered, marginal cost of production is equal to marginal revenue ; [1] price and average cost may have different values, but, if they have a common value, the price and average cost curves must be tangential at the equilibrium point. What of the longer period ? First, profit on fixed equipment must lie within the limits postulated by Mrs. Robinson. This condition need concern us no further. The second condition may be expressed in two ways which come to the same thing. The firm will use such an amount of fixed equipment that it produces the equilibrium output in the cheapest way (charging fixed equipment with a normal rate of profit as defined above). Put otherwise, the marginal revenue due to the marginal outlay on fixed equipment yields a normal rate of profit upon it.

I showed in the previous essay [2] that a firm's cost of production may be represented by a family of parabolas, each member of the family representing the cost of producing different amounts of output from a given amount of fixed

---

[1] Mrs. Robinson has re-christened my somewhat clumsy 'increment of aggregate demand curve' with the more elegant name, 'marginal revenue curve'. Cf. *Economic Journal*, June 1930, p. 238, and December 1932, p. 546.

[2] See above, p. 100.

equipment. The cheapest mode of producing any particular amount of output, $x_r$, is by using that amount of fixed equipment the parabola of which has the lowest ordinate of all the parabolas at $x_r$. Since in a long period a firm will tend to produce in the cheapest manner, the long-period cost curve is the envelope of the family.

In constructing each parabola, a normal rate of profit, as defined above, should be assumed. For it is precisely this rate of profit which determines the action of a firm, when deciding whether to extend (or reconstruct) its plant or not. It will regard extension of plant as the cheaper way of producing an increment $\Delta x$, when the extra prime cost required to produce $\Delta x$ without extra plant exceeds that required to do so with the extra plant by anything more than an amount yielding a normal rate of profit, as defined, on the extra plant.[1]

It follows that the second mode of stating the second condition for long-period equilibrium set out above comes to the same thing as the first mode. In long-period equilibrium the firm will be earning on its marginal outlay on fixed plant a rate of return which it regards as justifying fixed capital expenditure.

In long-period equilibrium the long-period cost curve and the curve showing total cost per unit of producing from the particular plant in use are tangential at the point of equilibrium output (*vide supra*). Are these curves also tangential to the demand curve?

If they are, the price is equal to the total cost of production per unit, which means that it yields an average rate of profit on the fixed plant that is equal to the rate used in constructing the cost curve, *i.e.* that the average rate of profit is equal to the normal and to the marginal rate. If, as Mrs. Robinson implies, the firm must earn a unique normal rate of profit on all its fixed equipment in long-period equilibrium, then her conclusion follows that the total cost per unit curve, which embodies this rate, must be tangential to the demand

---

[1] If the next biggest size of plant can only be achieved, not by the addition of an extra piece, but by radical reconstruction, the period under consideration is longer.

curve, and, since that has a negative gradient in an imperfect market, an equilibrium firm working for an imperfect market must show decreasing costs.[1] It is true that in equilibrium a firm's rate of profit on all its fixed equipment must be normal in her sense. It is not true that there is a unique normal rate of profit in this sense. Nor is it true that a firm must earn a normal rate of profit on all its fixed equipment in the unique sense defined above. It must earn a normal rate so defined on its marginal fixed equipment. If the price exceeds the total cost per unit, the average rate of profit on the firm's fixed equipment will exceed the marginal which is equal to the normal rate, and if the price falls short of the total cost per unit the average rate of profit in the firm will fall short of its marginal which is also its normal rate.

It seems to be true, therefore, that it is *not* a necessary condition of long-period equilibrium that the price should be equal to the total average cost per unit. If the price is greater than the total average cost per unit, the gradient of the demand curve has a greater negative value than that of the total cost per unit curve;[2] in this condition, therefore, the long-period cost curve may not have a negative gradient at all. If the price is equal to or less than the total average cost per unit, the long-period cost curve must have a negative gradient. It seems to follow from this that after a period of prolonged depression when firms are tending to reach a long-period equilibrium at a low level of output, prices and profits, long-period decreasing costs are more than usually likely to be present in firms that are in imperfect competition.

This analysis confirms the view of an earlier article,[3] that an equilibrium firm working in conditions of imperfect competition *may* be subject to decreasing long- and short-period costs in equilibrium. It is in conflict with the further contention that such a firm *must* be subject to decreasing costs.

[1] Cf. Robinson, *loc. cit.* p. 549.
[2] Since the marginal revenue curve and the marginal cost curve intersect at the point of equilibrium output, $x_r$, that average curve must have the greater negative gradient which has the greater value at $x_r$. Cf. the formula on p. 570, *Economic Journal*, December 1931.
[3] *Economic Journal*, December 1931.

## *A Further Note on Decreasing Costs*

Mrs. Robinson's theorem is consistent with a possible definition of normal profit, but not with that given above. The definition I have chosen may be defended on the grounds, first, that it is natural and conformable with general economic usage, and secondly, that the cost curve which it entails is the most appropriate one, if cost analysis is undertaken with an eye to supply price analysis. Mrs. Robinson has shown that changes of supply price in imperfect competition, depend on the nature of changes in demand. The simplest kind of change in demand to suppose seems to be that the particular demand curve, as it shifts its position, retains a constant elasticity for each value of $y$. In the face of such changes the supply price curve and the cost curve constructed in the manner suggested above both have a negative gradient, both have a positive gradient or are both horizontal.[1]

[1] The last two propositions were suggested to my mind by a hint given by Mrs. Robinson herself. She must not, however, be held responsible for them.

# THE EQUILIBRIUM OF DUOPOLY[1]

I PROPOSE a solution of the problem of duopoly in a perfect market [2] on the arbitrary assumption that the particular demands, with which each duopolist is confronted, are linear functions.

Represent the market demand by $F(x)$ and the particular demands by which the first and second duopolists are confronted by $f_a(x_a)$ and $f_b(x_b)$. It is required to determine the values of $f'_a$ and $f'_b$, the cost functions of the duopolists and the market demand being known.

The fall in the market price, due to the first duopolist increasing his output by $\Delta x$, is equal to the fall which occurs, when the total supply is increased by an amount $\Delta x$ less the amount by which the second duopolist restricts output in consequence of such a fall in price.

When the first duopolist increases output by $\Delta x$, the demand curve of the second duopolist moves to the left by an amount equal to $\Delta x$ throughout its range. If this demand curve has a linear function, the gradient of the marginal revenue curve correspondent to it may be represented by the expression $2f'_b(x_b)$.[3] Consequently, when the second duopolist's demand curve recedes by $\Delta x$ throughout its range, his correspondent marginal revenue curve recedes by $\frac{1}{2}\Delta x$.

[1] *Economic Journal*, June 1934.

[2] The expression 'perfect market' is used to indicate the rule of a single price and the absence of competitive marketing costs, in contradistinction to perfect competition when particular demand curves have infinite elasticity.

[3] The gradient of the marginal revenue curve is equal to

$$\frac{d\frac{d(x_b y)}{dx_b}}{dx_b}.$$

When the second differential is zero, this expression $= 2\frac{dy}{dx_b}$.

If $\phi_b(x_b)$ represents the cost function of the second duopolist, his restriction of output consequent on the increase of that of the first by $\Delta x$ is

$$\left\{ \frac{2f'_b(x_b)}{2f'_b(x_b) - \phi'_b(x_b)} \right\} \tfrac{1}{2}\Delta x.^1$$

Consequently the net increase of output is

$$\left\{ 1 - \tfrac{1}{2} \cdot \frac{2f'_b(x_b)}{2f'_b(x_b) - \phi'_b(x_b)} \right\} \Delta x = \left\{ \frac{f'_b(x_b) - \phi'_b(x_b)}{2f'_b(x_b) - \phi'_b(x_b)} \right\} \Delta x.$$

Therefore the particular demand for the product of the first duopolist is shown by the equation

$$f'_a(x_a) = F'(x) \left\{ \frac{f'_b(x_b) - \phi'_b(x_b)}{2f'_b(x_b) - \phi'_b(x_b)} \right\}. \qquad . \qquad (1)$$

---

¹ THE SECOND DUOPOLIST

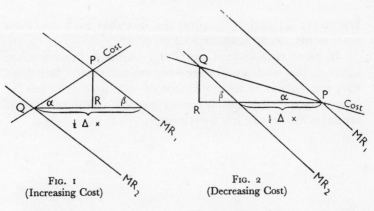

FIG. 1
(Increasing Cost)

FIG. 2
(Decreasing Cost)

In these figures the cost curve intersects the old marginal revenue curve ($MR_1$) at P and the new marginal revenue curve ($MR_2$) at Q. The horizontal distance between the MR curves is $\tfrac{1}{2}\Delta x$. The restriction of output in Fig. 1 is QR, that in Fig. 2 is PR. In Fig. 1 QR is equal to

$$\frac{\tan \beta}{\tan a + \tan \beta} \cdot \tfrac{1}{2}\Delta x = \frac{2f'_b(x_b)}{2f'_b(x_b) - \phi'_b(x_b)} \cdot \tfrac{1}{2}\Delta x.$$

In Fig. 2 PR is equal to

$$\frac{\tan \beta}{\tan \beta - \tan a} \cdot \tfrac{1}{2}\Delta x = \frac{2f'_b(x_b)}{2f'_b(x_b) - \phi'_b(x_b)} \cdot \tfrac{1}{2}\Delta x.$$

Thus the same expression serves for both cases.

Of these terms, $F'(x)$, the gradient of the market demand curve, and $\phi'_b(x_b)$, the gradient of the second duopolist's cost curve, are known; $f'_b$ is, however, unknown. But for this we have a second equation analogous to (1) above:

$$f'_b(x_b) = F'(x) \left\{ \frac{f'_a(x_a) - \phi'_a(x_a)}{2f'_a(x_a) - \phi'_a(x_a)} \right\}. \qquad . \qquad (2)$$

Thus we have two unknown quantities and two equations with two roots for each unknown.

If the gradients of the particular demand curves, $f'_a$ and $f'_b$, are known, the determination of the duopolists' position becomes a simple matter. It is required to find the price $(y)$ and the amounts produced by each duopolist, $x_a$ and $x_b$. For these three unknowns we have three equations:

$$y = F(x_a + x_b) \qquad . \qquad . \qquad . \qquad (3)$$
$$= \phi_a(x_a) - x_a f'_a(x_a) \qquad . \qquad . \qquad (4)$$
$$= \phi_b(x_b) - x_b f'_b(x_b) \qquad . \qquad . \qquad (5)$$

Equations (4) and (5) express the fact that each duopolist equates his cost to his marginal revenue.

If more complicated particular demand functions are allowed, the mathematics becomes less tractable. But there does not appear to be any reason of economic principle for supposing that the equilibrium of duopoly would on normal assumptions be any less determinate.

# DOCTRINES OF IMPERFECT COMPETITION[1]

1. It is my purpose in the following pages to set out what appear to me to be the principal points of significance for economic theory in the doctrines relating to Imperfect Competition that have been recently evolved.[2] I propose to divide this into three parts, their significance for equilibrium theory, their significance for the theory of the optimum, and their significance for trade cycle theory.

I

2. The starting point in the theory of imperfect competition is the proposition that individual sources of output are very frequently confronted with a downward sloping demand curve. With the aid of this premise many interesting conclusions may be deduced and many paradoxes resolved. But first it may be asked — how is the premise itself established?

3. The possibility of a particular source of supply being confronted by a downward sloping demand curve has always been recognised by economic theory, namely, in the case of absolute monopoly. The claim now advanced is that the phenomenon is far more widespread than has been commonly supposed or implied, and the chief basis of this claim is actual observation. This is a notable instance of the assistance which the inductive method may give to the course of *a priori* reasoning. The phenomenon occurs so frequently in fact as to suggest the framing of a theoretical structure into which it can easily be fitted.

[1] *Quarterly Journal of Economics*, May 1934.
[2] See especially J. Robinson, *Economics of Imperfect Competition*, and E. Chamberlin, *The Theory of Monopolistic Competition*.

4. Traditional theory has clear-cut conceptions with regard to the demand curve confronting a particular source of output in two cases, those of perfect competition and of absolute monopoly. An individual source of output working in conditions of perfect competition can always find a market for any amount of output it pleases at a price determined by forces outside itself. Variation in its own contribution to the supply of the commodity does not have an appreciable effect on its price. Two consequences follow from this.

(i) The particular source can never be subject, in the equilibrium of either the short or the long period, to decreasing costs of production. If the $(n+1)$th unit can be produced at a lower cost and sold at no less a price than the $n$th unit, then, if it is profitable to produce $n$ units, it is *a fortiori* profitable to produce $n+1$. Similarly with the $(n+2)$th unit, and so on, until the source of supply runs into a range of increasing costs. Therefore in equilibrium, even in that of the short period, it must be in a range of increasing costs. Consideration of external economies does not affect this. For if an increase of output is not sufficiently large in relation to the total output of the industry to have an effect on price it will not be sufficiently large by parity of reasoning to have an appreciable effect on external economies.

(ii) Sources tend to have their fixed means of production constructed on a scale which, having regard to technical considerations and the supply price of factors, is the one capable of producing most cheaply (the optimum). Since no increase of output will have an appreciable influence on price, the source is free to expand its plant to the scale at which it can produce most cheaply per unit. Short-period variations in demand are met by variations in the extent to which fixed means are exploited. Long-period variations in demand are met by an increase or diminution in the number of sources of supply. Each source of supply tends to have its fixed means of an optimum size independently of the state of demand.

5. The rather vague term, source of supply, has been used advisedly. Fixed aids to production may be divided into the material and the immaterial. The latter consist of knowledge, experience and connexions embodied in the person or

persons engaged in regulating production. It is convenient to call the material fixed equipment 'plant'. A plant is a congeries of fixed material aids to production situated together. The plant may or may not have associated with it persons constituting a storehouse of valuable experience. Such persons may be simultaneously associated with a number of plants, and the unit consisting of scattered groups of fixed material equipment all associated with the same immaterial fixed aids to production may be thought of as a firm. The peculiarity of a firm is that it comprises not merely entrepreneurial ability of a certain standing, but also, as soon as it has subsisted for any period of time, entre-preneurial experience, which is like the fixed plant in that it cannot readily be switched over to another occupation and applied with equal efficiency in it.

The expression, source of supply, used in the foregoing paragraphs, can be applied either to a plant or to a firm. The plant and the firm may be co-extensive, or a firm may include a number of plants, or it may even happen that a number of firms utilise a single plant. The propositions that sources in perfect competition cannot be subject to the law of decreasing costs and tend to be adjusted to the optimum size independently of the state of demand apply both to plants and to firms.

6. That there is still a wide area to which the notion of perfect competition is applicable need not be denied. The output of primary products is still generally subject to it. Even where attempts have been made to organise selling by the formation of rings, regulation of output has proved diffi-cult, and the individual source, rightly thinking that its own output would not affect the price, and not sufficiently controlled by the central organisation to be impeded, has continued to produce the output appropriate to perfect competition. Perfect competition is usually characterised by the presence of an organised exchange, through which sales can be effected, and by the complete homogeneity of the products of competing sources.

7. It is observation that has suggested that as soon as we move outside the area of primary products handled in

organised exchanges, individual sources are confronted with
downward sloping demand curves. What concepts has
traditional theory to offer for use in this field? There are
absolute monopoly and duopoly. In the case of absolute
monopoly the downward sloping curve is recognised. In the
case of duopoly traditional theory has failed to provide a
satisfactory solution.

Is it the lesson of experience that the concept of absolute
monopoly is really appropriate throughout a vast area, in
part of which competition in the ordinary sense of the word
would be deemed to be rampant? This view is too strong.
It has never been supposed that the monopolist was confronted with an absolutely inelastic demand, and it is
recognised that elasticity depends on the availability of
substitutes. There is hardly anything for which substitutes
cannot be found. Only a monopolist who controlled not
only the whole supply of one commodity, but that of a large
group of commodities, such as all foodstuffs, would find
himself in an absolutely dominating position. Otherwise his
absolutism is tempered.

We are driven to ask the question, what is a commodity?
Is there any certain distinction between different varieties
of a commodity and different commodities? Are dining
chairs and easy-chairs one, and only sofas different? Or if
the dining and easy-chairs are different, what of Chippendale
chairs? What of the particular design?

Some products are to all intents and purposes absolutely
homogeneous. If they are, an organised exchange is likely
to spring up and perfect competition to reign. If differences
of design and detail are possible, each producer may be
thought of as a monopolist of his own wares, but subject to
the substitution of his rivals'. His degree of monopoly may
be measured by the size of the gap in kind between his wares
and the most similar wares available from another source.
It must be recognised that no monopolist is absolute, but
that every producer of goods not absolutely homogeneous
with those of other producers is something of a monopolist
and likely to be confronted by a downward sloping demand
curve.

The traditional concept of the monopolist seems to suffice for the main part of the field of production outside that of perfect competition, provided it is recognised that the monopolist's position is never absolute and the elasticity of the demand for his product always greater than zero. It will indeed be shown that in equilibrium the elasticity of demand must be greater than one.

8. I shall now put forward as briefly as possible some technical apparatus of analysis (paras. *infra* 9-21). This seems necessary in order to justify certain generalisations which I wish to make. Limits of space entail compression and the severity of terseness.

9. (i) Contemplation of the downward sloping demand curve has suggested a simple labour-saving technique for determining monopolistic behaviour.[1] If the monopolist increases his output from $x$ to $(x+1)$ units, the additional revenue which he secures by doing so is equal to the price of one unit when he sells $x+1$ less the difference between the price of $x$ when he sells $x$ and the price of $x$ when he sells $x+1$. His sales must be thought of, as in all supply and demand analysis, as so much *per unit of time*. This additional revenue has been well called his marginal revenue.[2] The value of the marginal revenue for any amount of output may be derived from the demand schedule. If $x$ is the amount of output and $y$ the demand price, the marginal revenue is $\dfrac{d(xy)}{dx}$. If $\eta$ is the elasticity of demand,[3] the relation of the marginal revenue to the demand schedule may be shown as follows : $\dfrac{d(xy)}{dx} = y + \dfrac{xdy}{dx} = y - \dfrac{y}{\eta}$. If $\eta$ is one or less, there is no marginal revenue and the position is not one of equilibrium. If $\eta$ is infinite, the marginal revenue is equal to the price and the position is that of perfect competition (*i.e.* the demand curve is not downward sloping).

The monopolist extends his sales to the point at which

---

[1] Cf. above, pp. 84-6 and 94-9.

[2] See J. Robinson, *Economics of Imperfect Competition*, p. vii.

[3] Measured by the Marshallian formula $\dfrac{dx}{x} \div -\dfrac{dy}{y}$. Marshall, *Principles of Economics*, 8th ed., p. 839.

marginal cost is equal to marginal revenue. The value of $y$ corresponding to the value of $x$ at the intersection of the marginal cost and marginal revenue curves is the equilibrium monopoly price (see Fig. 1). This technique may well be used in place of that given by Marshall to represent monopolistic equilibrium.[1] It has the advantage of being less cumbrous and of only requiring knowledge of the elasticity and value of the demand curve at the equilibrium point. Moreover it represents perfect competition clearly as being the limiting case of monopoly, viz. when $\eta$ has risen

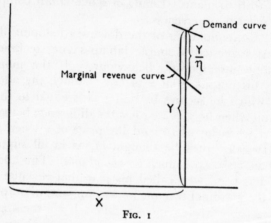

Fig. 1

to infinity. Only in this case will the marginal cost of production be as high as the price.

10. (ii) Next it may be well to define certain concepts in the realms of costs. In the short period it is usual to consider prime costs only. A curve showing the average prime cost per unit of producing $x$ units may be drawn for a certain range of values of $x$. This curve is of parabolic shape, descending in the range of low values of $x$, and later rising. Its shape is deduced from the principle that increasing quantities of some factors of production applied to a fixed quantity of others (the supplementary factors are taken in the short period to be fixed) yield first increasing and then diminishing returns per unit.

[1] *Op. cit.* pp. 479-480.

11. (iii) From the average prime cost curve, a marginal prime cost curve may be deduced by the same formula by which the marginal revenue curve is derived from the demand curve. If the average cost curve is downward sloping, the marginal cost curve lies below it; if the average cost curve is upward sloping, the marginal curve lies above it ($\eta$ then being negative [1]). At the point at which the average prime cost is lowest, it is equal to the marginal prime cost.

12. (iv) Though unusual, it is convenient for this analysis to entertain the concept of a short-period average total cost curve. Since in the short period the amount of fixed equipment is unalterable, the supplementary costs should be represented by a constant, $k$, and the supplementary cost per unit by $\frac{k}{x}$. The average total cost per unit is equal to the average prime cost plus $\frac{k}{x}$. The marginal curve derived from the average total cost curve by the formula for deriving marginal curves will be precisely coincident with the marginal curve derived from the average prime cost per unit. By parity of reasoning it will intersect the average total cost per unit curve at the lowest point of the latter. In other words, for the output at which the average total cost per unit is lowest, the marginal cost is equal to the average total cost per unit. This is the point at which it may be said that the fixed equipment is used at its optimum capacity.

13. (v) A long-period average total cost per unit curve may be drawn. In this case the amount of fixed equipment used is taken to vary as $x$ varies, an appropriate amount always being used. This curve is also of parabolic shape, but for reasons different from those which apply to the short-period curves. The downward slope in the early ranges is due to the increasing economies of large scale which may be utilised as the output of the source expands. The upward slope in the later stages is due to the increasing difficulties

[1] Though the same term, $\eta$, is used and the same formula for $\eta$, in the case of cost as in that of demand, it would be anomalous to call $\eta$ in the former case elasticity of cost.

of co-ordination and control. The universal validity of this second part of the assumption may indeed be challenged; it will appear that it is not necessary to make it in analysing the equilibrium of imperfect competition.

The output for which all economies of large scale can be utilised or all such as do not necessarily entail greater diseconomies of large scale, the output, that is, at which the long-period average total cost per unit curve reaches its lowest point, may be thought of as the optimum output of a source. And the fixed lay-out appropriate to such a scale of output may be thought of as the optimum lay-out.

The concept of a long-period cost curve implies that for any output $x$, the direction foresees that it will have to produce this amount and no other, and provides itself with the amount of lay-out most appropriate to this. In determining what is most appropriate, supplementary and prime costs have to be pitted against each other. For this purpose it is necessary to assume a specific rate of profit on the fixed equipment. The appropriate rate to assume is the lowest rate which constitutes an adequate inducement to the firm itself to invest in fixed equipment. This I shall call the standard rate of profit. It will bear a certain relation to the profit earned on circulating capital, but must contain an additional allowance for the greater element of risk which necessarily attaches to fixed investment. It will also bear some relation to the rate of profit which can be earned by the purchase of industrial shares in the open market bearing a corresponding schedule of risk.

14. (vi) From the long-period average total cost per unit curve a long-period marginal total cost per unit curve may be struck off in the ordinary way. A source will plan to produce on the scale indicated by the intersection of the long-period marginal total cost per unit curve and the prospective marginal revenue curve.

15. (vii) Next, it is necessary to understand the relation between the long-period cost curves and the short-period cost curves. In drawing the short-period average total cost per unit curve it is desirable to estimate $k$ on the basis of a 'standard' rate of profit. For every fixed quantity of lay-out

there is a short-period average total cost per unit parabola. For low values of $x$, as the lay-out is increased, the lowest point of the corresponding parabola is lower than the lowest points of the parabolas indicating costs with smaller fixed lay-out, owing to the economies of large scale. A family of short-period parabolas may be drawn (Fig. 2) with the lowest point of each member below the lowest point of the preceding one.[1]

It might be thought that the long-period average total cost per unit curve was the locus of the lowest points of these

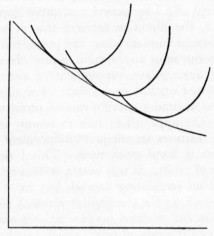

FIG. 2

parabolas. But that is not so. The long-period average total cost of producing $x$ units is the cost at which $x$ units can be produced most cheaply. The lowest cost of producing $x$ units is shown by the lowest point on any member of the family of parabolas for that value of $x$. The locus of these points is not the line joining the lowest points of the parabolas, but the envelope of the family [2] (see Fig. 2). If the

[1] To define this point it is proper to determine it on the principle explained in sections 13 and 15.

[2] Cf. Professor J. Viner, *Zeitschrift für Nationalökonomie*, Bd. III, September 1931, p. 36. The draughtsman, to his argument with whom Professor Viner refers in a footnote, was right in economics as well as in mathematics. Cf. also R. F. Harrod, *Economic Journal*, December 1931, p. 575.

prospective demand is for an output less than such as to employ the optimum lay-out to its optimum capacity, a lay-out less than that of the optimum scale will be employed. Moreover it will not be employed to its optimum capacity. The amount of lay-out indicated as correct by the long-period curve is that, the short-period cost parabola of which is tangential to the long-period curve at that point. If this curve is downward sloping at the point of prospective output, the short-period cost parabola will therefore be downward sloping also, *i.e.* if the demand is what is expected, the lay-out will not be used to its optimum capacity. It is economic in these circumstances to construct a rather more elaborate plant than it is possible to make the best use of.

If two average curves, as in this case, have the same gradient and the same value for a given value of $x$, their corresponding marginal curves will also have the same value for that value of $x$.[1] Consequently the long-period marginal total cost of a given amount of output is equal to the short-period marginal (prime) cost for that amount, when the lay-out has been made on this basis. The prospective output is indicated by the intersection of the long-period marginal cost curve with the marginal revenue curve; the actual output is indicated by the intersection of the marginal prime cost curve and the marginal revenue curve. Since these two marginal cost curves have, as we have shown, the same value for the prospective value of $x$, then, if the marginal revenue curve turns out to occupy the expected position, the actual output will be the same as the prospective output. The long-period total and the short-period total costs will be equal, and the long-period marginal and the short-period marginal costs will be equal also.

But if the actual demand is either greater or less than the prospective demand, the short-period average total cost will be greater than the long-period average total cost; if the demand is greater, the short-period marginal cost will be greater than that of the long period, while, if the demand is somewhat less, the short-period marginal cost will be less than that of the long-period.

[1] This follows from the formula set out in section 9 (i).

In Fig. 3 points $M_1$ and $M_2$ represent possible prospective outputs. The dotted curves are prospective marginal revenue curves, the starred curves are unexpected marginal revenue curves. The LA curve is that of long-period average total cost and the LM curve that of long-period marginal cost. $SA_1$ and $SA_2$ show short-period average total costs if the lay-out is designed for $M_1$ and $M_2$ respectively, and $SM_1$ and $SM_2$ the corresponding short-period marginal costs. For prospective outputs $M_1$ or $M_2$, the value of LA equals

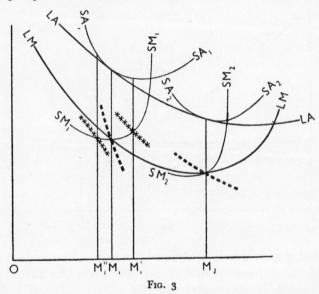

FIG. 3

that of $SA_1$, the value of LM equals that of $SM_1$, the value of LA equals that of $SA_2$ and the value of LM equals that of $SM_2$. But for the output $M'_1$, greater than that expected, the value of $SA_1$ exceeds that of LA and the value of $SM_1$ exceeds that of LM, while for output $M''_1$, less than that expected, $SA_1$ exceeds LA, but $SM_1$ is less than LM.[1]

[1] The gradient of the marginal curve depends on the second differential of the average; since the second differential of the short-period average curve is (arithmetically) less than that of the long-period average curve, the gradient of the short-period marginal curve will also be less than that of the long-period marginal curve; the long-period marginal will therefore intersect the short-period marginal in a downward direction at the equilibrium point.

16. (viii) In conditions of *perfect* competition, the scale of lay-out will tend to the optimum. This depends on the fact that an individual source can produce as much as it wishes without affecting the price of the unit and will tend to produce that amount which it can produce at the cheapest rate. If the business does not pay with the optimum lay-out, it will not pay at all. Fig. 4 represents the long-period equilibrium of a source in perfect competition, earning a standard rate of profit, with output OM, price PM, short-

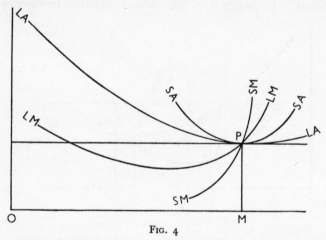

Fig. 4

period marginal cost (SM curve), long-period marginal cost (LM curve), short-period average total cost (SA curve) and long-period average total cost (LA curve) all equal to PM. The marginal revenue which is equal to the price is also equal to PM.

It does not follow that perfectly competitive sources always produce the optimum output. Demand may shift away from the prospective position. If it exceeds what is expected, the plant will be overworked (output $OM_1$ in Fig. 5); if it falls short of what is expected, plant will be used below capacity (output $OM_2$ in Fig. 5). The horizontal lines $D_1$ and $D_2$ show the demand schedules which would cause outputs $OM_1$ and $OM_2$. In the former case profits will exceed the standard rate by a gross amount, $P_1C_1 \times OM_1$, and in the latter case profits will fall short of the standard rate by a gross amount $P_2C_2 \times OM_2$.

Short-period changes in demand will be met by changes in the degree to which a given lay-out is exploited. Long-period changes in demand will be met by changes in the number of separate lay-outs. The word lay-out has been used as the correlative of source and includes immaterial as well as material fixed investment.

If excess profits are earned, new competitors will be attracted. If profits are sub-normal, existing competitors

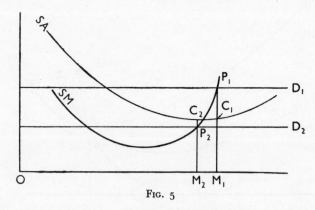

FIG. 5

will tend to be squeezed out. Long-period equilibrium implies a standard rate of profit. It need not be regarded as necessarily excluding the birth and death of particular firms. Marshall's proposition that a *representative* firm must be earning a standard rate of profit seems still to be of value.

In perfect competition a high rate of profit does not normally induce a competitor to increase his lay-out beyond the optimum scale. If he did so, he would be laying himself open to loss. To earn standard profit with an excessive lay-out, it is necessary to receive a price above the competitive level. This high price would attract fresh competitors, whose output would reduce the price back to the competitive level. If, however, some competitors have any *special advantages* in production — and this supposition is not necessarily inconsistent with perfect competition — it may be in their interest to extend their lay-out somewhat beyond what is for them the optimum scale.

17. (ix) In conditions of *imperfect* competition, the position is radically altered, because the downward sloping demand curve may restrict the output of a source even in the long period below the optimum level and because price exceeds marginal revenue.

It may be well to begin by supposing that owing to mere accident the demand schedule for the output of a particular source is such that it is able to use an optimum lay-out to its

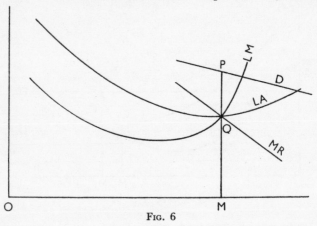

Fig. 6

optimum capacity. In this case the marginal revenue will be equal to the long- (as well as the short-) period average total and marginal costs and the price will exceed them. Consequently an excess rate of profit will be earned. This is shown in Fig. 6, in which the MR curve represents marginal revenue and the D curve price. Output is determined by the intersection of the marginal revenue and the marginal cost curve (Q). By hypothesis (that of optimum output) the average total cost is equal to the marginal cost, and the average total cost (which includes allowance for a standard rate of profit) falls short of the price. Excess profits of a gross amount PQ × OM will be earned.

18. (x) The position indicated by Fig. 6 is, in certain circumstances, consistent with long-period equilibrium.

It must be noticed in the first place that, although the source is earning excess profits, it is not tempted to extend its lay-out. For it is *not* earning excess profits on its marginal lay-out. This is shown by the fact that in this equilibrium, the marginal revenue has the same value as the long-period marginal total cost, which includes an allowance for a standard and not more than a standard rate of profit. Moreover, if the source expanded output, the marginal revenue would fall short of the marginal total cost, and any addition to its existing lay-out would therefore fail to earn the standard rate of profit.

19. (xi) The next question is, will not the spectacle of excess profits earned in a representative source attract fresh competitors and so disturb the equilibrium?

It is impossible to give a general answer to this question. For the answer depends on the details of the market structure which makes competition imperfect. The postulate of imperfection precludes the hypothesis of a new competitor capturing a large part of the existing producers' market by offering its wares at the ruling price or at a price infinitesimally less. A substantial price concession must be made by the new-comer, the more substantial the more he wishes to encroach on existing producers' customers. The encroachment must be considerable if he is to reach the optimum scale of output or even to take sufficient advantage of the economies of large scale to make any production at the standard rate of profit feasible. This being so, new-comers *may* be excluded, even if existing producers are making excess profits.

In that case the condition shown in Fig. 6 will be consistent with long-period equilibrium.

It must be emphasised at this point that the excess profits, shown in Fig. 6, are not a fortuitous phenomenon, but a necessary corollary of the adoption of optimum methods of production in imperfect competition. The surplus exists, if marginal revenue is to cover marginal cost, and cannot be conjured away.

20. (xii) The marginal revenue curve may cut the long-period marginal cost curve further to the right. In

that case the excess of price over average cost will be less, and the source will have a lay-out in excess of the optimum.

It was explained earlier (page 118) that the generalisation that long-period costs tend ultimately to rise, as the output of a source is increased, is not an absolutely safe one. If the cost curve shows constant costs for a long, even for an indefinite, range beyond the point at which the optimum is first reached, the main argument of the text is not affected.

If, on the other hand, costs do rise, and the individual is tempted to expand beyond the optimum point, he may remain in equilibrium; but this is less likely, since the incursion of new competitors, taking care not to over-expand, is more likely to be feasible on a profitable basis.

21. (xiii) On the other hand the marginal revenue curve may cut the marginal cost curve further to the left. In this case the lay-out will be below the optimum scale, and, as explained in para. (vii), it will be worked below optimum capacity.

It may be well to illustrate this with a case in which not more than standard profits are earned. This would represent long-period equilibrium in an industry on the unlikely condition that, in spite of imperfect competition, new competitors can enter the business and find a market as easily as pre-existent sources. In that event profits would tend to a standard level.

This is illustrated in Fig. 7. The long-period marginal cost curve intersects the marginal revenue curve at Q. OM is, therefore, the equilibrium output and MP the price. But, if a standard rate of profit is earned, MP must also be equal to the total cost per unit, which makes allowance for profit at this standard rate. The profit on the marginal lay-out is equal to the average profit on all the lay-out.

If the values of two marginal curves correspondent to two average curves are equal and if the values of the average curves are also equal at that point, the gradients of the average curves must also be equal at that point. It follows that average cost curve and the demand curve are tangential at the point of equilibrium output (P). The long-period and the short-period total cost curves are also tangential at the point and both downward sloping. It follows that in these circumstances the lay-out is of less than the optimum size and that what lay-out there is is not used to optimum capacity. This is a necessary corollary of long-period equilibrium with a standard rate of profits in imperfect competition.

This is the smallest output from a source that is consistent with long-period equilibrium. In the short-period output may, of course, recede further.

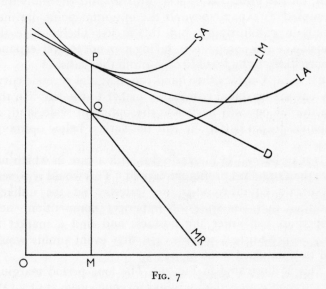

FIG. 7

22. (xiv) To summarise, in conditions of perfect competition, lay-out will tend to be of the optimum size, irrespective of the state of demand. Short-period fluctuations in demand will be met by variations in the degree to which the lay-outs are utilised. Long-period fluctuations in demand will be met by fluctuations in the number of sources.

In conditions of imperfect competition, long-period equilibrium is consistent with lay-outs of less than the optimum size and their exploitation below their optimum capacity. If not more than standard profits are earned in equilibrium, the lay-out *must* be too small and it *must* be worked below capacity. If, on the other hand, optimum conditions of production are achieved, profits *must* be above the standard level. In either case the price will be above the competitive level.

23. (xv) The analysis of imperfect competition may also be extended backwards to the market for factors of production. In perfect competition the supply price of factors is constant for any quantity of them demanded by a source of output. Consequently the price of each factor tends to equality with the increment of value due to it.

It should be noticed in passing that the proposition that the value of each factor tends to equality with its marginal net product is ambiguous. Marginal net product may mean (1) the value of the increment of the physical product due to the employment of the factor at the margin, or (2) the increment of the total value of the output of a source due to the employment of the factor at the margin. In conditions of perfect competition in the marketing of the product, value (1) and value (2) are in fact equal, since the price of the product is equal to the marginal revenue derived from the sale of it. But in conditions of imperfect competition value (2) is less than value (1); and it is to value (2) that the value of the factor tends to be equated.

This tendency to equality is only realised, however, if the market for the factor itself is subject to perfect competition. If a source demanding increasing quantities of a factor is confronted with a rising supply price schedule, a marginal curve may be struck off from the supply price curve by the ordinary formula. The increment of expenditure required to secure the $(x+1)$th unit of a factor of production at a source of output is equal to the price of a unit when $(x+1)$ units are demanded by the source, plus the difference between the price of $x$ units when $x$ units are demanded, and the price of $x$ units when $(x+1)$ units are demanded. This increment of expenditure may be called marginal outlay. It is to the marginal outlay on a factor that the marginal revenue accruing from the employment of that factor tends to be equated and, in conditions of imperfect competition for the factor, this marginal outlay exceeds the price of the factor.

Imperfect competition in the marketing of factors is

probably less widespread than in the marketing of com-modities. It should be observed that the collective bargaining of Trade Unions, Industrial Codes, etc., tend to make the labour market more perfect in the meaning of this analysis, because they substitute a constant supply price schedule of the factor to a particular source of output for a rising supply price schedule. This, as explained below, makes for a more economic distribution of productive resources.

II

24. In the foregoing section I have been concerned with the effects of the existence of imperfect competition on the equilibrium position. In this section I propose briefly to relate these results to the doctrine of the economic optimum.

It may be asserted with confidence that if an individual A can produce two commodities X and Y with equal effort, in the sense that he would undertake of these two jobs the one for which he could get a superior price, and if a second individual B prefers X, in the sense that if X and Y had the same price he would choose to purchase X, then if B is in fact induced by a lower price to purchase Y, the economic optimum is not achieved. This proposition does not imply that it is legitimate to compare the utilities accruing to different individuals with one another. Productive dis-utilities on the side of A are compared by an objective test and found to be equal, and consumptive utilities on the side of B are compared by an objective test and found to be unequal. The machinery of the market ought so to work that A is induced to produce X and not Y for B to consume. If the opposite result in fact occurs, it can be said unequi-vocally that the economic system is in this respect failing to secure the best allocation of productive resources.

25. With the aid of the doctrine of unverified probability the proposition of the last paragraph may be extended. A condition for the best allocation of productive resources is that the prices of various products should be proportional to the cost of producing them within any area in which factors can be freely allocated to the production of various wares.

This means that if there is a unit of productive service applicable alternatively in the production of commodity X or commodity Y, the ratio of the price of X to that of Y should be proportional to the ratio of the number of such units required for the production of X to that required for the production of Y. The various kinds of service employed are not, of course, homogeneous; but the same measuring rod for comparing them with one another should be used in the case of X and of Y. (By the law of comparative costs, this principle can be further extended to demonstrate the optimum kind and degree of trade between areas between which factors are not freely mobile.) Put otherwise, the principle states that productive resources should be so allocated to occupations that their marginal social net products are equal in each.

26. The backbone of the advocacy of *laissez-faire* has been the proposition that if the laws of supply and demand were allowed to operate freely, productive resources would in fact get themselves distributed among occupations in the required manner. Rewards for identical services would tend to be equal in different occupations and the price of each product, which must constitute the sum of the rewards to the productive services embodied in it, would be proportional to the amount of those services required for their production. This in fact happens if the markets for products and the markets for factors of production are both subject to conditions of perfect competition, but not otherwise. It happens if and only if the price of the product is equal to the marginal revenue derived from the sale of it and the supply price of each factor is equal to the marginal outlay upon it. The doctrines of imperfect competition thus make a large breach in the defence of *laissez-faire*.

27. It is, of course, clear that the best distribution of productive resources requires the equation of the marginal and not the average net product of resources in different occupations. And it might be imagined in haste that the equation of marginal revenue to marginal outlay in imperfect competition embodies a nice fulfilment of the marginal principle. But this is not so. For the price itself represents

a marginal quantity, viz. marginal utility, and marginal revenue, in the case of a downward sloping demand curve, is less than price and less, therefore, than marginal utility.

If productive resources are allocated so as to produce equi-marginal revenue in different occupations, they will not yield equi-marginal utility, except in the unlikely event of the demand curves confronting representative sources of supply in different lines of production having equal elasticity.

Similarly the supply price of a factor represents marginal disutility. If different occupations are confronted with supply price schedules of factors having different elasticities, there will be a corresponding distortion of the proper allocation of productive resources away from the optimum.

28. It would be wrong to dismiss the distortion away from the optimum allocation due to imperfect competition as unimportant. It would not be unreasonable to suppose that the injury done is at least as great as that due to the tariff systems of the world. The distorting power of a tariff of 50 per cent *ad valorem* may be compared to that of the presence of finite elasticity in a demand curve equal to 3, a tariff of 20 per cent to an elasticity equal to 6.

29. The moral of this is not, of course, that conditions of perfect competition should be 'restored'. For in most instances such conditions probably never have existed, nor in the nature of the case can exist. But it should render us more sceptical of the benefits of a 'free economy'. Price-fixing by a public authority would have the advantage of providing sources of supply with a horizontal demand curve ; but against this must be set : (i) the great difficulty such an authority would have in determining the cost, to which price should be equated, even if it was thoroughly imbued with true costing principles — which it might well not be ; and (ii) the fact that such a policy would not abolish marketing expenses, the presence of which, though space has forbidden the treatment of them in this article, entails precisely the same consequences and distortions as a downward-sloping demand curve.

But these doctrines do provide a strong case for the fixing of wage rates by public authority or other means, always provided that inequalities of wage rates for similar services are not set up between occupations among which labour would otherwise be fairly mobile.

A word should also be said about the situation that may arise, as described above, in which sources of supply are too many and units of lay-out too small and insufficiently exploited. The compatibility of such conditions with long-period equilibrium, which the theory of imperfect competition demonstrates, might be a valid ground for compulsory 'rationalisation'. If competition were always perfect, the advocate of compulsion would have to rest his case on the superior wisdom of the public authority compared with the profit-seeking individual. But in the case of imperfection he may have stronger grounds. If, in the above-mentioned situation, sources were grouped together, more efficient production would be achieved. This might entail the consequence of greater excess profits; but, since the community as a whole benefits by more efficient production and inequalities of wealth may be redressed by progressive taxation, the balance so far seems to be in favour of compulsory grouping. On the other hand the demand for the product of the group may have less elasticity than the previous demand curves confronting the individuals, and the grouping may thus lead to a larger repression of output of the product below the optimum level. It seems, therefore, that caution should be exercised in the introduction of compulsion, unless the public authority can also authorise a fixed price determined on the basis of cost.

III

30. It is only possible to speak very briefly of the importance of these doctrines for trade cycle theory. I believe this importance to be of the first order, but I shall confine myself to indicating the lines along which more elaborate exploration might be undertaken.

31. Ultimately trade cycle theory is concerned with the conditions which determine the equilibrium of the level of output as a whole in contradistinction to the particular

equilibria of each industry which are determined by the demand and cost conditions of each. In a recession many particular disequilibria may be set up, but the leading characteristic is a general running down of activity. It is the failure to understand precisely what factors determine this general equilibrium of output as a whole that is also responsible for perplexities concerning movements away from it or changes in it.

The key which the doctrines of imperfect competition provide for solving the mystery is that in long-period equilibrium industries may be subject to the law of decreasing costs (in the long *and* short periods).

32. Let us suppose that the economic system consists of two industries each producing one commodity and that in a given long-period equilibrium the cost of production in each may be represented by 1 and the ratio at which the commodities exchange against each other by 1 : 1.

First let us suppose that both the industries are subject to increasing costs of production. Now let it happen that, owing to no change in fundamental conditions (costs or demand), but to some miscalculation, misapprehension or mere chance, one of the industries, A, reduces its rate of output. In accordance with the law of demand, the value of a unit of its output rises in the first instance, and, by the law of increasing costs, the cost of a unit falls, so that the industry comes under a stimulus to re-expand and revert to its old equilibrium position. But let us suppose that before this has time to happen, the other industry, B, adjusts itself to the new position. In accordance with the law of demand industry B will in the first instance be getting a lower price per unit for its product and will be induced to restrict. Supposing that A has not yet re-expanded, how much will B be induced to restrict? There is a given amount of restriction, say *x* units, which, having regard to the elasticities of demand for A and B, will restore the ratio at which A exchanges for B to 1 : 1. If industry B restricted by *x* units the value received by it per unit of its output would be the same as before. The amount by which B will in fact restrict will be something less than *x* units. For, since it is subject to increasing costs, as soon as it begins to restrict, its cost per unit will be lower, and it will not, in consequence, require in the new equilibrium to get as much value per unit of its output as it did at the old level. Consequently it will reach equilibrium before the exchange ratio of A to B reaches 1 : 1, but at some previous point, *e.g.* when the ratio is 9 : 10.

Thus, if A restricts owing to some miscalculation in the first instance and waits, before reverting to its old output, for B to readjust itself to a new equilibrium position, it will still get more units of B per unit of its output than it did in the old equilibrium, say 10 for 9 (*vide supra*) instead of 1 for 1. But costs per unit in A will be lower. This being so and the value received for its product per unit being higher, even after it has given B time to restrict output to a new equilibrium level, it will be subject to a stimulus to re-expand; and when it does this, B will follow in its wake. They will both be tempted to revert to the old equilibrium position.

In other words, the old position of equilibrium will be a stable one. Any fortuitous contraction of either industry may induce a temporary contraction in the other but will set up forces impelling them both to revert to the old position. If they are both subject to increasing costs and if there is no fundamental change in demand or cost conditions, there is no level of output below the old equilibrium at which one or other will not be tempted to re-expand. The same argument applies, *mutatis mutandis*, to an expansion beyond the old equilibrium level. They will then be led to re-contract.

33. Now introduce the supposition that B is subject to decreasing costs. Examine the position in which A has made its original fortuitous contraction and B is considering how far it must restrict in order to adjust itself to the new conditions of the market. It will have to restrict by more than $x$ units. If it restricts by $x$, the price of its product will be the same as before, but its cost per unit higher. To attain equilibrium, it will therefore need to restrict by more than $x$, so as to raise the price of its product above the old equilibrium level, in accordance with its now higher cost.

What is the consequential position of A? When B has reached the new equilibrium, the value of the product of A will be lower than in the old equilibrium. The ratio at which A exchanges for B will not be 1 : 1, but something less favourable to A, say 10 : 9. Cost per unit in A is indeed lower than in the old equilibrium. But it may not be as much as 10 per cent lower. In this case it will be under a stimulus, not to expand, but to contract farther. B will be consequently induced to make a still greater contraction. Thus they may chase each other indefinitely until they chance upon some new equilibrium position at a level of output, which may be much lower than the old one. The old equilibrium will prove not to have been a stable one. The contraction of the decreasing cost industry (B) is likely to be considerably greater than that of A and the ratio of exchange is likely to move in favour of B.

This provides a rational explanation of the relatively greater contraction and relatively smaller fall of prices in industries subject to conditions of imperfect competition in a trade recession.

The argument from a two-industry situation may be extended by like reasoning to the situation in which there are a large number of industries.

So long as the decreasing cost industries are small and unimportant, their presence may not have an appreciable effect on the stability of a given long-period equilibrium. But if they are large and important, stability is *pro tanto* undermined. The relative growth of their importance in the world economy may well have been the principal factor making for an increase in the severity of trade oscillation, first after the industrial revolution, and secondly in very recent times.

34. Professor Pigou has set out very clearly the economics of long-period equilibrium when industries are subect to increasing costs. In view of the first-rate importance of the subject, quotation *in extenso* may be justified. He writes: [1]

A, thinking that B is about to be prosperous and so to exercise an increased real demand for his products, increases his output, and B, dominated by the corresponding thought about A, does

[1] A. C. Pigou, *Industrial Fluctuations*, pp. 77-78.

likewise. These increased outputs, created in error though they are, nevertheless constitute increased reciprocal demands for one another. Therefore, the argument runs, the fact of A's error causes A so to act that B's error becomes the truth ; and the fact of B's error causes B so to act that A's error becomes the truth. The fact that *all* expectations have been false causes *each* expectation to be true ! This reasoning, paradoxical as it is in form, is not obviously fallacious in substance. It is, however, in fact, fallacious. The nature of the fallacy involved can be set out as follows. It is perfectly true that an increase in the output of A, however caused, makes worth while some increase in the output of B. . . . The two false expectations jointly create for one another *some* justification, but not a *sufficient* justification. This can easily be proved. The general laws of demand inform us that A will be prepared to offer a lower real price per unit for B's goods the larger the quantity offered becomes ; and that B will stand in a like relation to A's goods. Hence if A thinks that B is going to offer twice his normal supply of goods, A will reply by producing, not twice his normal supply, but, say, one and a half times his normal supply ; and B, under the influence of a similar opinion about A, will act in the same way. Hence, both A and B, as a result of their false opinions, produce one and a half times their normal output. But, *ex hypothesi*, A is willing to give one and a half times his normal output in exchange, not for one and a half times, but for twice B's normal output ; and B is in like case. Hence, the error of the one, though it makes the error of the other less glaring than it would otherwise be, does not convert it into a truth. A and B are both disappointed and both find that their expansion of output was a mistake. The situation is exactly similar if each of A and B falsely expects the other to contract his output, and contracts his own in consequence.

This passage describes the economics of a stable equilibrium with admirable lucidity. But the limiting condition that the two industries must be subject to the laws of increasing costs is not stated. Indeed the expression 'the general laws of demand inform us' suggests that the description is not intended to be so limited but to have general validity. Such a suggestion is not illegitimate, if it is tacitly assumed, as has been customary in traditional economics, that industries are in perfect competition. For in that case they are subject to increasing costs in the short period (and usually to constant costs in the long). But, once it is assumed that an industry is as likely as not to be subject to imperfect competition, the postulate of increasing costs must be discarded for purposes of generalisation, and Professor Pigou's analysis becomes inapplicable to the economic system as a whole.

35. Recognition of the prevalence of decreasing costs makes a radical difference to our interpretation of the psychological theory of the trade cycle, to which Professor Pigou has himself made such an important contribution. So long as the equilibrium of output as a whole is regarded as stable, departures from it in one direction by conjoint action are essentially connected with the prevalence of *error*. The error is explained by an abnormal psychological condition. The continuance of a recession or over-expansion depends on the persistence of error. Once the error is clearly seen, the departure from the long-period position of stability is corrected. Other factors may indeed supervene upon the psychological one and be responsible for a longer duration of the departure than the psychological factor would alone account for. But to that extent the explanation of the cycle ceases to be a psychological one.

If, on the other hand, imperfect competition, decreasing costs and the absence of a stable equilibrium in the general level of output as a whole are recognised, the psychological theory becomes a valid explanation of trade cycle phenomena without reference to error at all. There being various levels at which, if industries attain them conjointly, they will be in equilibrium with one another, a depressed mentality leads to the choice of a lower instead of a higher level. The lower level is as rational as the higher one. Provided that a number of producers are depressed and recognise the existence of depression in each other, rational choice demands restriction by each. Nor do they subsequently recognise that their action was erroneous, for they attain an equilibrium at the new level and are under no stimulus to re-expand.

Or, if error is to play any part in the theory, it may be used to account for the initial step. One downward step having been taken by one individual or a group of individuals from error, the rest follows for logical and not psychological reasons. On this explanation error may be called in as a *deus ex machina* to explain the original impetus to a movement; thereafter its services can be dispensed with. While, if perfect competition is postulated, the *deus ex machina* has to be maintained in operation, until the reverse movement begins. The prolonged persistence of these errors is surely an unreasonable hypothesis.

It might be claimed that the hypothesis of persistent error is justified because it accounts for the subsequent reversal of the downward or upward movement. Against this it may be urged : (i) that neither form of the psychological theory claims to preclude all other factors making for oscillation ; and (ii) that on the hypothesis of unstable equilibrium the fortuitous occurrence of an error may, after the new temporary equilibrium has been reached, set up the reverse movement.

36. The significance of the doctrine of imperfect competition for trade cycle theory has been but briefly sketched. It seems that a wide field is open for further enquiry and analysis.

# THEORY OF IMPERFECT COMPETITION REVISED

THREE interconnected problems will be discussed in the following pages.

1. Are any of the doctrines of imperfect competition, as now generally accepted, insecurely based on the premises from which they purport to be derived?

2. Does empirical evidence suggest that entrepreneurs fail to any important degree to act under the pure motive of profit maximisation which the theory of imperfect competition assumes?

3. To what extent does the conduct of entrepreneurs in conditions of imperfect competition cause a maldistribution of productive resources as among their various employments?

The words 'doctrines of imperfect competition, as now generally accepted' need a gloss. In the last twenty years there has been much specialist writing on this topic. This has focused attention on many complexities inherent in the facts analysed and introduced new refinements of analysis. It cannot be said that in the process the conclusions have become more clear-cut; rather the contrary. An expert might raise the question whether there are now any 'generally accepted' doctrines.

The words in point are intended to refer not so much to these specialist writers as to the general body of economists, especially of the younger generation. The two great works on the subject, by Mrs. Robinson and Professor Chamberlin, made a strong impact on the minds of economists; certain broad conclusions seemed to have been successfully established and have come to constitute part of the mental furniture of most economists; they have even had some influence on thinking, if not on action, in regard to public policy.[1] The fact that specialist work has tended to show that the questions at issue are more difficult and doubtful than at first appeared has not substantially changed the position; the original conclusions continue to be accepted as rough approximations, subject no doubt to many qualifications; it seems better to work with these, however rough they may be, than to revert to earlier doctrines that are clearly false. They will tend to hold their place until better workable approximations of nearly equivalent simplicity are substituted for them.

I

## *Doctrine of Excess Capacity*

My first task is to submit that one of these rough approximations, which has played quite a notable part in the non-specialist literature, is altogether wrong, and should cease to be used by economists as a working assumption. I refer to the alleged tendency of conditions of imperfect competition regularly to give rise to the creation of excess capacity, especially when there is relative freedom of entry into the business. I do not wish to imply that such a tendency is never operative. In Essay 3 on this subject (see page 84 above) I gave reasons for holding that 'long-period equilibrium is compatible with there being too many sources, that is, too many centres with a core of permanent equipment, and every one or many of these centres working below their optimum capacity'. I see no reason to question the validity of the arguments (concerning *decreasing cost conditions*) that led to this conclusion. But the scope for this phenomenon, as there defined, is far narrower than that suggested by the arguments later developed by Mrs. Robinson and Professor Chamberlin, and the reasons for it brought forward by me are quite different from theirs.

[1] With all due apologies to Professor Chamberlin, I use the expression 'imperfect competition' in a broad sense, to comprehend some of the phenomena, for which he thinks the words 'monopolistic completion' a better description.

I would further concede that the tendency may occasionally operate outside the scope originally defined by me, but strongly challenge the view that it normally operates where there is imperfect competition and free entry. Considered as a roughly approximative account of what usually happens in such circumstances, it appears to me to be wrong.

The fact that Mrs. Robinson and Professor Chamberlin, working independently, approaching the same problem from different points of view and using different tools of analysis, reached the same conclusion in regard to excess capacity was singularly impressive. They both held that, in the normal course of events, firms in imperfect competition would find equilibrium at a point where their total cost curve had the same downward slope as the demand curve with which they were confronted (point of tangency); as this total cost curve must become horizontal at the point of the optimum use of the available equipment, production only up to a point at which the short-period total cost curve still had a sizable downward slope would clearly mean production well below that for which the plant was best suited. In the conspectus of the doctrines of imperfect competition which I wrote after studying these two treatises (pages 111-38 above) I incorporated this finding, albeit not without misgiving. I did not hold that this would be the normal position of equilibrium, but that it was a possible position only 'on the *unlikely* (italics not in original) condition that, in spite of imperfect competition, new competitors can enter the business and find a market as easily as pre-existent sources'. These words show that my misgivings in regard to this doctrine centred on the doubt whether 'free entry' was an appropriate assumption in the case of imperfect competition.

At this point I must burden the reader with a short digression on Mrs. Robinson's views. For the purpose of drawing a total cost curve it is needful to incorporate some figure for normal profit per unit of output. She chose to define normal profit as a rate of profit just high enough to attract (or, what is the same thing, not to attract) new entrants.[1] Thus there might be a rampant monopolist, well secured, who is able to obtain a very high rate of profit without fear of challenge; yet there must be some point at which even he, if sufficiently exorbitant in his charges, will eventually provoke competition. It is at this high level of profit that, according to Mrs. Robinson's definition, he is earning a 'normal' profit. This inflation of profit, if I may so call it, alters the shape of his total cost curve. Postulating a very high rate of profit on his fixed capital as 'normal' raises the amount of fixed cost that has to be spread over the output in computing total cost and causes the total cost curve to slope downwards over a much bigger range of output than it would if a more modest profit rate had been used in making the computation. Take the case of a monopolist who, if 'normal' profit is defined in a more modest way, is working his plant to optimum capacity, viz. at the point when total cost, including a normal profit per unit of capital, is at its lowest, and enjoying in addition to this normal profit a surplus monopoly profit His position is shown in Fig. 6 on page 124 above. But if his surplus profit, which he is able to continue to enjoy owing to the difficulty of others entering into competition with him, is reckoned as part of his 'normal' profit, then the diagram representing his position is automatically transformed into Fig. 7 on page 127; this inflation of normal profit and the inclusion of the high rate of profit as part of his cost makes it look as if he were using his plant below its optimum capacity. This is a mere trick. If we are concerned to show how imperfect competition may cause a waste of productive resources, it is most important to represent the monopolist as using his plant to full capacity and making a surplus profit (as in Fig. 6) and not as using his plant below capacity and earning a normal profit.

[1] In the article which challenged the utility of this definition of normal profit (printed on pp. 103-7 above), I made play with the fact that she stated that 'if profits are more than normal, new firms will tend to enter the industry, and if profits are less than normal, firms will tend to leave the industry'. I observed on this that normal profit so defined would not be a unique rate of profit but a wide range of possible rates. In the present text, however, I have not drawn attention to this weakness in Mrs. Robinson's definition, since it seems irrelevant to the matter in hand.

It was for this reason, among others, that I felt it needful, in controversy with Mrs. Robinson, to define normal profit in a different way and not simply as that profit, however high, which would, in circumstances however monopolistic, just not attract new entrants into the business. I chose to define it as the rate of profit which the entrepreneur would himself deem just sufficient in considering whether or not to undertake an extension of his plant. This is explained in the essay printed on pages 103-7 above.

This surely brings us back to the common-sense position that where there is free entry profit tends to be reduced to the normal level as defined by me, but that where there is not free entry a monopoly profit may be earned. The existence and amount of the monopolist's equilibrium profit thus depends, not on the slope of the demand curve with which he is confronted, but on the amount of impediment there is to the entry of rivals into competition with him. The possibility of monopoly profit when there are impediments to competitive rivals is old-established doctrine, in no wise dependent on the special analysis of 'imperfect competition'. One proviso must be made. Profit may stand above the normal level as defined without being such as to attract new entrants and without representing a monopolistic position, if it is the result of superior efficiency. This point should be borne in mind throughout the following analysis.

What in connexion with imperfect competition we have now to consider is whether, when there is free or relatively free entry, there is a tendency towards the creation of excess capacity and whether that tendency is stronger the more steeply downward sloping is the demand curve with which the individual source of supply is confronted. Under the influence of Mrs. Robinson and Professor Chamberlin I tended to acquiesce in the view that there is such a tendency, and focused my doubts on the question whether free entry would often be the correct assumption.

Subsequent study has not confirmed those doubts. This is a question of fact, not of analysis, and it is therefore proper to give weight to the testimony of practical persons. While field enquiry fully confirms the view that imperfect competition is widely prevalent, if not omnipresent, throughout the field of manufacturing industry, a lively fear of the possibility of the incursion of new entrants, should excessive prices be charged by those already producing a certain article, is very widespread. While there are many cases of fairly securely established monopolistic (or oligopolistic) positions, in the majority of cases it seems to be assumed that sustained high prices will attract new entrants. (An exception must be made for periods of continuing inflation.)

Mr. P. W. S. Andrews, who has recently been doing most valuable work in this field, has brought an important point into prominence. Having regard to the difficulties in modern conditions confronting one who would establish a new business on a large scale — and large scale is needed for production at a competitive price in many lines — some economists have been inclined to doubt whether it is easy for new entrants to come into business at all readily. Mr. Andrews has stressed the point that the 'new entrant' may often, indeed usually, be an existing firm which is induced to take on a line of production hitherto new to it. Most firms produce a number of products. It is comparatively easy for an established firm, with its permanent cadre of management in existence, its buying and selling organisation and its attachment of skilled and unskilled labour, to switch part of its organisation, which may only be a small part, to producing an article not before produced by it, and to do so on a scale quite adequate to secure the necessary cheapness of production. Sometimes this may simply be due to the firm's vexation at having to pay an undue price for a component that it needs. More often it is due to a vigilant look-out for profitable ways of expanding its operations. Its attention may first be drawn to a new profitable line by some fortuitous event in the course of its business dealings; accident plays some part in determining the direction of expansion of firms; it may accordingly decide to take on a new side-line. What begins as a side-line sometimes becomes the main line of a firm's output. Entrepreneurs usually have the notion that there is no lack of potential rivals, should they expose themselves by charging an unduly high price.

If the possibility of the relatively free entry of rivals is fairly widespread, it is clearly expedient to examine, with the sharpest tools available, the doctrine that this free entry tends, in conditions of imperfect competition, to create excess capacity.

In this connexion attention should be drawn to an article by Dr. Kaldor, published in *Economica* in February 1935, which challenged the excess capacity doctrine. Part of that article contains a line of thought which I now propose to develop.

The analysis of imperfect competition, beginning with the short period, postulates a source of supply having a given quantity of fixed equipment. This being given and known, it is able (in theory) to draw its own short-period marginal cost curve; it ascertains the point at which this intersects the marginal revenue curve with which it is confronted; it decides to produce a volume of output corresponding to this point of intersection, and charges a price which will secure the sale of that amount of output. This price may often exceed the total cost of production per unit, including normal profit, for that amount of output. Thus at this price the firm makes a surplus profit. If this position is typical, *i.e.* if the firm does not enjoy any advantages peculiar to itself, and if other firms act in a similar manner, new entrants are likely to come into this line of production — for free entry is the case we are considering. The increased supply thereby generated tends to reduce the price at which each and every firm can market a given volume of output of this kind; the particular demand curve confronting each such firm is pushed to the left and its marginal revenue curve also; this process continues until surplus profit is eliminated and with it the stimulus to new entrants. In this equilibrium position each firm, or perhaps we should say, the representative firm, makes no more than a normal profit. It is still guided in its output and pricing policy by the intersection of its short-period marginal cost curve and the marginal revenue curve with which it is confronted. This point will have moved to the left in consequence of the arrival of new competitors; the new price is exactly equal — by definition of the equilibrium — to total cost including normal profit per unit. The double condition thus required for equilibrium in these conditions that marginal cost is equal to marginal revenue, and that total cost, including normal profit, is equal to price, is satisfied when the demand curve with which the particular source of supply is confronted is tangential to its total cost curve (see Fig. 7 above). If the particular demand curve is downward sloping, as we suppose, the total cost curve of the firm must have a downward gradient. Whether before the incursion of the new competitors the firm in question was or was not producing to optimum capacity, it will certainly not be doing so in the new equilibrium; it will be further removed from its optimum capacity than it was before. Thus although the representative firm is not earning more than a normal profit, the supply to the consumer will be unduly restricted, in relation to the welfare optimum, and the price will be unduly high. The representative firm will be loading into its price an unduly high cost since, the volume of output being reduced in relation to optimum capacity, overheads cannot be so widely spread; but by hypothesis they are covered and a normal profit on capital earned. Since the representative firm and presumably the majority of the others are working below capacity, it can be said that there are too many firms in relation to the output that is being produced. The consumers are having to pay for an unnecessarily large amount of overheads in all. This is one of what I have called the 'generally accepted doctrines' of imperfect competition. It is deemed to apply wherever there is free entry and to a less degree when the impediments to new entrants are not severe.

*Prima facie* this seems a dubious story. It essentially depends on the decision of the firm, when in its initial position, to limit its output to the point at which the short-period marginal cost curve intersects the marginal revenue curve, and to charge a price appropriate to that decision. Even at this stage of the analysis we may ask whether a firm would think this the right thing to do. If aware of no advantage peculiar to itself, it must regard the prospect of maintaining its market at this price as likely to be short-lived (as 'accepted doctrine' deems that it in fact is). By charging the high price it forgoes the present opportunity of establishing itself in a somewhat larger market, and thus deliberately makes its position weaker for the time when it has to face the incursion of new entrants. Surely it will rather seek immediately to entrench itself in as large a market as it profitably can. But if the representative firm does this, the feared incursion of new entrants will not take place, and each firm will be able to retain its original market.

The case against supposing such a line of policy, which would seem to be the prudent one, may be put as follows. To take, for the sake of argument, the strong case of absolutely free entry, a firm has the following choice. If it is to entrench itself firmly in available markets before new competitors arrive, it must confine itself to a normal rate of profit. If, on the other hand, it charges a higher price, it can make a surplus profit while the sun is shining, and later, after its own market has been invaded by new entrants, it will enjoy a normal profit on its capital. Thus by one line of action it can only make a normal rate of profit on its capital throughout, while by the other it can make a surplus profit for an initial period and a normal rate of profit on its capital thereafter. Consequently, it is suggested, it will make more profit in total by the high pricing policy.

This is the argument, but it surely carries little weight. By all accounts and on all hypotheses, the future is largely uncertain. No firm, which is interested in a certain line of production, wishes to sacrifice markets available to it for the sake of a fleeting surplus profit. Such a sacrifice will tend to make it weaker in facing the various contingencies of an unforeseeable future. I submit that any experienced man of business would pronounce it most 'unsound' to make a temporary surplus profit by charging a high price at which it is known that sales are unlikely to be capable of being maintained in the long run. It is surely wrong for economists to insist, on the basis of a partial theory, that this is none the less what entrepreneurs normally do.

It is not in conflict with this conclusion to suppose that

there may be occasions on which entrepreneurs can and do seize a short-lived surplus profit. We are now concerned with the doctrines of excess capacity. The market conditions may temporarily be such that entrepreneurs can *safely* charge prices well above their costs including normal profit, safely in the sense that the temporary prevalence of such profits will *not* attract new competitors. A general willingness to snatch surplus profits that is confined to such cases has by hypothesis no tendency to create excess capacity. In times of persistent inflation, open or suppressed, this opportunity may be fairly protracted.

The argument against the tendency to excess capacity can be greatly strengthened, if we take a somewhat more extensive view. In the foregoing analysis the amount of fixed equipment was taken to be an unalterable datum in the situation, and the marginal cost curve was deemed to be computed by reference to it. But fixed equipment has to be created, and the intentions of the entrepreneur at the moment when he decides to make such equipment must be brought into the picture.

One must not regard most fixed equipment — though it is true of some — as having been created once and for all in a remote past, when the present was still shrouded in a thick mist of uncertainty. In most firms the existing fixed equipment has been built up by stages, with replacements made from time to time as deemed expedient. At each stage careful consideration is given to the use to which such extra plant will be put. What is the nature of such consideration?

The 'accepted doctrine' of imperfect competition is as follows. The entrepreneur assesses the marginal revenue curve with which he will be confronted; he also estimates his long-period marginal cost curve. Let $x$ stand for the amount of output indicated by the intersection of these curves. He will choose to install the amount of fixed equipment at which he can produce $x$ units most cheaply, using a normal rate of profit in computing and comparing the overhead costs required for each amount of output. The long-period marginal cost (which includes overheads and profit) of producing $x$ units will be identical with the short-period marginal cost of producing $x$ units. (Once the equipment is made, the short-period marginal cost of producing an amount other than $x$ will be higher than the longer period marginal cost.) The entrepreneur is deemed to contemplate that, when he has the equipment ready, he will, if the market conditions are precisely what he expected they would be, charge a price that enables him to sell $x$ units, neither more nor less. This price may be substantially higher than the cost per unit, including normal profit, of producing $x$ units. He will then become subject to the pressures of new competitors, which will prevent his maintaining such a surplus profit in the long run. And he will only be able to obtain a normal profit by producing less output than that for which his capacity was designed.

What I have so far set out is the 'accepted doctrine'. But has it not an internal inconsistency? If the entrepreneur foresees the trend of events, which will in due course limit his profitable output to $x - y$ units, why not plan to have a plant that will produce $x - y$ units most cheaply, rather than encumber himself with excess capacity? To plan a plant for producing $x$ units, while knowing that it will only be possible to maintain an output of $x - y$ units, is surely to suffer from schizophrenia.

What, then, should he plan to do? To have a plant which gives him the lowest cost of production per unit for $x - y$ units only? Thereby he would save a futile waste of capital outlay and make a bigger profit on the $x - y$ units to which he finally settles down, than he could if he had a plant designed to produce $x$. This, however, will not save him from inconsistency, if he persists in the maxim of equating short-period marginal cost to marginal revenue; if he does this, he will charge a price that cannot be sustained in the long run without loss of market. As his market shrinks, he will find thereafter that he can only profitably sell $x - y - z$ units. This argument may be extended to show that, however small the plant he designs, he will always be pushed backwards, so that it will be redundant. Apparently it is impossible to be an entrepreneur and not suffer from schizophrenia!

It must by now have become plain that the radical flaw lies in the way in which the equation of marginal cost to marginal revenue has been interpreted. It is necessary to have a consistent integrated concept of the entrepreneur's plan in regard to the plant he creates and the pricing policy that he will adopt when he has obtained it. The whole of the foregoing argument implies that the entrepreneur pays attention only to the *short-period* marginal revenue. But when he plans his plant the concept of *long-period* marginal revenue is indispensable. In planning his plant he certainly has in mind long-period marginal cost (viz. cost including overheads and normal profit) and he must relate this to long-period marginal revenue, viz. the proceeds that he can hope to get during the expected life of the plant, to the best of his ability to calculate them, having regard among other things to potential competition. The radical mistake is in assuming that as soon as he has his plant he forgets about long-period marginal revenue. In fact when he has the plant, he will continue to adapt his pricing policy to the potentialities of long-period marginal revenue.

There is an asymmetry here, which is probably at the root of the confusion. Once the plant is constructed, long-period marginal cost is irrelevant, since the decision to have the plant is irreversible; short-period marginal cost is the sole guide for policy. But the difference between short-period marginal revenue and long-period marginal revenue relates to the future and long-period considerations on the demand side remain just as relevant to day-to-day pricing policy, after the plant has been constructed as it was before. What the entrepreneur has to consider is not what the revenue is that he can get by fully exploiting the situation to-day or this week, but what the revenue is that he can get and maintain. He must have had this longer period in view on the supply side in deciding on the size of plant; he should equally have had it in view on the demand side and should retain it in view on that side if he is to avoid the charge of schizophrenia. Long-period marginal revenue, relating to any given price, is the revenue which will continue to accrue in response to that price. If a price is charged that new competitors can undercut, the loss of potential revenue due to the consequent loss of market must be subtracted from the immediate revenue yielded by the price charged.

The long-period demand curve has greater elasticity than the short-period curve, just as the long-period cost curve has less slope than the short-period curves. Consequently the long-period marginal revenue curve will cut all the cost curves at points further to the right than does the short-period marginal revenue curve; consequently the entrepreneur will plan to have a *larger* fixed equipment, if he has regard to the long-period marginal revenue curve, than he would if he had regard to the short-period marginal revenue curve.

The conclusion is that, if there is free or relatively free entry, the entrepreneur, if he is to avoid schizophrenia, will plan to charge a price yielding only a normal profit, save to the extent that he is aware of possessing an advantage peculiar to himself, will plan to have equipment on a scale that gives the lowest cost for producing what he can sell at such a price, and, having acquired the equipment, will sell at that price, even although the short-period marginal revenue yielded by such a policy is less than the marginal cost. The equipment required for this policy will be larger and the price charged lower, and nearer (though not necessarily equal to) the social optimum than those entailed by 'accepted doctrine'.

It is to be observed that the foregoing reasoning does not imply that an individual entrepreneur can himself by his own pricing policy affect the appearance or non-appearance of new competitors, *i.e.* the analysis does not imply oligopoly. If he pursues a prudent pricing policy and his existing competitors do not, his individual action will not prevent the arrival of new competitors, and this may damage him. But what he can do to mitigate the ill effects of the short-sighted policies of his competitors is by charging a low price from the beginning, to make his own market less vulnerable. It is of the essence of imperfect competition that the markets of each firm are subject to separate influences.

But the analysis takes us further than this. If the considerations which I have set out are those which would normally actuate an entrepreneur in his investment and pricing policy, we can conceive of the representative entrepreneur being so actuated. But if the representative entrepreneur is so actuated, new competitors will not normally appear. Thus no excess capacity will be created.

This conclusion is derived exclusively from theoretical premises. No support has had to be drawn from the testimony of entrepreneurs about what in fact they do. It is theoretically proper that an entrepreneur should consider long-period marginal revenue in deciding on the size of his plant, since the plant is expected to have a long life in this sense. It is theoretically correct that, even after his plant is constructed, he should in his pricing policy continue to have regard to long-period marginal revenue.

I conclude that there is no foundation in theory for the view that imperfect competition combined with free entry usually tends to create excess capacity. I make an exception for the special case referred to on page 84 and page 140 above. No one, I believe, claims that imperfect competition without free entry usually tends to create excess capacity. Consequently we may conclude that imperfect competition does not usually tend to create excess capacity. Economists should therefore discard the 'generally accepted' doctrine to the contrary effect.

The doctrines of imperfect competition were developed rather rapidly in the years from 1930. A number of important British industries had for a considerable time been suffering from excess capacity for some special reasons that are well known. After 1929 most industries in the world were suffering from excess capacity owing to the world slump. It is possible that this particular doctrine of imperfect competition (viz. its tendency to excess capacity) was accepted more readily than it would otherwise have been, because any additional explanation of an evil so widespread was apt to the times and therefore assimilable. It does not follow that the explanation provided was correct. Sufficient explanations of the excess capacity present in those years may be derived from other considerations.

The foregoing theory has assumed that entrepreneurs are able to calculate long-period marginal revenue. Very great practical difficulties beset any attempt to calculate short-period marginal revenue. These difficulties would have to be considered very seriously, if we retained the assumption on which the previously 'accepted' doctrine, now rejected, was based, viz. that entrepreneurs use a calculated short-period marginal revenue in determining their investment and pricing policies. It might be supposed that it would be no less difficult to calculate long-period marginal revenue. This matter will be dealt with in the next section.

One further point remains to be considered before we finally dismiss the doctrine of excess capacity. It might be objected that the foregoing argument assumes that entrepreneurs know to what extent a given price will make their market vulnerable to new competitors, whereas in fact they have no such knowledge. It may be admitted that their opinions on this matter may be little more than 'hunches'.

It has been much debated to what extent equilibrium theorists should assume knowledge on the part of the individual. In some cases the matter is easily settled. Many future developments, *e.g.* technological changes, are in principle unforeseeable, and in these cases the correct assumption is ignorance. The theory of profit rests essentially on this assumption. At the other extreme one might cite the case of an arbitrageur. He has certain quotations before him and can readily calculate that by effecting two or more operations he can make a clear gain. The economist can quite safely assume that he acts accordingly. If it were in fact theoretically proper for entrepreneurs in the circumstances envisaged to relate policy to the value of short-period marginal revenue — but we have shown that it is *not* — this would be a borderline case.

It is to be stressed that the great majority of entrepreneurs have scarcely any knowledge about the value of short-period marginal revenue. This applies even to those who conduct intensive market research. There appear to be few cases in which an entrepreneur could decide with confidence whether a drop in price of 10 per cent would cause, other things being equal, an increase of sales of 10 per cent or 15 per cent or 20 per cent. While there might be a vague opinion that the increase of sales would not be likely to lie far outside these limits, there might be complete uncertainty as between 10 per cent and 20 per cent. Yet this would make the difference between a marginal revenue consisting of a loss per unit of one-ninth of the price and a positive marginal revenue consisting of four-ninths of the price. No little difference.

The prevalence of ignorance in regard to short-period marginal revenue is commonly understood. It is not as well appreciated that ignorance in regard to short-period marginal cost, while not quite so devastating, is great enough to make fine calculation impossible. Fig. 1 provides what may be regarded as a typical realistic marginal cost curve.

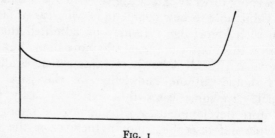

Fig. 1

About the range in which the line runs horizontally there may be fairly good knowledge. This is the cost accountants' direct cost. If the theorist, however, insists on including Keynes's 'user cost' in short-period marginal cost, the computation of it becomes much more complicated and probably impracticable. But imperfect competition analysis is mainly concerned with the range in which the curve is moving upwards. About the values in this range the entrepreneur is very much in the dark. The rise is due to sundry bottle-necks and breakdowns that occur when the plant is working near its maximum capacity. The entrepreneur will be lucky if he gets a precise account at the end of a period of the extra direct costs due to high-pressure working. It is most unlikely that he will be able to translate that information into a curve giving the true values of marginal cost as a function of the level of output. This problem is immensely more complicated in the usual case of a multi-product firm, since there is then the problem of imputing the high pressure to the various products. To make an approximate prognostication of the upward slope of the curve would be still more difficult.

In this kind of case the theorist is inclined to assume that the entrepreneur will, despite his ignorance, somehow gravitate, by hunches, by trial and error, even by the survival of the fittest, to the highest profit position. In certain circumstances, when nothing better is available, such an assumption may have its uses. A sharp distinction, however, should always be drawn between an equilibrium which will be reached through the use of knowledge that actually exists, as in the case of arbitrageurs, and an equilibrium which will only be achieved on the more doubtful assumption that trial and error will be an adequate substitute for knowledge.

We now turn back to the question whether it is proper to assume that entrepreneurs usually know, when it is in fact true, that prices above a certain level will render their markets vulnerable to new competitors, and also whether it is proper to assume that they will base their pricing policy on this knowledge. Theorists of excess capacity postulate that certain prices will in fact make markets vulnerable to new entrants. The question is whether it is proper to assume that entrepreneurs will also perceive the likelihood of this development and shape their pricing policy by reference to it. These same theorists are content to assume that entrepreneurs tend to act as they would if they knew the values of short-period marginal revenue and cost, although in fact they have not this knowledge; then surely they ought, by parity of methodological procedure, to assume that the entrepreneurs will act as though they knew the extent to which a certain price is likely to make their markets vulnerable to new entrants, whether they have this knowledge or not.

Whether it is proper to assume that in the absence of full knowledge entrepreneurs tend by inscrutable processes towards the position they would take up if they had this knowledge, may depend on how complete and blank their ignorance in fact is. Now how complete their ignorance is on any topic is a question of fact; the theorist, as such, has no special qualifications for assessing the degree of ignorance. On such a point it may therefore be appropriate to question a sample of entrepreneurs.

At this the fur of the theorists tends to rise and they become cynical and indignant. 'The entrepreneurs', they cry, 'do not understand what they do or why they do it.' This attitude may be appropriate in certain cases. If entrepreneurs claim to adopt a policy which the theorist can indeed show to be likely to involve loss, it is proper to consider carefully whether the entrepreneur may not be deceiving himself or failing to understand all the bearings of the type of action he claims to be describing, or even have a sinister motive for deceiving his questioner. But in the case in point, namely how ignorant entrepreneurs normally are about certain classes of fact, such a sceptical attitude about their testimony is quite out of order.

The vast majority of entrepreneurs claim that they are completely ignorant about the value of short-period marginal revenue — when the meaning of that esoteric expression has been explained to them — and that they do not, because they cannot, act by reference to it. They often express a wish that they did know it; they would give much money for the information, but are aware of no means of obtaining it. *Per contra* they usually claim that they have a very good idea, although not of course precise knowledge, about the extent to which a given price is likely to render a market vulnerable to new competitors, and that they are continually adapting their policy in the light of their opinions on this matter.

The theoretical exponents of the doctrine of excess capacity assume that entrepreneurs tend to act as though they knew the value of short-period marginal revenue; the entrepreneurs on the whole claim that their ignorance of its value is blank and deny conscious adaptation of policy by conjectures about that value. These same exponents assume that the entrepreneurs do not act as if they had knowledge about the long-run vulnerability of a given price; the entrepreneurs usually claim that they do have shrewd and fairly reliable ideas on this topic and are constantly guiding their policy in the light of them.

We may conclude that the particular combination of two assumptions by which the doctrine of the tendency to excess capacity is reached is perverse. It assumes that entrepreneurs know, or, lacking knowledge, strive to base their policy decisions on their best guess about matters in regard to which they deny having knowledge or basing their decisions on their best guess; it assumes that they are ignorant and do not strive to base their policy decisions on their best guess about matters, in regard to which they deny that they are ignorant and affirm that they do base their policy decisions on such knowledge as they have. Accordingly the doctrine of excess capacity may be finally rejected.

II

## Full Cost Principle

Among the British entrepreneurs interviewed by the Oxford Economists Research group, a majority explained that they were normally in the habit of arriving at prices of their products for quotation by assessing their direct cost and average overhead cost of production, including in the latter, or by making a further addition to it, a proportionate share of the overhead costs of the firm and some allowance for profit. I define this procedure as adhering to the full cost principle.[1] It cannot be claimed that this rule was adopted by all or that those who adopted it did so rigidly or without sometimes departing from it. The testimony was, however, such that one could fairly say, by way of rough approximation, that this is the most usual procedure in British manufacturing business.

The economist lays down that in fixing a price with a view to maximising profit overhead cost is an irrelevant

---

[1] This does not imply that the entrepreneur always gets his full cost; all depends on the market and on the procedure for determining the average overheads, for which see p. 165 below.

consideration; on the cost side all that need be taken into account in pricing is short-period marginal cost. Attention must also be paid to marginal revenue so as to determine how far above marginal cost to fix the price. This should be done so as to limit sales to the amount of product indicated by the intersection of the marginal cost and marginal revenue curves. This price may be above direct plus average overhead cost or, in adverse circumstances, below it. An entrepreneur, it is claimed, cannot do better for himself than charge such a price and will suffer needless sacrifice of profit or needless additional loss if he fails to do so.

The marginal principle must in general be accepted as correct.

If entrepreneurs habitually adopt another criterion in pricing, it appears at first sight that they must make a needless sacrifice of gain, and this, it is claimed, is hardly to be believed. Does it follow that there is something wrong in the entrepreneurial testimony? It is not to be dismissed lightly. It is necessary to examine how the 'full cost' principle works out by reference to a variety of possible cases.

In the following pages, which profess to give a realistic, although, of course, greatly over-simplified, account of entrepreneurial behaviour, it is assumed that the producer fixes his own price for quotation. This contrasts with perfect competition where the price is fixed in an organised market. This assumption may seem to jar with a situation which, though probably not obtaining in the majority of cases, is very typical and widespread. Entrepreneurs often claim that although there is no organised market and sales have to be promoted through the firm's own channels or by advertisement, none the less the market does dictate a price from which the entrepreneur will deviate at his peril. This does not mean that he can sell any amount he pleases at that price, as with perfect competition; far from it. This seems to imply that the producer is doubly a prisoner, both as to the price he must charge and the amount he can sell. But in fact he has room for manœuvre in two respects, namely, in the quality of the article which he offers at the price imposed on him and, in certain cases, in his expenditure on selling. I do not propose to examine the causes or consequences of this type of case. My object is to concentrate on the full cost principle and to consider its consequences both for the normal equilibrium position and for deviations from the social optimum, and, in order to do so, I shall assume that the entrepreneur has the liberty to quote his own price. I suggest that the same consequences would emerge if, instead of assuming that the entrepreneur decides what he wants to produce and bases his price on the full cost of producing it, we assume that he accepts a ruling market price for a certain general kind of article and then decides what quality of article he can produce at that price so as to cover his full cost. In both cases the intention to sell at approximately full cost is the actuating principle governing his size of plant and pricing policy. The following arguments should apply *mutatis mutandis* to the case where the entrepreneur has to accept a market price. In the real world situations may be a subtle blend of the two types distinguished above. The entrepreneur may begin with an idea of the article he would like to produce and then, having assessed his full cost, modify his idea somewhat if the price looks unsuitable. I return to the variety of possible cases.

First we take the class of cases where the entrepreneur anticipates that there will be absolutely free entry and that he will have no special advantage in production compared with representative competitors. He then has to anticipate that if he plans to charge and does charge a price which gives him more than a normal profit — save in consequence of superior efficiency — he will render himself vulnerable to new competitors and his projected output will not continue to be sellable at the projected price. Within this class we take the case where the condition of the market is identical with that anticipated when it was decided to install the fixed equipment.

In order to decide on his proper size of plant, the entrepreneur, basing himself on the full cost principle, cannot avoid considering the various prices which he would get and the various costs he would incur, according to whether he plans to operate on a smaller or larger scale; to arrive at a correct decision about the right size of plant he cannot avoid having to compare these two sets of quantities, a set of prices and a set of costs. In principle he has to solve two simultaneous equations (cost as function of amount produced and sales as a function of price) ; no doubt the matter is not usually so formally schematised in his mind, and his solutions can only be approximate. He may have fairly accurate data about the various costs. It is to be noted that the rate of the upward slope of the short-period marginal cost curve, which is so difficult to determine and would present an intractable problem to anyone having to compute the values of a short-period marginal cost curve in this range of it, will not greatly affect the slope of the long-period curve, with which alone he is (on any theory) concerned when deciding on the scale of equipment. He will be hazy about demand and make the best guess he can. Again it is to be noted that this uncertainty will not reduce him to the impasse of one who had to compute short-period marginal revenue. A mistaken estimate of prospective demand of 10 per cent either way will prove no great disaster. A similar mistake made in the calculation of short-period marginal revenue might easily show that revenue to be two or three times greater than it really is.

It would not be reasonable for an entrepreneur to assume, when he orders fixed plant, that he will be producing a given fixed amount of output per unit of time throughout the life of the plant. He will anticipate fluctuations and may also anticipate a growth of orders at a given price with the mere procession of time. The latter point will be especially important, if he is putting forth a new product.

For the purpose of a simplified analysis we may assume that he plans a plant which will give the cheapest possible cost for the mean quantity per unit of time that he anticipates producing, which I shall call $x_e$. It is in this sense that I shall refer in what follows to his plant having been designed to produce $x_e$ units. It should be noticed that, if his output is subject to the law of increasing returns, the plant that produces $x_e$ units most cheaply would produce a larger number of units more cheaply (see Fig. 2 on page 100 above).

If, when he has produced his plant, the market proves to

be what he had expected when he planned it, he will be able to quote a price that covers his overhead costs and gives a normal profit — more if he has superior efficiency — and be able to sell on average, taking good times and bad, $x_e$ units per unit of time.

Now this price at which he can sell $x_e$ units is in fact an equilibrium one. There is no need for him to refer to short-period marginal cost or marginal revenue. It does not follow that the doctrine of equalising these marginal values is invalid. It so happens that in the circumstances of free entry — which may be frequent in the realm of imperfect competition — he can find a shorter and more manageable way of reaching the same result as he would if he could assess these elusive quantities, as I must now explain.

The proposition is that if he raises the price appreciably above direct plus overhead cost he will render his market vulnerable; the demand for his own product will recede in due course and he will finally be driven back to a position of lower output at which he can make no more profit on his capital than he could if he had been content to charge a 'full cost' price for $x_e$ units. It is true that he might for a brief interval enjoy a higher rate of profit. It is assumed, in accordance with the arguments of the foregoing pages (pages 146-8), that he will not choose to do this (i) because he will be in a weaker position to meet the uncertainties of the future if in consequence of snatching a temporary profit he only maintains thereafter a regular market for $x_e - y$ units instead of one for $x_e$ units, and (ii) because, had he intended to allow this recession of market to happen he would never have wasted his capital on plant designed to produce as many as $x_e$ units. Accordingly it is assumed that he will think any restriction of output involving a backward movement along the demand curve from the position of producing $x_e$ units disadvantageous to himself. This may be expressed by drawing a long-period demand curve, which takes account of the vulnerability of his market if he charges a higher price. This long-period demand curve is flatter than the short-period demand curve.

If the entrepreneur plans as I have suggested, he must

anticipate that at a price covering full cost the long-period demand curve has a value $x_e$. During the life of the plant the short-period demand curve will move to and fro; its average value at the anticipated price will also be $x_e$, if the market proves to be what was anticipated.

If it is assumed that any backward movement up the short-period demand curve from $x_e$, which would be entailed by charging a higher price, is disadvantageous in the long run, it follows that the long-period demand curve does not rise to the left of $x_e$ above the long-period cost. Nor does it rise to the right above the long-period cost. If it did so, the entrepreneur would have planned a higher output than $x_e$. Therefore at the level of output $x_e$ the long-period demand curve is tangential to the long-period cost curve; therefore it is also tangential to the short-period cost curve, since these are tangential to one another at $x_e$. Therefore at $x_e$ the long-period marginal revenue curve and the short-period marginal cost curve will intersect at $x_e$. Therefore $x_e$ is the true equilibrium level of output. So long, therefore, as we are subject to the proviso that the entrepreneur dare not charge a price above full cost without rendering his market vulnerable, the 'full cost' criterion gives the same answer as the marginal criterion. The difference is that the former provides a practicable criterion for calculation, while the latter does not. But it is important to show that the latter criterion is also fulfilled, for, if it were not, the entrepreneur would always be tending to move away from the price yielded by the former, however practical for purposes of calculation it might be.

Thus we have to come to a new form of a doctrine of equilibrium in which the demand curve is tangential to the full cost curve. But in this situation equilibrium does not entail the presence of excess capacity. The old doctrine was partial and, as it turns out, incorrect, because it considered pricing policy in isolation from investment policy. The new doctrine rests on an integrated theory of investment and pricing policy.

The new doctrine, in this not differing from the old, is schematic, and thereby gives a simplified picture of a complex reality. It need not be denied that there is often much jiggery-pokery in the fixing of prices. It is only claimed that our account provides the best approximation to the truth at the level of simplification inevitable in this kind of analysis.

While so far only one sub-class of cases has been investigated, it is important to observe that it is one of central importance. If the full cost principle of pricing is valid in this sub-class, then it should occupy a leading place in any general exposition of the theory of imperfect competition.

We must next turn to the cases where the market deviates from expectation, so that if the planned price is charged, more or less than $x_e$ units will be sold.

Before proceeding it may be well to emphasise the point that there is often a strong bias in favour of maintaining a stable price in the face of changes that are not too great. I do not refer to the reasons represented in the famous Hall-Hitch kinked demand curve. These have their importance, but it is not needful for me to go over the ground so well explored by those authors. Their argument implies some degree of oligopoly, a matter with which I am not directly concerned.

I refer rather to the maintenance of good-will, which is important in imperfect competition. This militates both against an upward movement of price and also against a downward movement, if it is anticipated that this may have to be followed by an upward movement later; thus it militates against any short-period change in price, unless this can be justified by some public event, such as the change in the price of an important raw material or, notably, a change of excise duty. It must be admitted that this constancy of price is sometimes only a façade. An entrepreneur may adapt himself to a change of circumstances by reducing the quality, or, it is to be hoped, on appropriate occasions, by improving the quality of his commodity, and this is equivalent to a price change.

Still greater emphasis should be placed on the need for maintaining a uniform mode of arriving at a price quotation. Some manufacturers have to get out catalogues at intervals quoting prices for thousands of items; others have to answer enquiries relating to a large variety of items each with its own particular specification. Fairly simple rules for arriving at a quotation are indispensable. It need hardly be repeated that it would be impossible for an office in fixing the prices of a large number of items to make a full marginal analysis in each case — if indeed that were possible at all. The marginal cost of each item depends on the amount produced and thereby on the price and thereby on the marginal cost of every other. If there were a thousand items in regular production, this would involve solving two thousand simultaneous equations — and the correct coefficients in them are often not exactly known — to arrive at the price of any one. A simpler procedure has to be adopted. It is no use complaining of this as being a mere 'ritual'. Some ritual there must be, and it is up to the objector to a particular ritual to state what other he proposes to put in its place. Reference to marginal cost and marginal revenue is not a feasible procedure in practice. Furthermore it is highly useful to the economic theorist to know what rituals are commonly adopted, since this will assist him in his analysis. Of course if it can be shown that in certain circumstances the full cost principle has a systematic bias against the most profitable policy, then it is reasonable to expect that entrepreneurs will modify the rule in those circumstances, presumably by the substitution of a somewhat different ritual. It is not a valid complaint against any particular ritual that it does not in each case give precisely the right answer. Any loss resulting therefrom might well be small compared with the loss due to the chaos that would ensue if there were no ritual at all. To neglect the fact that a ritual is and has to be adopted in many cases would show just as serious a lack of realism on the part of a theorist as if he were to assume that all markets were perfect.

One further point must be made in connexion with the need for a ritual. Direct cost is usually precisely ascertainable over the range where the short-period marginal cost is running horizontally, but only very roughly, if at all, in the range where the short-period marginal cost curve is rising. True oncost, by which I mean the proportionate share of all overheads to be attributed to one unit, depends on the volume of output. This in turn depends on the price charged. We are brought back to the simultaneous equations that had in principle to be solved, however roughly, when the decision to install plant was made. One may assume a mental process roughly equivalent to solving the equations to take place on the occasion of decisions to install new plant. If the market proceeds to fluctuate thereafter, some simpler procedure, even if it is of the nature of a ritual, may be preferred to reiterated attempts to solve these equations.

Entrepreneurs, testifying to the Oxford economists, described their varying methods of deciding on the volume of output to be used in calculating oncost per unit; most of these had what theorists would regard as a 'ritualistic' flavour. One stated — and his practice was not widely dissimilar from that of the others — that he had a standing rule by which, for purposes of calculating oncost, it was assumed that his plant would be working to 80 per cent of capacity. If 100 per cent of capacity is taken to be the point of cheapest output per unit,[1] beyond which short-period marginal cost per unit rises above total cost per unit, 80 per cent of capacity might well represent a level of output not far removed from $x_e$, viz. the level of output for which the plant was designed. If this were so, this entrepreneur could be regarded as one who, in the face of moderate fluctuations of demand, calculated cost per unit on the assumption that he would produce $x_e$ units. One might at least say of his attitude that it was not altogether untypical. This formula may be regarded as a ritualistic modification of the full cost principle *stricto sensu*. More generally it may be said that entrepreneurs are not ready to modify their oncost percentage in response to small changes of output. This may be linked with the fact that $x_e$ is not conceived as a level at which output will run steadily, but rather as the mean value of a range of fluctuating outputs. If this anticipation is correct and the entrepreneur calculates his oncost on the basis of $x_e$, he will be charging a true oncost, taking good times with

[1] Cf. p. 100 above. It may often be that the point of cheapest output is somewhat less than the official 100 per cent capacity.

bad, and neither jeopardising his hold on his market on the one hand nor running into loss on the other.

We may now consider more closely the range of output between $x_e$ and 100 per cent of capacity, as defined by me.

In this range full cost *stricto sensu* is falling gently. This decline may be too nice a point to be considered at all in the rough-and-tumble of price-fixing. It is to be noted that the decline of full cost in this whole range (from $x_e$ to 100 per cent of capacity) is not so great as the difference between total overheads divided into 100 units and total overheads divided into 80 units, since in at least part of this range the decline in overheads per unit is partly offset by the rise in short-period marginal costs per unit. All the arguments in favour of a stable price will make the entrepreneur reluctant to make the fine change called for by a strict interpretation of the full cost principle.

There are further reasons. It seems on the face of it somewhat against nature to reduce a price at once in the face of an unexpected increase in demand. There is reason for this. If demand at the old price is carrying sales above $x_e$ units, there is danger that further stimulation of them by price-lowering may carry demand into the range beyond 100 per cent of capacity and this is attended with great difficulties, shortly to be explained.

If it is believed that the increase of demand is temporary only, the entrepreneur will not fear that the small surplus profit due to maintaining a stable price and over-covering overheads will stimulate new entrants. If, on the other hand, it is believed that the increase is permanent, he will already be planning an increase of equipment If he is subject to increasing returns, he will then contemplate the possibility of a substantial lowering of price when he has the equipment in. He will be likely to await this opportunity of making a sizable price reduction, in accordance with his ritual, rather than make a small reduction which may stimulate demand beyond the point at which he is ready to meet it.

I conclude that the entrepreneur is not likely to depart from the price appropriate to $x_e$ units in the range between $x$

units and 100 per cent of capacity; this means that he will continue to apply the full cost principle as slightly modified by 'ritual'. This range of output is, in normal times, an important one in the sense that actual output will often lie within it. If the full cost principle holds within it, this reinforces the case for affirming that importance should be attached to that principle.

Beyond 100 per cent of capacity, short-period marginal costs are likely to rise steeply. It is to be noticed that in this range the prices determined by the various criteria stand in a different order from that which they do in the lower ranges of output. Up to 100 per cent of capacity, the price indicated by the pure principle of equating short-period marginal cost to short-period marginal revenue is usually the highest, the full cost price comes next and the social optimum price is the lowest. Beyond 100 per cent of capacity, the social optimum price (= marginal cost) moves above the full cost price. A point may come when the short-period marginal cost curve begins to rise vertically — nothing more at all can be extracted out of the existing equipment. Then the price indicated by the intersection of short-period marginal cost and short-period marginal revenue and social optimum price become identical; it is in fact simply a question of producing the greatest possible amount and charging a price high enough to clear the market. But a partly 'ritualistic' full cost price may remain below the other two. While we must suppose that even the most conservative entrepreneur will tend to let his price move upwards, he may hold it well below the level indicated by the intersection of the demand and supply curves, whether marginal or average. How, then, can he satisfy the market?

He may establish a waiting list. He may continue to charge a price below that required for short-period market equilibrium, and delay delivery to his customers. Waiting lists have been widespread since 1939. They suffice to prove that entrepreneurs do not always or even usually base their prices on short-period considerations alone. In certain cases there may have been price controls or profiteering legislation rendering the prices required for market equilibrium illegal. But the phenomenon is too prevalent for this explanation to suffice. Entrepreneurs have in many cases deliberately preferred a conservative pricing policy.

Fear of competition is a two-edged argument in this connexion. High prices might stimulate competition; but so also might the waiting lists, if rivals could acquire the necessary materials and machines. I have no analysis to offer in regard to this choice, but merely note the low-pricing policy as a fact.

The social welfare criterion is not unambiguously on the side of high prices. Waiting lists, by allowing available supplies to go where the need is less great, cause a deviation from the optimum position; where the articles are components in a further productive process, the lists may gravely reduce productive efficiency. But there is a social argument on the other side. High prices have a tendency, not shared by waiting lists, to cause a 'spiral' of wages and prices. It may be often a nice point whether the admitted evils of suppressed inflation (waiting lists) are or are not greater than that involved in the danger of spiralling. To proceed further with these considerations relating to an inflationary situation would take me away from the matters with which we are primarily concerned in the analysis of imperfect competition.

Outputs below $x_e$ must next be studied. It is to be observed that while the full cost pricing principle may be regarded as a 'ritual', it is one which in the case first chosen for consideration (free entry and demand proving to be that expected when the plant was installed) gives precisely the right answer, viz. the price required by the intersection of the long-period marginal revenue curve and the short-period marginal cost curve. Onto the ritual of full cost pricing entrepreneurs have some tendency to impose a further ritual, already described; they do not re-calculate the oncost percentage for every moderate fluctuation in their own output, but have some tendency to maintain a stable percentage. If they took the full cost ritual literally, *i.e.* without superimposing a further ritual, they would lower prices as short-period demand increased and raise them as short-period demand weakened. This they do not normally do. We have already considered what is done in the range above $x_e$. What happens below?

It is commonly observed that manufacturers often reduce prices when a recession occurs. This does not necessarily mean that they reduce the oncost percentage. If the recession is part of a general slump, raw material prices will be falling and this fall will be transmitted to semi-processed components. The prices of these components and of fully processed articles may fall in accordance with the full cost principle, not because the oncost percentage has been reduced, but owing to the reduction in direct costs. In what follows, in order to concentrate on the oncost percentage, I shall assume that direct costs remain constant.

When the market recedes, so that $x_e$ units can no longer be sold at the previous price, the need to render markets invulnerable to new entrants becomes less prominent and the struggle to avoid loss (or the shrinkage of profit below normal) more so. One would therefore expect the full cost principle to give way to short-period marginal considerations, obscure though these may be.

Experience suggests, however, that the full cost principle, as ritualistically modified in the way already described, is maintained in the face of moderate recessions in demand, and only gives way in the face of very severe recessions. There is a good theoretical explanation of this phenomenon, which may most easily be shown diagrammatically.

In the figure on page 170 a price $y$ is charged in normal times in accordance with the full cost principle, and $x$ units are sold. Short-period marginal revenue (Q) is below the marginal cost of $x$ units (but long-period marginal revenue is not, owing to the long-period demand curve, not here represented, being flatter than the short-period demand curve, and tangential to the full cost curve). The dotted lines represent the short-period demand and marginal revenue curves after a recession in the market. If the price is maintained at $y$, $(x - a)$ units can be sold at that price; short-period marginal revenue (at R) will still be below short-period marginal cost (at S); therefore short-period marginal considerations call for no reduction in price below $y$.

Demand must recede much further before the marginal cost exceeds short-period marginal revenue at the amount of output corresponding to $y$ on the demand curve. This situation will be expedited, however, if during the recession the short-period demand curve gets flatter [1] and the marginal revenue curve is raised in consequence. Once this situation is reached, short-period marginal revenue becomes all-important. The fact that short-period considerations do not call for a reduction of price for a range of outputs below $x_e$ is the

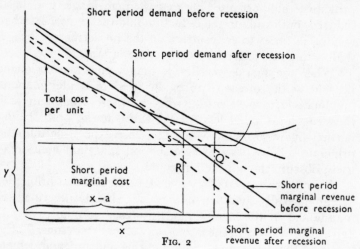

Fig. 2

direct and necessary consequence of the short-period demand curve having been steeper than the long-period demand curve at $x_e$ and the previous price having been adapted to the latter.

Thus, theory suggests that the full cost principle gives a good working approximation for the policy required for profit maximisation in the lower range, except in the case of a very severe depression in the firm's market. This seems to accord with experience. In moderate recessions the entrepreneur maintains his normal pricing procedure; only when facing loss does he reconsider his oncost percentage; he then takes short-period marginal considerations into account and willy-nilly has to have resort to guesswork as regards short-period marginal revenue, being prepared, at

[1] See R. F. Harrod, *Trade Cycle*, pp. 15-21.

the worst, to move his price downwards towards short-period marginal cost.

Thus in regard to the whole field where there is free entry (and the case of nearly free entry may be assimilated to this), it seems that the full cost principle may be justified on analytic grounds in times of normal or fairly normal business, but that deviations may be expected where there is a very big departure of the market from the level for which the fixed equipment was designed.

We now have to turn to the different case where there is no free entry. We lack a vocabulary that is both well-established and appropriate. I believe that it is not appropriate — *pace* Professor Chamberlin — to apply the word monopolistic in a field in which the producer dare not continue for a substantial period to earn a profit above normal (allowing, however, reasonable limits of tolerance, including a margin for superior efficiency) for fear of provoking competition. An exception must be allowed, of course, for a period of continuing inflation. I believe it would be more conformable to what is ordinarily understood by monopoly to confine the use of that word to conditions in which there is not free entry. I shall do so in what follows.

When there is free entry, investment policy and pricing policy, in so far as these are governed by demand, depend on long-period considerations. Where there are hindrances to new entrants, long-period considerations must still play a part, but there is more scope for short-period considerations to have influence. In this case, long-period considerations provide a belt of indeterminary within which short-period considerations may operate. The entrepreneur will not undertake investment if the likely return is below a certain level; if there is free entry, this minimum return is also the maximum for which he dares plan, although with good management he may get something more; he is imprisoned by potential competition and dare not deliberately aim at a surplus profit. If there are obstructions to entry, on the other hand, there is a higher rate of profit at which he may feel that he can aim without courting danger. For instance, he may regard 5 per cent net profit on turnover as the minimum rate which would make an investment worth undertaking, while believing that he could safely take 25 per cent without the slightest danger that a new competitor would enter the business. Twenty-five per cent is available to him, so far as competitive considerations are concerned. It does not follow that he will be able to get 25 per cent, for the short-period demand curve and its correspondent marginal revenue curve may be such that he cannot by any methods of expansion or restriction get more than 10 per cent. In this case the short-period considerations would be those effectively limiting his price.

The situation might be the opposite of this. If the short-period demand was fairly inelastic, he might find that he could easily charge a price and get sales yielding 40 per cent on his turnover; but he would not go for this, since, although he has greater freedom than the entrepreneur where there is free entry, who dare not plan for more than 5 per cent, he may reckon that it is unsafe even for him to charge a price yielding more than 25 per cent. In this case he, like the entrepreneur working where there is free entry, is ultimately governed in his pricing policy by long-term considerations.

Thus if there are hindrances to entry, pricing policy may be governed either by short-term considerations (short-period marginal revenue) or by long-period considerations (danger of market being invaded by new competitors). The entrepreneur would confine himself to the maximum return governed by either set of considerations, whichever is lower; he cannot get more than the short-period situation allows and would be unwise to get more than the long-period considerations allow.

It would seem natural to use the expression 'degree of monopoly' for the size of the impediment to the appearance of competitors to a given entrepreneur; this 'degree of monopoly' would be measured by the rate of profit that could be safely earned without provoking competition; with free entry the degree of monopoly thus defined would be zero, whatever the slope of the particular short-period demand curve. Refining, one might refer to this as the 'degree of potential monopoly', and use the expression 'degree of actual monopoly' for the profit that could in fact be earned in a certain market having regard to the short-period marginal revenue curve; in the long period the degree of actual monopoly could not be greater than the degree of potential monopoly, but it could continue for a long period to be less.

We may now consider how the monopolistic competitor stands in relation to the full cost principle. Whatever calculations he may choose to make in regard to short-period marginal cost, it is needful for him to estimate his full cost, in order to guide his policy in the face of potential competition. The surplus which may, if it rises too high, attract new entrants is not the surplus of price over marginal cost but the surplus of receipts over full cost, for it is on this latter surplus that the potential new entrant has his eye fixed; he will have to incur full costs if he is to come in.

Thus the monopolistic competitor will need to establish the value of his own full cost, in order to assess the price which gives the greatest surplus above full cost that he dare allow to accrue to himself. If the market is such that he is able to secure such a surplus in full, he need pay no regard to marginal revenue. He can get the highest surplus that he dare get in view of long-period considerations; it would be as foolish for him as for the entrepreneur subject to free entry to aim at a short-period rate of surplus above this level.

But it may be that the market does not allow him to enjoy so high a surplus as the maximum that his safety from new competitors would allow him to enjoy. In this case short-period considerations, which may be schematised in the marginal revenue curve, will be the limiting factor. He may have a very vague idea as to the precise values of the short-period marginal revenue curve. That curve gives formal expression to the restraining influence of the elasticity of demand, when it prevents a monopolist charging so high a price as he might, if he only had to consider the limit where new entrants would begin to be attracted.

In the whole of the foregoing analysis the short-period marginal revenue has appeared as the governing consideration in two sets of circumstances : (i) where there is free entry and market demand is far below that anticipated when the fixed plant was ordered, and (ii) where there are impediments to entry sufficiently great to make short-period considerations impose a lower limit to price than that provided by the fear of eventual competition. The latter case is the modern version of the hoary principle that the elasticity of market demand may protect the consumer from the worst excesses of the monopolist.

One final point, which is important, must be made in this context. All entrepreneurs, even those enjoying a considerable degree of potential monopoly, have in mind the vast uncertainties of a relatively distant future. The best method of insuring against them is to attach to oneself by ties of goodwill as large a market as possible as quickly as possible. If one can get a substantially larger market by earning no more than a normal profit than one could get by earning a surplus profit — even without fear of attracting new competitors — one may well choose to do the former, as an insurance against future uncertainties. Paradoxically the producer in imperfect competition is more anxious to expand his market than the producer in perfect competition ; the latter knows that an unlimited market will always be there, good or bad, independently of how much he markets now. Marketing a large quantity now at a questionable profit will in itself bring in no future return ; the entrepreneur in perfect competition should therefore be most careful at no time to let his marginal cost exceed the price. But for the imperfect competitor present sales improve future prospects and have their own importance on this account. This uncertainty in regard to the future is always operative in tempering the price policy of those in imperfect competition, including those in monopolistic competition.

### III

#### *Increasing Returns*

The 'Law of Increasing Returns' played an important part in the origins of thought about imperfect competition ;

there may have been some tendency more recently to give it less attention than it should have in this connexion.

Alfred Marshall and Professor Pigou both held that in a competitive economy the output of articles produced in conditions of increasing returns would be below the social optimum. This doctrine led to the quest for a sharper analysis of the equilibrium position under increasing returns. This matter was brought to a head by the famous article of Mr. P. Sraffa which roundly declared that increasing returns were incompatible with competitive equilibrium. There were also older problems raised by the marginal productivity formulations of the eighteen-seventies concerning the distribution of the product of a firm among the factors of productions, and these had not been solved to the satisfaction of economists.

The marginal revenue concept provided a double clarification, first in respect to the possibility of equilibrium under increasing returns, and secondly in respect to the distribution of the product among the factors.

1. A distinction was drawn between perfect competition, when each producer could sell as much of his product as he wished at a price quite independent of the volume of his own supply, and imperfect competition, when the sales outlets were so organised that this was not possible. Product differentiation was stressed as one of the factors which made the achievement of perfect competition difficult or impossible. Under perfect competition marginal revenue would be equal to the price, but under imperfect competition less. Recently there has been some tendency to multiply the conditions required for the concept of perfect competition; this has led to confusion. Until the very recent growth of organised restriction schemes, most food and raw materials in the world — a sizable part of total production — were produced in conditions of perfect competition. The area in which perfect competition operates is still important and may well become more so in future. Perfect competition may continue even if there are subsidies or other forms of government interference — all depending on the modes of operation of the interferences. It has been vexatiously

suggested that perfect competition implies complete knowledge and foresight.[1] On the contrary, uncertainty about the future is usually greater in conditions of perfect competition than in those of imperfect competition, and fluctuations between profit and loss — the specific rewards and penalties of uncertainty-bearing — are often greater in the former sphere.

Increasing returns are compatible with imperfect, but not with perfect, competition.

There has been a tendency, having taken perfect competition as the limit in which the particular demand curve is horizontal and the marginal revenue curve coincident with it, to class together all other cases as to some extent monopolistic, the degree of monopoly being measured inversely by the elasticity of the particular short-period demand curve confronting the firm. I suggest that this is unfortunate.

2. The second problem in regard to which the marginal revenue concept yielded clarification concerns the distribution of the product among the factors when increasing returns are present. If the reward of each factor is equal to its marginal product, will the whole product be divided among the factors without residue, plus or minus? If returns are diminishing or constant, it can be shown with the aid of appropriate concepts of rent and profit that the product will under the marginal productivity principle be divided without residue. But if there are increasing returns and each factor is to be paid at the rate of its marginal product, there will be over-payment to the factors and the entrepreneur must make a steady loss. (This is precisely the loss which public enterprises are now exhorted by some to incur.) But entrepreneurs are not usually willing to continue to make steady losses. Professor G. Cassel, no doubt with this problem in mind, boldly declared that, in conditions of increasing returns, the price would be equated not to the marginal but to the average cost.[2] Such an unexplained

[1] It is to be noted that Professor Chamberlin uses perfect competition for this unrealised and unrealisable state of affairs, reserving 'pure' competition for the frequently realised and practically important state of affairs which I have designated perfect competition in the text. I justify this because perfect competition so defined is the alternative possibility to imperfect competition.

[2] *Theory of Social Economy*, p. 101.

abrogation of the marginal principle is not acceptable. The marginal revenue concept satisfactorily solves this problem.[1] The entrepreneur recoups his loss out of the excess of price over marginal revenue.

I now wish to focus attention upon the conditions in which imperfect competition distorts the level of output away from the optimum. It is ancient doctrine that, where a monopolist or semi-monopolist secures a steady monopoly profit, output is unduly restricted. This doctrine is supported and clarified by the imperfect competition analysis and is not to be challenged. It may be worth, however, restating the point made at the conclusion of the second section above,[2] that the uncertainties of the future have a tendency to restrain the monopolist from raising his price much above a competitive level, even if all known factors indicate that he could do so with safety.

Further to this ancient doctrine, we have, prior to the elaboration of imperfect competition theory, the position held by Marshall and Professor Pigou that the output of industries subject to increasing returns will tend to be restricted below the optimum level. I believe this position also to be correct.

Next we must squarely face the question whether the existence of a downward-sloping particular short-period demand curve provides an independent cause, additional to those already specified, for a distortion of output away from the optimum. I believe it to be widely supposed that it does, but that this belief is due to confusion of thought, and that there is no such additional independent cause of distortion.

It may at once be objected that I have posed a meaningless question, on the ground that wherever there is a downward-sloping particular short-period demand curve for a firm's output there must be some degree of monopoly and that this admittedly causes distortion. On this view the doctrine of imperfect competition does not provide a new independent cause of distortion, but gives a schematic account of the cause resident in monopoly (or quasi-monopoly)

---

[1] Cf. pp. 93-6 above.      [2] P. 174.

itself, and also points to this monopoly cause being far more pervasive than was previously supposed. For since the whole of manufacturing industry and most of the services of distribution are confronted with downward-sloping particular short-period demand curves, the distortions due to monopoly must be correspondingly widespread. This position I do not accept.

It is needful to revert to the distinction between the cases where the entry of new competitors is free and those in which it is not. The latter cases fall naturally within the concept of monopoly (or quasi-monopoly) as entertained prior to the doctrines of imperfect competition. Now in the early literature of imperfect competition it is, I believe, commonly implied that the downward-sloping particular short-period demand curve will always cause a distortion of the level of output away from the optimum position, whether there is free entry or not. If this were correct then we should indeed have a new additional cause of distortion, for the older traditional doctrine did not contemplate any distortion occurring save where there was restricted entry.

It is easy to understand why initially it was supposed that the downward-sloping particular short-period demand curve would give rise to distortion, whether there was free entry or not. For, according to this initial doctrine, a downward-sloping particular demand curve would in conditions of free entry give rise to the creation of excess capacity in accordance with the principles discussed in the first section of this essay. Given a downward-sloping particular demand curve, there would, with restricted entry, be distortion on ordinary monopolistic principles, and, with free entry, there would be distortion owing to the inevitable tendency to the creation of excess capacity.

But, if we discard the doctrine of the tendency to excess capacity, a radical revision of the doctrine of distortion is needed by way of corollary.

I have already suggested that the expression monopolistic competition should be confined to cases where there are substantial impediments to new entrants. If imperfect competition is used for all cases other than perfect competition, as appears to be logical, we have no commonly accepted expression for the cases of imperfect competition with free entry. 'Free competition' is an expression often used in popular literature, and it might be convenient to adapt this for technical purposes. It would be natural to use it for all cases where there is unrestricted (or relatively unrestricted) entry, and these would be divided into those of free competition with a perfect market and those of free competition with an imperfect market (downward-sloping short-period particular demand curve). There would then be an overlap between free competition and imperfect perfection — which is not necessarily objectionable — both applying to the sphere in which there is free entry but imperfect markets. It is to this sphere, which may be a very important one, that I will now direct attention.

It has been noted that increasing returns in equilibrium and perfect competition are incompatible; but constant returns and imperfect competition are quite compatible (and probably frequent). I hold that with increasing returns at an existing equilibrium position — this implies a downward-sloping short-period particular downward demand curve — output will be restricted below the social optimum, in accordance with the doctrine of Marshall and Professor Pigou. I further hold that, with constant returns in equilibrium and a downward-sloping short-period particular demand curve, output will normally attain the social optimum level. This last proposition is, I believe, in conflict with doctrine that has become current since the formulation of imperfect competition theory.

I assume that if there is free entry the entrepreneur will plan to fix his price — except after a large unexpected fluctuation of the market — at his full cost, and that he will plan to have a plant of the size best adapted to the sales expected at such a price. It is needful to pay particular attention to the long-period average and marginal cost curves.

In the figure on page 180 I have drawn a long-period average cost curve which does not eventually slope upwards. There has been some controversy about this eventual upward slope. It is quite possible that, even if there is an eventual upward slope, the long-period curve has a flat bottom for a considerable range of output, and it is not necessary for our purpose to go beyond this.

If the entrepreneur whose position is represented in the figure has succeeded in achieving a market represented by demand curve A, he can realise all economies of scale and

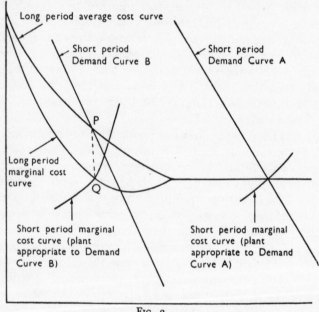

Fig. 3

produce under conditions of constant returns. In these conditions the long-period average cost is equal to the long-period marginal cost. If the total cost of producing $n$ units is $y$, the average cost will be $\frac{y}{n}$. With constant returns the total cost of producing $(n+1)$ units will be $\frac{(n+1)}{n}y$ and the average cost $\frac{y}{n}$. The marginal cost of producing the $(n+1)$th unit will be $\frac{(n+1)}{n}y - y = \frac{y}{n}$.

If the entrepreneur charges a price equal to the average

cost (full cost principle) — and he dare go no higher in conditions of free entry — he will be charging a price equal to marginal cost. Therefore despite the downward-sloping short-period particular demand curve there will be no distortion.

But if his market is more restricted, as shown by the Demand Curve B, he will charge a price shown by P on the diagram although his long-period marginal cost (which includes normal profit) is only Q. This involves a distortion.

What comes out clearly is that in conditions of free entry the cause of the distortion, if there is a distortion, is the existence of increasing returns at the equilibrium position, and not the downward slope of the particular short-period demand curve; for where the particular short-period demand curve has a downward slope and there are constant returns at the equilibrium position, there is no distortion.

It is true that a downward-sloping particular short-period demand curve is a necessary condition for distortion; that is because it is a necessary condition for the existence of increasing returns in equilibrium. It is not true that a downward-sloping particular short-period demand curve by itself entails distortion, for where this is present but there are constant returns, there will be no distortion.

Thus the Marshall-Pigou position remains intact. The downward-sloping particular short-period demand curve does not provide a new independent cause of distortion, but merely explains how increasing returns (which cause the distortions) are consistent with equilibrium.

A further point is brought out by this diagram and should be emphasised. Increasing returns are an independent cause of restriction of output below the social optimum (as suggested by Marshall and Pigou), which has nothing to do with monopoly. In neither of the cases represented in the diagram is there monopoly, but there is distortion in one (increasing returns) and not the other (constant returns). The lumping together of all cases other than those of perfect competition as imperfect (monopolistic?) competition has tended to obscure the part played by increasing returns. Since it came to be held that there was some kind of monopolistic element in all these cases, it tended to be assumed that the distortions which occur are all due to this monopolistic element. But in fact they are not. Where there are impediments to entry there will be distortions due to the monopolistic element and these may exist in conditions of constant returns. But where there is free entry, the distortions, if any, are due to the presence of increasing returns at equilibrium, and to that alone. Some specialists in this subject may insist, despite my plea to the contrary, in holding that every case where there is a downward-sloping short-period particular demand curve should be *called* monopolistic (because, for instance, they might hold that some degree of product differentiation was involved); that advances us not at all; for if that were the right use of the word 'monopolistic', it would only follow that 'monopoly' does not in itself cause distortion.

The amount by which price exceeds long-period marginal cost gives a *prima facie* index of the amount of distortion away from the social optimum. A more thoroughgoing analysis would require reference to consumers' surplus or indifference curves. I shall not attempt this.

In conditions of free entry the excess of the long-period average cost and thereby price over long-period marginal cost depends on the elasticity of the long-period average cost curve. The elasticity of the particular short-period demand curve plays no part.

If there is a monopolistic element the distortion due to it is over and above that due to increasing returns. If the entrepreneur represented in the above figure had, when confronted with demand curve B, an assurance that there were serious obstacles to the entry of new competitors, he could gain a surplus profit by raising his price above P (his 'full cost'). The size of this additional distortion would depend in the first instance on what was called above his 'degree of potential monopoly'. The elasticity of the short-period demand curve might play a part if it was such as to limit the amount of monopoly profit actually realisable to something less than that allowed by the degree of potential monopoly.

Thus, the elasticity of the short-period particular demand curve plays no part in determining the amount of distortion if there is free entry. If there is restricted entry this elasticity will play a part if, and only if, it is great enough to make the realisation of the profit as determined by the 'degree of potential monopoly' unobtainable.

In the foregoing discussion 'increasing returns' has been used in the analytic sense; there is in economics a time-honoured distinction between an instantaneous cost curve representing the existing condition of productive and managerial techniques and showing the amount of output per unit of cost as an increasing function of the amount of output produced on the one hand, and an increase of output per unit of cost through time in consequence of improving techniques on the other. There is, however, a kind of increasing returns which it is difficult to assign unambiguously to either category. This must be explained.

Many entrepreneurs testify that if they were in a position to produce twice (or ten times) as much as they actually produce, they could do so at a substantially lower cost per unit. When asked why they do not at once put themselves into this more favourable position by increasing their scale of operations, their answers are diverse. One answer, which, although characteristic, only represents a minority of cases, is that they simply have not the market. It is to this class of cases that the concepts of the downward-sloping particular demand curve and the marginal revenue curve are particularly appropriate. Thought may be given to the possibilities of public interference, such as compulsory standardisation, rationalisation, etc., and to the rationality or irrationality of consumers' preferences for product differentiation.

Another typical answer, also only representing a minority position, is that finance is lacking. It has long been recognised that a perfect market for the supply of capital to particular enterprises should not be assumed, and Mr. Kalecki has expounded the 'principle of increasing risk'. More important is the entrepreneur's fear of loss of control. To obtain too high a proportion of capital on a fixed interest basis is dangerous; to obtain it on an equity basis may involve loss of control. This obstruction to expansion cannot be fully overcome by the public provision of funds or by corporations constituted to assist small enterprises. The entrepreneur may only be willing to expand if he can do so mainly with his own money.[1] This is partly based on a rational fear of the injurious interference of new-comers lacking experience of the firm's particular problems, still more to the entrepreneur's belief, which may often be irrational, that no other person can guide his business as well as himself. Although this belief may well not be founded on fact, it would be feather-headed for public policy to ignore it or seek to frustrate it; for it is one of the greatest engines of economic progress. It may well be that the desire to maximise profit and the love of business power, of which much is heard, are motives to strenuous endeavour of less force than a man's belief that he can do a particular job better than anyone else. The accrual of profit may be one criterion in his mind, but it will not usually be the only one, for whether the job is being well done. This very strong human motive, which we may call by the unflattering name of vanity, should be harnessed to the cause of economic welfare. Pernicious when it actuates a dictator, it can be turned to good account when it actuates a private entrepreneur. It is true that the value of the service it causes him to render may not be as great as he deems it; none the less the service is normally of substantial value, and consequently frustration of its motive, which is likely to cause the entrepreneur in question to relapse into a cushy life, will tend to reduce national income. This has an important bearing on taxation policy, including death duties.

The preponderating answer to the question why an entrepreneur does not move forward along his increasing returns curve is somewhat different. The entrepreneur avers that he could in principle and indeed hopes in practice to produce twice (or ten times) his present output at a sub-

---

[1] The deleterious effect of high death duties should be noticed in connexion with this. Some firms deliberately restrict their scale of operations so as not to attract death duties at a rate so high as to involve loss of family control.

stantially lower cost per unit, but cannot do so immediately. His enterprise is a delicate organism with complicated labour relations and managerial relations. There is an optimum rate at which labour can be diluted and management formalised in the way required for larger scale ; to accelerate beyond this rate would not yield increasing returns. It is somewhat difficult to categorise this condition, which is widely prevalent. From the point of view of the economy as a whole, it is an instance of analytic increasing returns ; the various techniques and types of skilled labour or management are immediately available and could in principle be brought together as required for the larger scale of operation ; this is quite a different case from those 'historical' increasing returns which can only eventuate as and when still undiscovered technological inventions are made. But for the particular source of supply — and all supply comes from one or other particular source — this happy combination of the relevant factors can only be made by a process which takes considerable time ; the higher returns are not immediately available. It is doubtful, therefore, whether, when we apply 'increasing returns' to a firm which cannot achieve higher returns per unit of cost save by a slow process of growth, these are increasing returns in the strict analytical sense.

When we assert that much of British Industry is here and now subject to the law of Increasing Returns, it may be that a substantial proportion of the area referred to is subject to them in this intermediate sense. It is clear that quite a different remedy is appropriate in this case. Where a firm could here and now produce on a larger and cheaper scale if only it had the market or the finance, it is possible that some policy could be devised for securing a quick transition. But if the increasing returns are of the other sort, then nothing can be done save to encourage the study and application of techniques for the solution of the complex labour and managerial problems that arise when rapid growth is attempted. I have referred to this point because imperfect competition doctrine with its concentration on marketing problems, which are extremely important, might suggest the wrong inference that the limited market is the sole or principal cause holding firms back from larger scale production at lower unit cost.

It is needful to summarise this third section.

1. I define imperfect competition as the condition in which a particular source of supply is confronted by a downward-sloping particular demand curve.
2. I divide imperfect competition into free competition (which also includes perfect competition) and monopolistic competition. A source is in free competition if it cannot hope for long to enjoy a supernormal rate of profit, save in consequence of superior efficiency.[1] I define a normal rate of profit as one the contemplation of which would be deemed by the source itself to make a marginal investment in plant extension just worth while.
3. Increasing returns are compatible with any kind of imperfect competition, but not with perfect competition. But increasing returns are not necessarily present in imperfect competition.
4. A monopolistic element may normally be expected to restrict the level of output below the social optimum.
5. I measure the degree of potential monopoly by the level of profit that is the highest that the monopolist should expect to be able to enjoy without provoking an invasion of his monopolistic position.
6. The maximum price which a monopolist would normally charge would be governed either (a) by his degree of potential monopoly or (b) by the short-period marginal revenue curve confronting him, whichever price was lower. Thus if the degree of potential monopoly is sufficiently great, but not otherwise, the amount of restriction will be governed by the slope of the short-period demand curve. A wise monopolist, however, having regard to the uncertainties of the future and the desirability of entrenching himself in as large a market as possible, may set a price that is lower than either of the

[1] It would only darken counsel to define the possession of a superior efficiency as the possession of a kind of monopolistic element.

maxima enjoined by the considerations mentioned above. (It may also be possible to have a 'conscientious' monopolist, who charges a lower price because he considers that it is right to do so. Cf. pages 208-17 below.)

7. In the case of imperfect but free competition there will normally be no restriction of output below the social optimum, save if increasing returns obtain in the equilibrium position. In this case the amount of restriction will be related to the rate of increase of returns. For the purpose of the last two propositions 'increasing returns' should be taken in the narrow sense, viz. should be limited to those realisable (if only a sufficient market were present) as soon as additional plant was constructed and labour recruited.

# THEORY OF PROFIT

THIS essay is closely related to those on imperfect competition which precede it. Its central purpose is to relate the theory regarding profit under imperfect competition to the general theory of profit. It seems that, since the elaboration of the doctrines of imperfect competition, some confusion regarding profit has arisen, anyhow in the minds of students. As an examiner, both in my own university and others, I have found the following tendency. Candidates, having set out some general theory of profit, for instance on the lines of Professor Knight's classic analysis, are apt then to affirm that *in addition to* the profit arising for the reasons thus specified, there is another different kind of profit which occurs owing to the presence of monopolistic elements. I shall argue that this is quite erroneous, that monopolistic profit is not an additional profit, but part of the global profit in the economy that tends to secure an equilibrium between the demand and supply of uncertainty-bearing. It may happen that for a short period or a long one global profit in an economy exceeds that required to secure this equilibrium. But there is no necessary connexion between such a phenomenon and the presence of elements of monopoly profit. This phenomenon might occur in an economy in which there were no elements of monopoly profit. *Per contra* there might be an economy showing a large total volume of monopoly profit, in which none the less total profit, including the monopoly profit, was inadequate to sustain the amount of uncertainty-bearing required for equilibrium. *A priori* neither of these alternatives can be regarded as more probable than the other. In order to unravel this story I shall have to re-examine, albeit briefly, familiar territory.

Profit is essentially connected with the time interval

between the input of productive services and the consequent output of goods or services required by the consumer, and with the uncertainty at the moment of input as to what the value of the output will be when it occurs. In regard to how this uncertainty might be dealt with, I select three possibilities. (1) An article might be produced under a 'co-operative' system in the fullest sense of that word, by which all factors put in their services gratis for the time being and waited patiently for the eventuation of the value of output (which in the case of such things as houses and railway tracks might be spread over a number of years), dividing this value among themselves in accordance with the amount and value of their original input. (2) The bearing of uncertainty may be concentrated upon one of the factors of production, namely the person or persons responsible for the top direction of the enterprise, other factors being paid more or less simultaneously with their input of service in accordance with its current value. The uncertainty-bearer not only 'puts in' his own service at risk, but also the money required to pay the other factors at their current values. (3) Specialisation may be carried one stage further, the uncertainty being carried by a person or persons who put in the money and do nothing else whatever, as in a company wholly financed, both for its fixed and circulating capital, by the issue of ordinary shares to the general public.

We call an economy which deals with most of its uncertainty in the second or third ways, including an admixture of the two, a capitalist economy.

I have omitted from my list a fully socialist economy. The fact of uncertainty and its concomitant, the eventuation of profit (or loss), remain present under such a system, but the burden, if it is a burden, of uncertainty is put onto the shoulders of the consumers or the taxpayers. For instance, consumers may get the benefit of new products at low prices from the government workshops, in cases where capitalists would hold up the prices for a time to pay themselves for having carried the risk of a new invention; alternatively the consumers may have to suffer a detriment by continuing to consume obsolete articles in cases where capitalists would have been compelled to withdraw them, writing off a loss on their productive equipment. Alternatively the government may act more like capitalists, retaining a profit on new lines to the relief of the taxpayers and accepting losses on old ones at the expense of the taxpayers.

It is sometimes argued that socialist organisation would reduce the aggregate amount of uncertainty that had to be carried. It would only reduce those uncertainties due to changes in technology or taste at the price of being less progressive and repressing the standard of living. If it understood the causes of the trade cycle sufficiently to cure them, that might entail much reduction of uncertainty; it is arguable that with this knowledge the central authorities would be as well able, or nearly as well able, to iron out the cycle in a free enterprise economy, and reduce uncertainty in that way. Greatest stress is laid on the reduction of those uncertainties which are due to ignorance on the part of one competitor about what another is doing. This, however, is disputable. In principle the supreme authority should know from day to day what all its subordinate branches are doing and adjust the activity of each with accuracy to those of the others. In practice it may well be the case, as is argued by some, that private entrepreneurs with their ears to the ground and the fear of loss constantly actuating them, may adapt themselves more quickly to changes in the environment due to changes in the activities of their competitors, customers or suppliers, than a slowly grinding central government department trying to co-ordinate the activities of its multifarious sub-branches. If adaptation was less rapid in a socialist system, the amount of uncertainty in the economy as a whole would be increased, since there would be a less close fitting together of the various productive activities and more deviations of realised values from those hoped for when each activity was set going.

In the case of my first possibility, an idealised co-operative system, it may be analytically possible to divide the share in the product finally accruing into that representing the value of the service originally rendered and the residue, plus or minus, representing profit or loss. This would be practically feasible in the case of a co-operative enterprise working in a predominantly capitalist economy, since the values of various kinds of service would be roughly established in the capitalist section. But where the whole economy was co-operative it might be extremely difficult to establish the current market value of each service at the time of input, and one might have to content oneself by drawing a schedule giving in order of magnitude the values of the returns in the production of each article to each type of factor. This would fail to show profit or loss as an absolute amount, save by some arbitrary convention such as that labour on an article half-way (or three-quarters of the way) down the list was receiving a standard rate of pay, surpluses and shortfalls on the other articles being represented as profits and losses.

This point has its importance for the second and third more realistic possibilities also. In the case of the third, while the whole dividend is commonly regarded as profit, it may be desirable to divide it into interest considered as the payment for parting with value for a certain time and profit, positive or negative, as the return due to carrying a specific uncertainty. If there is a market of substantial size for the National Debt or similar type of security, the current yield ruling in that market may be regarded as the interest obtainable for safe loans; the return for bearing a specific uncertainty may then be regarded as the difference, positive or negative, between that return and the gilt-edged rate of interest prevailing in the market at the time when the investment was made. Keynes's theory that all interest is in some sense a payment for uncertainty — uncertainty about the future course of the gilt-edged market — does not conflict with this analysis. The uncertainty in the Keynes theory is not connected with any doubt as to whether the borrower will in fact pay the promised interest and redeem the capital at the specified date if any. The important point is that, under it, the gilt-edged rate of interest remains the reward for parting with liquidity in general on safe terms and may therefore be used as a yardstick for measuring the return on money parted with for a specific project.

In the case of the second possibility, a further problem arises, namely of separating that part of the return attributable to the devotion by the entrepreneur of his time and skill to the top direction of the business. It may be thought that an answer can be found by referring to the salary he could earn as a hired manager of business. There are some thorny difficulties in this case. There is no perfect market, like the Stock Exchange, for such services. Furthermore, we are in the presence of a heterogeneous factor, like land, but more minutely subdivided. We should have to undertake a fine grading of the managerial capacities of entrepreneurs; one might reach the point, especially at a high level, where each man was the sole member of his class. There is an analogy in the case of the sale of the services of barristers or best-selling authors.

There are still more radical problems. Edgeworth suggested that the combination of capital and business ability of a certain kind in the ownership of the same person may have a higher product than the sum of the products of each where the ownership is different. This may be due to the fact that a man's knowledge that he is working with his own money elicits powers that would not otherwise be brought into play. The efficient conduct of business is a complex matter requiring a subtle combination of qualities. In some cases the opposite of the Edgeworth dictum may be true, a man being able to do his best work only in the service of others. All depends on temperament, which is supremely important in this connexion. Whichever way the matter goes, there is the same difficulty in dividing an entrepreneur's return into that due and that not due to his own special powers.

In value theory it has proved expedient to relate profit specifically to uncertainty-bearing, ability to direct a business being easily assimilable in theory to the category of highly skilled labour. Analysis of its value proceeds on the usual lines where there is a heterogeneous factor. For simplicity of illustration, let us suppose that men of business ability may be divided into discrete groups, A, B, C, etc. Let us suppose that there are ten men in group A. They will be employed by the ten companies who set the highest value to the addition to the product that could be secured by having a managing director of class A rather than one of class B. This value will be differently assessed by the ten companies. The salary of any managing director in group A (assuming this to be a homogeneous group) will exceed that of one in group B by the amount of the addition to the product assessed as attributable to a managing director of this class by the company that makes the *lowest* assessment of this addition (the marginal company).

If the payment for top direction could be separated out in this way, the profit of the owner-entrepreneur would be the residue, plus or minus, of his returns after subtracting what he could get in such a market for managing directors. This narrowing of the concept of profit, so that it becomes the consequence of good luck solely and not at all of good management, jars with popular usage, by which profit is regarded as being in part at least attributable to the efficient direction of a business. There is some value in the popular usage, and it may be that economists should use the expression 'return for uncertainty-bearing' for profit in the narrower sense.

Two further important points are to be noted in connexion with the fusion in practice of the return due to efficient direction and the return due to a risk turning out favourably. It might be argued that with modern company development, the area of operation by the owner-entrepreneur is ever narrowing, so that the division of the proceeds required for analytic purposes is being realised more and more in practice also, ordinary shareholders receiving the return for uncertainty-bearing and the managing directors salaried rewards for their skilled labour. It will be readily understood that this practical result is not achieved if the company is merely the legal form of operation of what is in effect still a family business. More important is the fact that although the coverage of genuine company organisation with impersonalised ownership may be large, yet it may cover a much smaller proportion of the area in which the degree of risk attaching to the investment is great. We have to think of the early phase of a business enterprise, still small and growing; it is usually in this phase that high degrees of risk are to be found, and these go with the combination of ownership of capital and direction.

Secondly, even where there is company organisation in the full sense, there may still be some fusion of reward for direction and return to risk. Individuals at the top level of direction may invest their abilities in a business in the sense that their ultimate salaries may depend on its success. I do not refer only to special schemes for relating bonuses to profits realised by the firm. The salaries payable at the top level at a future date will depend on how much the business has grown and thrived. In the course of time, those at high levels acquire a value to their business which depends on their special knowledge of detailed matters relating to that business and exceeds their potential value in an open market for managers; if they go elsewhere some of this special knowledge will be of no service; how great the value of that knowledge is inside the business will depend on the prosperity of the business. Consider two men of equal ability in different businesses, each of whom has acquired the same volume of knowledge — if only this could be measured! — in his own business. If one business has thrived while the other has not — and this may be due to the luck of the game and not to differences in efficiency of management — the man attached to the former will be worth more to it than the man attached to the other. Men who attach themselves to a particular business put themselves to some extent in a different category from, say, barristers, film stars or journalists, who keep themselves free from attachments and, as their experience and reputation increase, can command appropriate incomes at market valuation. The man who attaches himself for long to a particular firm invests his earning capacity in that firm, and his eventual return will be in part payment for his general capacity and in part a profit in the narrower sense, viz. a return for investing his talent in that specific form of uncertainty-bearing. In practice these payments will be fused and it will not be possible to say how much of the total payment is attributable to each element. The valuation of such a man in the outside market for managers is no criterion.

Where there is a fusion of payments in practice, we have to resort to an averaging process. We may take a fairly large group of entrepreneurs and imagine them graded according to their true abilities, which for the sake of argument we suppose assessable apart from their achievements. Having divided the graded list into two parts, we may expect to find the average return in the top half higher than that in the bottom half. But we might well find that the ablest one of all had made nothing and lost all his money, while the biggest fool of all had had the biggest success. To the extent that the future is genuinely inscrutable, the finest ability is powerless and the outcome depends on luck. Actual business decisions can to some extent be guided by good judgment but must contain an element of guess-work.

In what follows I shall be considering mainly profit in the narrow sense, viz. the return to uncertainty-bearing. First, let us consider the supply price of this factor. We have to view the matter as seen by the potential investor. I use supply in the widest sense, conflating, where there is a separation between the capitalist and the entrepreneur, the willingness of the saver to invest money in certain ordinary shares with the willingness of the company to buy certain equipment. I use supply in this sense in contrast to demand, where the demand consists in the consumers' demand for those goods and services the provision of which has involved risk-bearing.

It is well recognised that this problem of supply is exceedingly complex, owing to the variety of prospects with which an investor may be confronted. He may be fairly sure that his profit will not exceed a certain sum nor his loss exceed another sum, but be quite vague about the possibilities between these points. Or he may be able to make some assessment of the shape of the frequency curve of possibilities between these points. There may be fairly high probability, according to his assessment, that the outcome will lie within a narrow range, but complete vagueness beyond the range, for instance if some particular condition assumed with good reason to be likely to hold should break down. There may be a wide spread with the possibility of drawing a sensible frequency curve or a narrow spread but with no possibility of drawing a frequency curve. And so on. I put down these points without order as reminders only, because it is not germane to my purpose to consider them more elaborately, as one might do, using, for example, the refined apparatus recently constructed by Professor G. L. S. Shackle.

There may well be as many different types of prospect as there are investment projects. I beg leave to abstract from all these complexities.

Alfred Marshall considered that if men act prudently, those engaging in risky investment should, as a group, have a premium on average over the gilt-edged rate of interest, on the basis that the diminishing utility of income makes it bad business to spin a coin for double or quits. This premium is calculated by adding together the profits of a sufficiently large group of entrepreneurs, subtracting all their losses, and assessing the residue as a percentage on all capital invested, including that lost. The premium is the excess of this percentage over the gilt-edged rate at the time of the investments.

It might be held in consequence that in the long run suppliers of risk-bearing would achieve a premium over the suppliers of riskless waiting. Such a conclusion would imply two propositions. (1) It would imply that suppliers of risk do as a body, or anyhow at the margin, have the prudent point of view regarded as rational by Marshall. (2) It would imply that on the average, although not of course in each particular case, out-turns corresponded with expectations. These propositions must be considered in turn.

1. The question must be raised whether investors as a class are as rational as the Marshallian doctrine implies. The investors on the tables of Monte Carlo know well that the average premium accruing to those who take this risk is negative. Some may be regarded as deliberately paying this premium for their recreation. Are some actually attracted

by the pattern which comprises an actuarial certainty of loss with the possibility of glittering prizes? This must not be ruled out. Nor can the possibility of such an attitude of mind among industrial investors be ruled out *a priori*. It may be argued that Monte Carlo selects gamblers and that the sample of people attracted to its tables are less prudent than the average investor. This may well be so. I would only point out that the greater prudence of investors cannot be assumed as a necessary truth. It may be that the attitude of mind of the representative or marginal investor in this regard varies from time to time, for instance from phase to phase of the trade cycle or in accordance with the national climate of feeling. If we had regard to the various sub-classes of risk prospect mentioned above, we might find that some of these sub-classes which belong to the Monte Carlo type do actually attract investment, simply because there is a limited number of people of this type of mind. From the point of view of economic welfare it is presumably desirable that the Marshallian attitude should prevail. It is to be noted, however, that, subject to what is said in the following paragraph, the prevalence of a more risk-loving attitude would lead to a lower average rate of profit, which should be a source of satisfaction to those who dislike that particular kind of income.

2. We next have to ask whether suppliers of risk will in the long run enforce their will upon the market, so that, for instance, if a certain average premium is required as an inducement, it will accrue. We normally assume that where a productive service can be withheld, and risk-bearing clearly can be, the suppliers can in the long run exact their terms by withdrawing the marginal supply. But in this case all we can say is that the prospects, as assessed by the suppliers, must be sufficiently good. These prospects are by definition uncertain.

In many cases, perhaps in most cases, the prospects are wrongly assessed. Is it legitimate to assume that, if we take a large number of investors, errors of over-assessment will cancel errors of under-assessment, so that, despite the uncertainty, out-turns will on average correspond with assessment? I am doubtful if such an assumption can be justified.

In that case we might get the result that the average risk premium on existing capital exceeded that amount the prospect of which was required to actuate the investments at the time they were made, or conversely. According to traditional analysis this maladjustment should be corrected in a longer period. The high premium experienced should cause investors to make more optimistic forecasts and so stimulate investment, and conversely.

Unhappily we cannot rest in this conclusion. In the case of profit it seems that the traditional theory of rewards to factors has to be modified by the Keynesian and post-Keynesian analysis of the forces determining the level of activity as a whole. We have to bring into the picture the familiar vicious circles of inflation and depression. If the current rate of investment is high by reference to the current propensity to consume, profit will be high and investment stimulated ; this calling forth of an additional supply of risk-bearing — which need not entail any additional saving — will not tend to reduce profit but will have a contrary effect. Conversely in the case of depression.

To pursue this line of thought further would take us far from our immediate subject matter. Suffice it to say that global profit in a period may yield an average risk premium that is excessive or deficient in relation to the assessments made when the investments were undertaken and that the question of eventual adjustment belongs to the theory of dynamic economics, which has not yet been brought into a satisfactory condition.

We must now revert to the distribution of global profit among the various types of risk-bearer. The ownership of existing capital assets may be changed, sometimes not without difficulty, but with great ease in the case of a large company with marketable shares. The value of such assets is determined in the market, where an assessment of prospective returns is made. The prospect is assessed anew from day to day by the market and the current value of the asset likewise. The same perplexities beset the market for

existing assets as beset the man who created them in the
first place. There are all the same patterns of uncertainty
in regard to what the future returns will be. The attractiveness of the various patterns to the potential buyers or holders
of the assets will vary from time to time. It may safely be
said that in reaching a valuation the market has regard only
to the kind of pattern of uncertainty represented and
amounts of return involved in this pattern. The rate of
profit, considered as a percentage of the present value of
the asset, which its holder can obtain, is governed (i) by the
current market valuation and (ii) by the actual return which
eventuates. The lower the market valuation and the higher
the return, the greater the rate of profit will be.

If the market had much accurate and precise information
about the future returns, it would give the assets a high
valuation, so that at the limit of complete certainty the rate
of profit on the existing valuation would be equal to the gilt-
edged rate of interest. If there is a high degree of assurance
but not complete certainty that the return will be $£x$ a year,
the market valuation is usually such that $£x$ a year, if
realised, gives a yield on it of a little more than the gilt-
edged rate of interest. This statement probably implies that
the market has a Marshallian outlook, but not necessarily,
since the possibilities of divergence from $£x$ a year consisting
of greater profit than $£x$ a year or less profit (which may
involve total loss of capital), may not be symmetrically
disposed around $£x$ a year.

Of one thing we may be quite sure, and that is that the
market does not arrange its valuations so as to give holders
of assets whose products enjoy some monopolistic advantage
a higher return. In making its valuation it has regard to the
probable amount of return and the pattern of uncertainty
only. The question of a monopolistic element does not
come into the reckoning save to the extent that this
affects the pattern of uncertainty. Consequently the
holders of assets embodying a monopolistic element do not
as such get a higher rate of profit than the holders of other
assets.

If one leaves out the 'as such' and seeks to generalise,

one may conclude that the owners of monopolistic shares get a somewhat lower rate of profit. For if there is some monopolistic element this usually carries with it some measure of assurance in regard to prospects; it is strong competition, perfect competition not least, that is usually surrounded with the greatest uncertainty. Therefore the market, if it has any Marshallian tendency at all, will tend to value a monopolistic share so that their holders get a lower rate of return on capital — this being the price of the relative certainty that they enjoy — than the holders of shares in highly competitive concerns. It is a matter of common experience that the dividends of great concerns supposed to enjoy monopolistic advantages show a low yield on the market valuation of their shares. Of course a monopolistic concern may declare an unexpectedly high dividend and a holder of its shares enjoy a relatively high profit; but so may a highly competitive concern; the stock market has no tendency to ignore the possibility of dividend increases in the case of monopolies while taking it into account in the case of competitive concerns; the investor has no greater chance of unexpected windfalls by investing in monopolies. In both cases the result may deviate upwards or downwards from the assessment of the market. The profit obtainable by buying or holding existing assets is governed entirely by the uncertainty theory and the monopoly element does not come into the picture. There is certainly no additional monopoly profit.

How is this to be reconciled with the cost and demand theory of price determination, which shows the possibility of a higher rate of profit, if a monopolistic element is present? To understand this it is necessary to look back to the history of the firm enjoying such a monopolistic element.

A firm does not usually enjoy an assured monopolistic position *ab ovo*. This may have happened in the old days when the Crown granted a monopoly in return for services rendered or for political reasons. Such cases may indeed involve a monopoly profit quite unrelated to the terms demanded by suppliers of uncertainty-bearing; they belong to a separate category and need not be considered in the analysis of monopoly as it exists in modern capitalist economies.

At the moment that a firm begins life, through an individual (or group of individuals) making a certain input of resources, the value of the investment is equal to the value of the resources put in. It might conceivably happen that in a very short period of time, say a day afterwards, it was universally recognised that the individual (or group) by having made this particular input had acquired the assurance of making a monopoly profit for a period lasting into the foreseeable future. It might, for instance, be judged in the case of an input based on a patent that, before the patent expired, the owners would be likely to acquire such a dominant position in the market as to make the entry of competitors extremely difficult. To take an extreme case, the business world might judge that the accrual of a monopoly profit on this investment *sine die* was absolutely certain.

In such a case the investor would be able to sell his investment on the next day at a capital value computed by regarding the prospective monopoly revenue as gilt-edged interest on the investment. This capital value might greatly exceed the value of the resources put into the investment the day before. The correct analysis is that the investor in question makes a true profit in the form of a capital gain on the first day and from then on draws a gilt-edged rate of interest on his property. It makes no difference to the analysis whether he decides to sell his asset on the next day or not.

In the real world a monopoly position is not usually created in a day, but rather over a term of years. The same analysis applies. A new firm may make a high rate of profit from the very beginning and this may be intrinsically due to the presence of a monopolistic element. But if the business world is not convinced that the current rate of income can be relied on to continue, the owner will be unable to capitalise a gain by selling the asset above its cost price. To schematise and simplify, one may suppose that for thirty years the business world remains completely sceptical and that during that period the assets cannot be sold above the value of the resources put in, and that one fine day at the end of this period the business world is convinced and is prepared to treat the prospect of continuance of the income as safe. (In practice, of course, the conversion of the business world will be a gradual process spread over the thirty years.) During the thirty years the owner enjoys a high return on the value of the original input; but all this time he is bearing risk. The well-informed world regards it as uncertain whether this income can be maintained or the original capital kept intact. At the end of the thirty years the risk comes to an end and he makes a large capital gain. His reward for having borne risk is twofold, namely (i) the high return during the period when uncertainty was present, and (ii) the capital gain at the end of that period. Beyond that there is no further reward for uncertainty-bearing because there is no further uncertainty. The owner, whether he retain his assets or sells them and invests the proceeds in gilt-edged securities, gets a gilt-edged rate on his capital. His monopoly profit comes to an end at the same point of time. The monopoly income due to accrue after the date when certainty is established is capitalised at that date and goes into the pocket of the owner at that date. The owner of the asset after that date, whether the same in person as the owner before that date or not, gets no monopoly profit — that has already been capitalised and accrued—but merely a gilt-edged rate of interest on the value of the assets as currently assessed. In practice of course, uncertainty is never entirely eliminated and a somewhat higher rate of return on the capital will continue to accrue. But the height of this rate will not depend at all on the presence or absence of a monopoly element but solely on the market valuation of the degree and pattern of uncertainty still inhering in the income-producing quality of the assets.

Thus the paradox is resolved. On the one hand analysis of cost and demand curves and the potentiality of competition reveals that a given firm is able to enjoy a monopoly profit in the sense of getting a price which exceeds cost plus normal profit. On the other hand it can be shown that the owners of the assets of this same firm may enjoy no more than a normal rate of profit on their capital. The essential point is that the whole monopoly element in profit as revealed by the former analysis is capitalised when uncertainty comes to an end (more or less), and goes in the form of a capital gain to the original owner who bore the uncertainty.

From this we deduce that monopoly profit is not a separate and additional element in the system, but one part of the global reward in the economy for uncertainty-bearing.

This is related to another proposition, namely that in a free enterprise economy total profit usually includes capital gain, whether there is a monopoly element or not. To establish the net profit of a group of entrepreneurs, capital losses, which are usually extensive, should be deducted, and capital gains included. Textbooks often imply that profit is always, or normally, to be regarded as an annual income. If capital gains are referred to at all, they are apt to be treated as occasional and incidental. In fact they are an essential and important part of the system.

The presence of a monopoly element does not necessarily involve capital gain; income that is due to a monopolistic position may accrue for a time, but well-informed opinion may regard it as so precarious that the owners could not raise a penny on the prospect of its continuance. A capital gain can only be obtained to the extent that the monopoly has begun to enjoy an assured position. A capital gain or a succession of capital gains may be obtained, as and when the monopoly position becomes progressively recognised as more secure. In the limit when the monopoly position is regarded as absolutely safe the whole income due to the monopoly element is capitalised, and the proprietors thereafter enjoy no monopoly element in their income.

If monopoly (of a precarious kind) can continue for a time without capital gain, conversely capital gains may accrue in the absence of any monopoly element at all. Capital gains may occur when there is free competition (in the sense defined above),[1] whether perfect or imperfect. Indeed capital gain may from one point of view be regarded

[1] Cf. p. 179.

as the most characteristic feature of free enterprise.

It may be well, in order to illustrate this point, to revert to profit in the wider sense as a subtle blend of the reward for efficiency and the return to uncertainty-bearing, and to consider particularly the former of the two elements in this blend. An efficient entrepreneur who initiates or takes over a business does not expect to receive in the early years a reward commensurate with his ability. The fruits of efficiency do not ripen in a single season. It may take a decade, or indeed several decades, before practical genius can engender the most efficient system of production of which it is capable. In the course of years profit may rise without any capital gain necessarily accruing. In the long run, if efficiency is maintained and the factor of luck is neutral, a capital gain normally occurs. This happens when it is judged that the efficient entrepreneur has built his ideas into the system by which his firm operates. Certain principles in regard to labour relations, to managerial problems, to the utilisation of research, to buying and selling problems, become established and traditional in the firm; in fine the business is well run, and a point may be reached when it is believed that the good methods can and will be maintained even should their initiator or initiators pass from the scene. At this point the high profit of the firm can be capitalised in the stock market. The capital gain involved is in no sense a windfall but a deferred once-over payment for efficient entrepreneurship.

This phenomenon is entirely consistent in theory and practice not only with free but imperfect competition, but also with perfect competition itself. If it is somewhat less frequent in the case of perfect competition, that may be because farming, the main area in the past of perfect competition, is not so susceptible to built-in methods of efficiency as manufacturing or distributive enterprise. Farmers differ widely in efficiency and farming profits differ likewise. But there may not be so much scope for the farmer, as for the manufacturer, so to implant his efficient methods in his farm, that there is general confidence that the farm will continue to be efficiently run, whether the particular farmer in question continues to run it or not. Efficient manufacturers have been able to make large capital gains precisely because they have been able to make upon their businesses an impress which, if not indelible, will at least not be quickly rubbed out.

Thus while the establishment of an assured monopolistic position entails capital gain, the accrual of capital gain cannot be taken as a sign that a monopolistic position has been established. Capital gains, whether due to a monopoly element or not, are a part of the global profit which constitute the incentive to uncertainty-bearing.

It remains finally to ask the question whether global profit over a period in the life of an economy during which a number of assured monopolistic positions have been established is likely to be greater than the global profit over a similar period in the life of an economy in which no such positions have been built up, when the amount of uncertainty-bearing investment in the two cases has been the same, and the attitude of investors to uncertainty-bearing has also been the same.

In answering this it is necessary to revert to a problem already posed. Can we assume that within a period of reasonable length the bearers of uncertainty will be able to enforce their offer price for this service on the purchasers of goods and services produced in conditions of uncertainty? It is obvious, from the very nature of uncertainty, that no single bearer is able to exact his terms. It might be argued, I will not say conclusively, that over a period of reasonable length uncertainty-bearers will in the aggregate be able to exact their terms, like other factors of production, in the sense that the average net return on uncertainty-bearing will be equal to the gilt-edged rate of interest plus such premium, positive or negative, for uncertainty-bearing as the attitude of mind of the marginal bearer requires. This must of course be positive, if he is of a Marshallian temperament.

If the answer to this question is in the affirmative, it follows at once that the creation of assured monopolistic positions adds nothing to the global profit accruing in the economy. In the case of the two periods referred to above, the one in which it is impossible to build up monopolistic positions will have a higher rate of average profit in the sphere of free competition, this being the condition for making the global profit up to a sufficient figure to attract the investment that occurs. It was assumed that the amount of investment and the willingness to bear uncertainty was the same in the two periods. Where the structure of industry is such that monopolistic positions can normally be built up, the possibility of doing this (with the consequent gain) is one of the factors that some investors have in mind in making their investments. If in the nature of things they cannot have the prospect of this possibility in mind, they must have something else correspondingly gainful to take its place, viz. a higher average rate of profit in competitive industry generally.

It must be admitted, however, that the proposition that the suppliers of uncertainty are able to exact their terms in a reasonably long run is unsafe. These suppliers may accustom themselves to the normal ups and downs of the trade cycle. But the economy may run into a secular phase of chronic depression (or inflation) and average expectations may be persistently belied over a very long period. In a fairly steady economy errors of over-estimate of the actuarial value of a given investment project would be likely to cancel errors of under-estimate, so that by and large suppliers of uncertainty-bearing would get their offer prices. But chronic depression or inflation might continue to take them by surprise.

Excess profit may be said to accrue in an economy in a period, if the global profit that accrues on investments made in the period is greater than the sum of the actuarial equivalents of the expectations of all those who made the investments. Thus we come at last to the question — is excess profit more likely to occur or likely to be larger in an economy in a period in which monopolistic positions are being built up than in one in which they are not? We must divide the analysis into two parts.

1. If in the period in question it proves possible to build up more (or more lucrative) monopoly positions than

was anticipated by the investors, it may be argued that global profit, which will include the profits due to these positions, will exceed the sum of expectations. It is not necessary to consider the validity of this argument, because, even if valid, it is of no avail. We have also to consider the possibility that it proves possible to build up less (or less lucrative) monopoly positions than was anticipated by the investors. Whether the number of positions built up exceeds or falls short of expectations has no necessary or probable connexion with the number of positions built up. Therefore this approach does not yield the conclusion that there is any connexion between the existence of excess profit, when that exists, and the number (and lucrativeness) of the monopoly positions that it is possible to build up.

2. Another approach is to assume that excess (or deficient) profit is likely to be connected with chronic inflation (or depression), *i.e.* with the values of the propensity to consume and of the marginal productivity of capital schedule. The building up of monopoly positions is not likely *prima facie* to increase the propensity to consume nor to move the marginal productivity of capital schedule to the right. Therefore it does not appear that the building up of monopoly positions is likely to be connected with a tendency to chronic inflation.

I conclude (i) that the monopoly element in profit is part of the total profit that rewards uncertainty-bearers and is not a profit additional thereto, and (ii) that, while in a fairly long period global profit accruing may exceed the sum of the actuarial equivalents of the expectations giving rise to the investments that occur, there is no known connexion between the existence of such a phenomenon and the fact, where it is a fact, that a certain number of monopoly positions have been built up in the period in question.

# PROFITEERING: AN ETHICAL STUDY

I PROPOSE to revert to certain ideas which were published some years ago but have made no impact.[1] I submit that there does exist a moral sentiment, although a weak one, against profiteering,[2] and that this sentiment has some influence on action. The entrepreneurs who testified at Oxford defended their adherence to the 'full cost principle', when they did adhere to it, on economic grounds — to depart from it would entail economic loss in the long run. But it was also possible to detect a recurrent note of moral support for the principle; there was a distinct sense among some of the witnesses — perhaps a minority — that there was something morally unsavoury in a consistent policy of charging a price substantially above cost.

When this is reported, the economist is apt to dismiss it summarily. He takes it to be a mere archaic survival, a relic of obsolete and intellectually disreputable mediaeval ideas of a fair price, or, more probably, mere humbug. Has not Adam Smith shown — and he ought to know, since he is the historic vindicator of free enterprise — that it is in seeking maximum profit for himself that the producer can secure the greatest wealth for the society? Adam Smith did not say anything about restraint in favour of the full cost principle . . . . Yet it is to be doubted if all entrepreneurs are as deeply versed in Adam Smith as perhaps they should be; they may have somewhat different ideas, based on the logic of their own thinking and related to the world of to-day.

We may be sure that there is a superabundance of humbug in the world, and whoever advances the charge may consider himself on a safe wicket. Actually humbug is not

[1] *Oxford Economic Papers*, No. 2, 1939.
[2] And also against cut-throat selling.

easy to detect; much that appears sincere is humbug, and conversely; it requires profound psychology to unravel this. Economists are apt to display some vexation in dismissing the suggestion of a moral sentiment; this vexation is tell-tale, for it is usually symptomatic of a suppressed doubt whether the rejected proposition may not after all have some truth in it.

Of course there is plenty of moral reprobation against profiteering in the press and on the platform. But this is usually dismissed wholesale by thinking people, as mere verbiage or dust thrown in our eyes — by politicians seeking to cast the blame elsewhere for an inflation due to their own bad policy, or by low agitators seeking to stir up hatred and rancour. There is undoubtedly much truth in this diagnosis. None the less there may be just a grain of sense in the popular sentiment. Many British producers have shown great restraint in the face of the unprecedented temptations of inflation since the war, while others have made hay. It may be argued that the former have shown restraint because of legal barriers or market conditions or because so much of any extra profit would be taken by the government, while the profiteers were simply those in a position to pocket their profits. Is this quite the whole truth? May it not also have been the case that some of those who have shown restraint may be distinguished from the price-racketeers by having had a touch of moral scruple?

The wickedness of monopoly is often denounced. To reach a monopolistic position by sheer efficiency is not in itself wicked, but only to exploit that position in an anti-social way. Is it possible that some monopolists have not sunk to this particular kind of wickedness, but have endeavoured to provide goods at prices related to their costs? At this suggestion loud howls will arise from certain intellectuals. It is absolutely ludicrous, it will be said, the apotheosis of nonsense, to suppose that a man enjoying *de facto* a monopolistic position will refrain from monopolistic exploitation. . . . Is not this a little cynical? Monopolistic exploitation of the public is universally admitted to be bad. Is it not just possible that men who have achieved such a position by honest toil and inventive enterprise will refrain from exploiting the public owing to some moral scruple and proper human self-respect?

I do not wish to exaggerate. I do not suggest that the moral sentiment in regard to profiteering is more than a poor, feeble thing, the weakest reed in the world. But it has an interest and significance far beyond the quantitative effect of its present-day operation. In the first place it is of great, I would say exciting, intellectual interest to ascertain why it exists. Secondly the fact that it can exist, if it does exist, could be of great moment for future policy. If we are to build our society mainly on free enterprise rather than detailed central instructions to producers — this is not the place to enumerate the many advantages of the former plan — it may be important to supplement incentive by a stronger moral code of individual behaviour than we have at present. Therefore I regard the question of whether a moral sentiment does exist, however weak it may be, as quite a crucial matter.

The issues in this case, involving the relations between ethics and economics, are complex.

It is unfortunate that not much help in unravelling them can be expected from present-day moral philosophy. I would say, with respect, that it is in the doldrums. A prevailing current fashion is that moral judgments are merely emotive noises. Earlier we had a phase of intuitionism. Neither would be likely to take us far in discovering whether the moral sentiment against profiteering is correct. The emotive noise school clearly have nothing to say on this matter and I suspect that the intuitionist school could not take us very far.

Nor are the economists more helpful. They are frequently attacked from two sides. One school upbraids them for falsely setting up material well-being as the supreme end of human endeavour; according to this school, economists are implicitly interfering in matters that do not concern them by implying that material considerations should be the sole guide of conduct, anyhow in the whole field of production and trade. The economists have long been in the habit of

making a forthright rebuttal : they are not concerned with
the ends of endeavour, a matter they are perfectly willing
to hand over to the wise discretion of the moral philosophers,
but with the means for realising the ends to the greatest
extent possible with the limited quantity of resources at our
disposal. I do not think that this is a wholly satisfactory
account of what the economists do, but it is much nearer the
truth than the contention of their anti-materialist critics.

The other school has an opposite criticism. It holds
that it is the economists' very endeavour to delimit their
activities from those of other social students, and to make
them, so to speak, morally neutral that is wrong. Economic
matters must be considered jointly with other social phenomena ; economics should be integrated into a wider social
science ; any attempt to draw a line between economic and
non-economic causes and consequences is likely to lead to
fallacious conclusions. Confronted with attacks on this
flank, economists are apt to shrug their shoulders. It is for
the sociologists to be more explicit, to offer some point for
consideration. As they seldom do this, economists are
inclined to infer that their adjurations are due to their
bankruptcy of precise ideas in their own field.

In the argument which I shall now develop, ethical and
economic reasonings are interlocked. Each practitioner
must concern himself with the subject-matter of the other
study in an unwonted manner. Thus this essay is a contribution towards that integration within social studies which
sociologists so often desiderate ; but I am afraid that the
type of reasoning I shall employ will not be to their taste.

In what follows I shall be concerned with the concept of
moral obligation. This only covers part of the ground of
ethics. Another part of ethics is concerned with altruism,
or, to use more humane words, kindness and unselfishness ;
in that field we are concerned with more or less, from the
extreme altruism of the saintly man who gives his whole life
to the service of others, by successive stages to the ordinary
man who thinks much of self but achieves a measure of
kindness and self-sacrifice, onwards to the selfish brute at
the other extreme.

In the sphere of moral obligation we are not usually confronted with such gradations; there is a certain thing that ought to be done — to be truthful, for example, when speaking; and not to do it is wrong. To all such classes of obligation there are likely to be exceptions.

Although the concept of moral obligation implies a fixed rule, unlike the gradations of general kindliness, there may be gradations in the strength of moral sentiment supporting the fixed rule. To charge a price equal to cost of production including normal profit is the kind of behaviour that might in principle be a moral obligation; it is, so to speak, a candidate for admission to the class of moral obligations, but, as I have repeated, the moral sentiment in its favour is weak.

It is now needful for me to outline a theory of moral obligation. In doing so I shall not be reporting the views of others, but advancing my own temerariously.[1] My treatment will be one of extreme brevity and focused upon the matter in hand. No doubt for a full treatment of the theory of moral obligation, certain other principles and modifications would have to be introduced.

I hold that a rule of conduct in a certain type of situation is morally obligatory in a given society if the following three propositions are true of it:

1. Most members of the society regard it as morally obligatory.

2. The advantage to society consequent upon most members observing the rule is substantial, and substantially greater than the sum of each of the advantages that would accrue if each separately acted upon it while the others did not.

3. If there are a number of alternative possibilities of choice in a given situation, the rule must provide a unique solution in regard to what should be done.

These three criteria are all fulfilled in the great historic rules of conduct universally recognised as morally obligatory in civilised society. I give as examples truth-telling, honouring promises, serving one's country in war-time.

I draw attention to the complex second criterion. It marks within the ethical sphere the distinction between the

[1] For a fuller treatment, see *Mind*, April 1936, 'Utilitarianism Revised', by R. F. Harrod.

kinds of action to which the words right and wrong are applied, and the kinds to which the words good and bad (or unselfish and selfish) are appropriate. In the latter case the merits of each separate act can be judged on its own, albeit taking into account its remotest foreseeable consequences, without reference to whether other people are acting in a similar way; in the former case reference to the contemporary actions of others is necessary.

It must not be inferred from the presence of the first criterion that I hold that what makes a kind of action a moral obligation is merely that people think it so. This would take me perilously near to the 'emotive noise' schools, whose doctrines I repudiate, on the one hand, and to certain kinds of German idealism on the other. Throughout history sundry rules have been generally held to be obligatory, but were not so in fact, because they failed under the *second* criterion. Some rules may fulfil the second criterion if the surrounding circumstances of the society are of a certain kind, but fail under it when those circumstances change; it is then that reformers should come forward, to persuade people to alter their ideas. There may also be cases which would come nearer to the 'thinking makes it so' position, where the benefits under criterion 2 can be obtained only if there is a rule, but can equally well be obtained under several alternative rules; in such cases, which rule was obligatory would depend simply on the first criterion.

But although the first criterion is not sufficient to constitute a moral obligation, it is necessary. The individual will not feel himself bound by a rule — fulfilment of which in certain cases may have net harmful consequences to himself and others — if most of the fellow members of his community do not recognise or observe it. There is then no point in his observing it either, especially when it is positively injurious to himself and others for him to do so.

If a rule fulfils the second and third criteria but not the first, there is scope for the moralist or preacher to endeavour to get the first criterion fulfilled also. There is a difficulty here, however. He cannot validly castigate those who do not observe the rule, so long as most do not. How, then, persuade most to do so? There seems to be a vicious circle, which may in fact be the greatest impediment to man's moral progress. The 'international anarchy' is a case in point. Many nations would gladly observe certain codes of international behaviour, if only a sufficient number were of like mind. Yet, if there are not enough of like mind, those striving for international order may feel unable to regard the rules as in all cases binding on themselves. And this very fact confirms the non-conformists in their scepticism.

If there is a rule to which the second and third criteria clearly apply, one may think of it as a moral obligation in embryo. In such cases there may be a strong or weak moral sentiment in its favour; let the sentiment become strong enough, and the rule automatically becomes obligatory. The embryo may struggle forward to maturity. Or the environment may change and nothing more may be heard of the rule.

I have suggested that there is a weak moral sentiment in favour of fixing a price in relation to cost. This sentiment may grow weaker and eventually disappear. On the other hand it is conceivable that it might grow stronger. The sentiment seems to be too weak, and action in accordance with it too irregular, for us to regard the first criterion as fulfilled or to dub the man who pursues a high-price policy as, without qualification, a wicked fellow

We must turn to the second criterion. None of this moral sentiment is of any importance or potential validity if the second criterion is not fulfilled. This brings me to the crucial point. It is the economist, and the economist only, who can say whether it is fulfilled. This brings the economist right into the middle of the field of ethics. If the economist pronounces that the second criterion is fulfilled, then he should give a lead to public opinion to try to get the first criterion fulfilled also. But if the second criterion is not fulfilled, then any hue-and-cry in favour of the first is a mere waste of time. Thus the economist by his answer will, if public opinion responds, be acting as a moral legislator. His verdict will create a new kind of moral offence. He should not hesitate to do this, because, if he does not, no one else can. And it may be that the society would gain much from the introduction of this new moral rule. Thus in this case it is the economist's task to pronounce on whether a certain moral obligation exists, not tentatively and with deference to moral philosophers, but aggressively, in his own right and in the proper discharge of his special function.

Surely economists will in fact answer in the affirmative. If only a few producers price by cost, that will not by itself improve the distribution of resources among users; indeed, if monopolistic price-fixing is widespread, it may worsen the distribution. But if most producers observe the rule, that will indeed get a better distribution of productive resources. Thus the advantage that occurs if most observe the rule is greater than the sum of each of the separate advantages that occur when one observes the rule, but most do not. This is precisely the second criterion for the existence of a moral obligation.

The question may be raised how — if the basis of the common moral rules of conduct is really as complex as that stated in the second criterion — man ever came to adopt these rules so widely. This may be something of a mystery, but is not peculiar to the field of moral obligation. Modern science has taught us to expect fairly rigorous proofs of conclusions to be accepted. But before the dawn of modern science man had already progressed far in complex technology and social arrangements, sustained on accepted conclusions, for which the proofs were not forthcoming. Did the conclusions win dominance by some process of individual or social natural selection, so that, so far as the individual or society were concerned they were in effect innate ideas? Or was there all the time some half-conscious apprehension of the premises? Even in branches of modern science proofs are not always rigorous.

In the case of some moral rules, such as truthfulness, the implicit argument is not very difficult. If there were no obligation to be truthful, one would tell the truth when the consequences of doing so, as far as they could be traced, were advantageous to oneself and others, and would tell lies in the opposite case. This would have disastrous consequences, since the great abundance of lies would undermine confidence in those purporting to convey information; communication between members of a society, which is so valuable, might become entirely impossible; communication cannot exist in the absence of all confidence in the truthfulness of what is stated. This fact justifies a sentiment in favour of truth-telling even in cases where its direct effects, as traceable, are harmful to all concerned. In calling the sentiment arising in such a kind of case moral, I am defining the word 'moral'.

It does not follow that there can be no exceptions to a moral rule. We may be able to divide a category of occasions of behaviour into sub-classes, and, if we find in the case of some sub-classes considered by themselves (*e.g.* in the case of communicating information, matters concerning lethal diseases, defence secrets, etc.) that the second criterion does not apply, then we may exempt these sub-classes from the general rule, provided that this exemption does not seriously detract from the benefits conveyed by the general rule. In the case of communication we must not make the exceptions to truthfulness sufficiently numerous to have any appreciable effect in undermining confidence in communication.

If one has to allow too many exceptions, this may not only jeopardise the benefits obtainable under the second criterion, but also the maintenance of the first criterion. It is not easy to maintain a strong moral sentiment in favour of a type of action while subjecting it to numerous exceptions. Unfortunately the cost-price principle would have to be so subjected. In the case of a temporary expansion of the market it may be good that the price should be raised, so as to get the best use of scarce supplies and keep the economy running smoothly. It is difficult to set a limit to what is 'temporary' in this connexion. When there is a long-drawn-out inflation we have seen that it may not be clear whether price-raising is better than allowing waiting lists to develop. Again, it may be good that an entrepreneur who strives to expand his business quickly should charge high prices for the time being, so as to have a high profit to plough back. And no doubt there are other exceptions.

The third criterion is fulfilled for producers under imperfect competition, but not for those under perfect competition.[1]

This essay offers no dogmatic conclusion. Its aim has been to present a new type of discussion.

[1] I owe the perception of this cardinal point to Mr. Hitch.

# III

# EMPLOYMENT

ESSAY 11

# THE EXPANSION OF CREDIT IN AN
## ADVANCING COMMUNITY[1]

THE question has been much discussed recently whether
in an advancing community it is desirable that the general
level of prices should remain constant or fall in proportion
to the increase in the flow of goods.  Grave difficulties beset
any attempt to define the general level of prices, and these
apply in connexion with either desideratum.  When a fall
of prices is considered, the weights used in the index number
of prices should, of course, be the same as those used in
defining the increase in the flow of goods.

The following essay is divided into two parts.  The
first contains a brief summary of the considerations affecting the choice between the two alternatives.  The second is
concerned with some misconceptions with regard to the distorting effect on sectional price levels that an increase in the
quantity of money by an extension of producers' credits has
been supposed to produce.

It may be observed that this is not primarily an essay
in trade cycle analysis.  It is an enquiry into the relation

---

[1] *Economica*, August 1934. [Although the name of Professor F. A. von
Hayek is not mentioned in this essay, it was intended to be a refutation of
certain ideas set forth by him in his *Prices and Production*, which had considerable influence in the following years.

My main reason, however, for including it in this collection is that it is
an essay in dynamic economics, in the sense in which I have ever since
urged that that expression be used and that subject studied (cf. pp. 252-6).
Even now this method of approach remains somewhat rare in economic
literature, and an example of its exercise may be illuminating.  It bears marks
of having been written before the appearance of Keynes's *General Theory* and
suffers from that.  But for all the path-breaking importance of that great
work, it is in one respect retrograde by comparison with this essay; for, dealing
with the subject also dealt with in this essay, namely the balance between
saving and investment, which can only validly be tackled in dynamic terms,
it uses static concepts.  1952.]

between the rates of increase in a regularly advancing society, with a view to determining what kind of system would allow the full potentialities of progress to be realised while being internally self-consistent. The second section professes to throw some light on trade cycle theory by demonstrating that an alleged cause of fluctuation is not a true cause.

I

It is not proposed to go outside the limits of a stable price system on the one hand and a system in which the quantity of money is kept constant on the other. Since the hypothesis of an advancing community seems to preclude a diminishing flow of goods, a rising price system will not be considered. A constant money system is defined as one in which the flow of money is such that the general price level moves down at the same rate that real aggregate income increases, it being assumed that changes in the velocity of circulation or changes in the amount of work that money has to do through vertical integrations or disintegrations in the productive process are offset by appropriate changes in the supply of money.

It is possible that the true desideratum lies between the extremes set forth in the foregoing paragraph, and this will be considered.

If the constant money system is adopted two difficulties arise, which will be called the primary difficulty and the secondary difficulty. It is not suggested, however, that in the real world the secondary difficulty is the less important.

The primary difficulty is that connected with the fact that certain rewards to factors, *e.g.* to debenture holders, are contractually fixed in money for long periods. The secondary difficulty is that connected with the fact that factors, whose money rewards are legally and in principle adjustable, *e.g.* wage-earners, are often unwilling to agree to a downward revision. The difficulties arise when, under a falling price system, the consequential rise of real rewards to these factors in the absence of a monetary adjustment is greater than the rise in their real productivity per unit.

The secondary difficulty is so named because it is possible in principle, though it may not be in practice, to overcome it within the structure of our economic system, by persuading the factors themselves to agree to suitable revisions; while the primary difficulty is so named because it cannot be overcome without a change in the structure of the economic system under which we live. It is proposed to examine, first, the consequences of these difficulties when they do arise and, secondly, the conditions in which they are likely to arise.

1. The secondary difficulty arises when the productivity per unit of a factor, such as labour, does not increase at so great a rate as prices are falling. Under a constant money system this would occur when the productivity of labour per unit is not increasing as rapidly as aggregate income. Its consequences are well known and need not be dwelt upon here. Unless a downward revision of monetary rates of reward can be secured, it becomes impossible for the factor to obtain full employment and the regular economic advance of the community is impeded.

The consequences of the primary difficulty require more detailed scrutiny. Owners of fixed means of production are divided into two classes, those whose lien on the product of the fixed instruments is contractually fixed in terms of money over a long period, and those whose titles secure to them the remainder of the product. The primary difficulty arises when the fall of prices proceeds more quickly than the productivity, per unit, of the fixed instruments increases. Under a constant money system this happens, when aggregate income increases more rapidly than the productivity, per unit, of fixed instruments of production. The 'fixed interests' then become entitled to a rising share in the product of the fixed instruments.

The occurrence of the primary difficulty entails two consequences, both of which retard to a serious degree the normal advance of the community. (i) The rate of bankruptcies is increased. (ii) The proportion of firms not earning a normal rate of profit is increased.

(i) Bankruptcy normally performs two important functions in our system. (*a*) It puts out of operation sources of production, the output of which, owing to unforeseen changes in the conditions of supply and demand, is no longer worth producing. (*b*) It eliminates the less efficient producers, thus tending to the survival of the fittest. The expression 'healthy bankruptcy' has had some vogue recently. It is a valuable one if the adjective is used selectively to distinguish the bankruptcies which discharge these two functions from those which do not. It is misleading when the adjective is used as an undiscriminating tribute to all bankruptcies, as such.

The swelling up of the value of fixed money charges through a rise in the value of money increases the number of bankruptcies. Now it is well known that the existence of fixed money charges has economic disadvantages; ideally the whole ownership of fixed means of production ought to be of the 'equity' form. For it is economically sound that fixed means should continue to be exploited, so long as the value of the product exceeds the prime costs. The existence of fixed money charges brings the operation of firms to a premature end, if and when the value of the product, while exceeding prime costs, does not exceed them sufficiently to meet the fixed charges. The system of incurring fixed money charges, though it may be best suited to eliciting the required supply of means of production, has the demerit of entailing premature death in many cases. The swelling up of the fixed money charge renders the deaths still more premature and must be set down as a notable disadvantage of a system of falling prices, if and in so far as that system causes the primary difficulty to arise.

It may be objected that the fixed assets of a firm can be sold on liquidation, and set to work again relieved of all or part of the fixed charges. But this is not necessarily so. Fixed means of production are of two kinds, the material and the immaterial, the latter consisting of the knowledge and experience embodied in the enterprise attached to the firm. The break-up of the firm divorces one form of fixed asset from another, and it may happen that neither can be profitably exploited without the other. Moreover, the immaterial asset is sensibly damaged by the discredit attaching to failure. It may be impossible for those who have to assess the value of the immaterial asset with a view to future collaboration to determine how far a falling price system and how far inefficiency was the cause of failure. And valuable entrepreneurial ability may, in consequence, be lost to the economic system and run to waste.

(ii) The second consequence of the swelling up in the value of fixed money charges is probably still more detrimental. The number of firms earning subnormal profits is increased. These firms are not likely to be able to secure capital for expansion. Opportunities may offer allowing a normal or supernormal return on the additional outlay designed to take advantage of them, but, if a firm is waterlogged by reason of fixed charges incurred in the past, it will have to let them go by. Even in spheres in which competition is 'perfect', this may retard progress, for much enterprise being attached to the waterlogged forms, the supply of enterprise available outside them to co-operate with other factors of production is severely restricted; a section of the community's productive resources which should normally be available is put out of action. When competition is imperfect, the situation is worse. For the firms, or some of the firms, to whom alone the fresh opportunities offer, may be precisely those which are unable, by reason of their past obligations, to obtain fresh capital.

The patience and kindness of creditors and banks, while tending to ease the situation with regard to bankruptcies, does nothing to alleviate the evil due to the prevalence of subnormal profits.

2. Next it is necessary to examine the conditions in which the primary and secondary difficulties might arise. Falling prices are associated with a rising aggregate real income. This can only be due to an increase in either (*a*) the quantity or (*b*) the power of the factors of production. It is required to find the probable relation between an increase of income due to either cause and an increase in the productivity of the factor, the money rewards to which are not adjusted.

Consider first the primary difficulty. For a brief summary, it may be sufficient to use the classification of factors into natural resources, capital and labour. On the side of quantity of factors, income may increase owing to an increase in the quantity of capital and/or labour. A proportional increase of both increases national income, but does not normally increase the productivity per unit of existing fixed instruments. Then under any system other than a stable price system, the primary difficulty arises. If there is an increase in the quantity of capital greater than that in the quantity of labour, aggregate income rises, but the productivity of fixed instruments tends to be affected unfavourably. Again the primary difficulty arises. The reverse effect ensues, if labour is increasing more rapidly than capital. But I propose to rule that possibility out as being inconsistent with the hypothesis of an advancing community. Any increase of income, then, due to an increase in the quantity of factors, gives rise to the primary difficulty, except under a stable price policy.

An increase in the power of factors, due to forces, which may be characterised by the generic expression 'technological advance', increases aggregate income. Now this technological advance may increase the productivity of existing instruments. Broadly, however, it is of the nature of a technological advance to be biased against pre-existing instruments. It is possible that it will not increase the productivity of pre-existing instruments at all; it is unlikely to increase their productivity as much as it increases the productivity of the community generally. Accordingly it is possible in these circumstances that the primary difficulty will arise under any system except that of stable prices; and it is very probable that it will arise under the system of constant money.

To summarise, an increase of aggregate income due to an increase in the quantity of factors — and this increase occurs even with a stationary population, if any net annual saving is occurring — will entail the primary difficulty under any system except that of stable prices. And an increase of aggregate income due to an increase in the power of factors *may* give rise to the primary difficulty under any system except that of stable prices and *is likely to* give rise to it under a system of constant money. In a normally advancing society in which the increase is due to both causes, the constant money system must give rise to the primary difficulty, but under a system in which prices fall at a considerably slower rate than income increases, it may be possible to avoid it.

At this stage it may be well to examine a possibility that has not so far been considered. It may happen that some of the fixed money charges have been incurred in a way that admits of 'conversion' on to a lower interest basis. Make the supposition most favourable to a régime of falling prices, that *all* fixed money charges may, when occasion offers, be so converted. As this is an analysis of the economics of a regularly advancing community, it is proper to suppose that the market rate of interest is equal to the natural rate, and that conversion is only possible if there is a fall in the natural rate.

It is worth giving brief attention to the fallacy that a fall in prices is a sufficient condition for the possibility of conversion. If all prices fall, it might be argued crudely, the price of capital will fall too! But interest is 'money for money', and a change in the value of money by itself makes no difference in the rate. If, for instance, capital and labour were increasing *pari passu*, and the only technological change was one which increased the power of natural resources in such wise as to leave the marginal productivity of capital and labour constant, aggregate income would also rise and prices under a constant money system would fall. The marginal productivity of capital and therefore the rate of interest would remain unchanged. But, it might be objected, the capital market may discount the future fall of prices and the money rate may stand below the natural rate by an amount sufficient to offset the prospective increase in the value of money. This is true, but irrelevant. If a fall of prices is confidently anticipated, the money rate will be *permanently* lower than it otherwise would be. But it will have no tendency to fall! And therefore no possibility of conversion will arise from this cause.

Possibilities of conversion will indeed arise, if forces

operate to reduce the natural rate of interest. This may happen through an excess rate of increase of capital or through 'capital-saving' technological improvements. It can be shown, however, that the existence of these possibilities does not affect the arguments of the foregoing paragraphs. For forces, tending to reduce the productivity of capital generally, are likely to reduce in similar measure the productivity of existing instruments of production. There may not be an exact parallelism; existing instruments may be more or they may be less injured than capital generally. It is fair to assume in the absence of special knowledge with regard to the change of circumstances, that it will affect both equally. But, if that is so, the possibility of conversion will not prevent the primary difficulty from arising. For the conversion will only reduce the fixed money claims in the same proportion that the real productivity of the fixed instruments is reduced. It will not also reduce them in proportion to the fall in the money returns accruing to a unit of real productivity. It will, therefore, do nothing to offset the tendency of the proportion of the return to fixed instruments, that has to be paid to the fixed money claims, to swell owing to the fall in prices.

It is important that this point should be clearly apprehended. The joint money income of the owners of fixed instruments is falling in the circumstances supposed, owing to two causes, (i) the fall in prices and (ii) the fall in the real productivity of the fixed instruments. Conversion can only reduce the money income of 'fixed interests' in proportion to the fall in the real productivity of fixed instruments. There is no reduction in the income of 'fixed interests' to correspond with the fall in prices. Consequently the share of the total investment income which goes to the 'fixed interests' rises. Considerations, therefore, connected with conversion possibilities leave the conclusions of the foregoing paragraphs with their validity unimpaired.

It remains to examine the conditions which give rise to the secondary difficulty. (i) *Quantity*. If the quantity of labour and capital are increasing *pari passu*, the equilibrium real wage does not normally increase, and the secondary difficulty will arise under any system except that of stable prices. If capital is increasing in quantity more quickly than labour, there is some increase in the equilibrium real wage, and some fall of prices is consistent with avoidance of the secondary difficulty. The condition for avoiding it, however, with a constant money system and a stationary population is that the elasticity of substitution of capital should not be greater than one.

(ii) *Power*. The secondary difficulty can only be avoided with falling prices, if the increase of power raises the marginal productivity of labour. With a constant money system it can be avoided only if the productivity of labour rises as much as aggregate income, *i.e.* if the technological advance is not on balance of a 'labour-saving' kind.

*Summary*. If the increase of income is due to an increase in the quantity of the factors, the primary difficulty can only be avoided by a system of stable prices and the secondary difficulty by one in which prices do not fall more than the marginal productivity of labour increases. If the increase of income is due to an increase in the power of the factors, to avoid the primary difficulty it is necessary that prices should not fall more than the productivity of fixed instruments increases, and to avoid the secondary difficulty it is necessary that prices should not fall more than the marginal productivity of labour increases. It appears that if both difficulties are to be avoided, there is only a narrow range of technological improvements, the increase of income due to which can be allowed to entail a corresponding fall in prices. Put otherwise, if both difficulties are to be avoided, the maximum rate at which prices can be allowed to fall is the rate at which the productivity of fixed instruments per unit is increasing or the rate at which the productivity of labour per unit is increasing, whichever is smaller. And if the primary difficulty is to be avoided the system of constant money is not allowable, if any net saving at all is occurring.

So far no difficulties connected with the stable price system have been considered. If this were really free of all difficulty, then surely it ought to be preferred, both for its simplicity and by reason of the doubts which must always be present in a real situation as to whether the conditions, under which falling prices will not give rise to the primary or secondary difficulties, are fulfilled.

There are two principal difficulties which, it has been suggested, may arise in connexion with the stable price system. The first is concerned with the disturbance to sectional price levels caused by the infusion of new money. This difficulty, which is examined in section II of this paper, I believe to be illusory. The second is concerned with the failure, on occasion, of rewards to factors of production to move upward in the manner which the preservation of equilibrium requires, and the consequent inflation of profit. This is really an inverse form of the secondary difficulty referred to above.

It should be observed at once that the inverse secondary difficulty is not such a weighty matter as the direct secondary difficulty. Both are due to a certain inertia in the economic system. In a régime of *laissez-faire*, trouble may arise because factors of production stubbornly resist downward revisions of their monetary payments, or because they are sluggish in pressing for those payments which the conditions of supply and demand enable them to obtain. To put the second alternative more strongly, we may write — because employers resist an upward revision of rates of payment to their employees. If now the community wishes for the equilibrium of regular advance to be maintained, it can urge, through the organs which give effect to its will, that employees should consent to a downward revision or that employers should consent to an upward revision, as the case may be. The chances of this persuasion being effective are clearly less in the former case than in the latter, especially when it is remembered that on occasions when an upward revision is urged, the higher level is consistent, by hypothesis, with the earning by employers of normal rates of profit on balance.

It may be thought that, besides an inverse secondary difficulty, an inverse primary difficulty might arise. This, if it were right to suppose that it would arise at all, would do so much less frequently than the inverse secondary difficulty, only, in fact, when technological improvements were making existing instruments of production more productive on balance. But in fact it will not arise at all. The disturbance which is thought to result from the inverse difficulty, arises because entrepreneurs are led to embark on projects, which can only be profitable while real rewards to factors are below the equilibrium level and may subsequently prove, if real rewards are restored, to have been ill-advised and wasteful. But the level of rewards to the 'fixed interests' is an irrelevant consideration in the decision to embark on fresh projects. An abnormally low level of rewards to these, if it has an influence in this connexion, will tend to check rather than to stimulate the formation of new *firms*, by rendering the existing firms more solvent. But this tendency is desirable, in accordance with a principle that has already been explained (pages 224-5 above). There is, consequently, no inverse primary difficulty.

The inverse secondary difficulty cannot occur under a system of stable prices when a departure from that system would give rise to the direct secondary difficulty. It only occurs when a fall of prices would not provoke the direct secondary difficulty. Now there are occasions when a fall would not provoke the secondary but would provoke the primary difficulty. Consequently it is possible to imagine situations in which a conflict occurs between secondary and primary considerations, when it is impossible to avoid the primary difficulty without incurring the inverse secondary difficulty and vice versa. What should be done then remains an open question. It must be borne in mind that it is possible to overcome the inverse secondary but impossible to overcome the primary difficulty within our existing economic structure. *Per contra* the magnitude of the inverse secondary difficulty which in practice occurs may be greater than that of the primary difficulty, and policy should be shaped accordingly.

Finally, it should be noted that the lag of real wages behind the advance of labour productivity should cause no trouble provided that the lag is constant.

From these considerations it appears that the ideal

system in a community advancing in a normal and regular way might be consistent with some fall of prices, but not with keeping the quantity of money constant in the sense defined at the outset. It is unlikely that the fall of prices should be nearly as great as the increase of aggregate income, or as great as the increase of income per head.

II

It remains to consider the troubles which have been supposed to be due to the infusion by producers' credits of such new money as is required for the maintenance of the desired price policy. This infusion has been supposed to necessitate the depression of the market below the natural rate of interest with a consequent disturbance of sectional price levels.

In examining this contention it is only proper to analyse what occurs when a regular advance is under way. If irregularities and discontinuities occur, there will be sectional disturbances under *any* system. The correct mode of procedure is to determine what are the relative rates of increase of the various quantities in the system and ascertain whether these rates are mutually consistent. It appears probable that whatever system is most stable in the absence of discontinuities will absorb the shock of discontinuities with least subsequent disturbance.

Consider the case of a rising aggregate income and a stable price level. On the assumption of constant velocity the community will require to add to its monetary holdings, at the same rate that income is increasing. Suppose, to take the extreme case, that all money consists of banking obligations — notes and deposits — and that the assets held against these obligations consist exclusively of producers' credits. The rate at which credit must be expanded in order to maintain the system is equal to the rate at which aggregate income is increasing.

The natural rate of interest is that which causes real capital to be increased at a rate equal to that at which the aggregate savings of the community increase. The savings of the community in any period may be defined as the difference between the value of its total income and the value of the consumable goods purchased therewith. It is required to determine whether the banking system will be obliged, in its effort to infuse new money, to depress the market rate of interest below this.

Let X be the total stock of money in existence at any time and $x$ the new money that is to be injected in the succeeding unit period. $x/X$ = the rate at which aggregate income is increasing. The community may be divided into two sections, the business section and the income receivers. The business section sells consumable goods and securities to income receivers and buys the services of income receivers as factors of production; members of the business section also buy and sell goods from and to each other. The income receivers sell their services as factors of production to the business section and buy goods and securities from it. Individual members of the community may belong to both sections in their respective capacities of entrepreneurs and income receivers.

The distribution of the stock of money between the two classes may be constant or changing. In either case we may suppose that $qx$ is the increment in a given unit period that the business section requires and $(1-q)x$ consequently the increment that income receivers require in the same unit period. $q$ may be zero, in the case in which all members of the business section are overdrawn.

In the unit period income receivers pay to the business community $(1-q)x$ less units of money by the purchase of goods and securities than they receive from it as factors. Consequently, unless it is replenished from some other source, the monetary holding of the business section will run down by $(1-q)x$. But the business section wishes to increase it by $qx$. If it is to do this, it will have to receive money from some other source equal to $(1-q)x + qx = x$. And this is equal to the amount of new money injected by the banking system. It need not be supposed that any of the individual borrowers from the banks use any portion of the borrowed money to add to their monetary holdings; it suffices for the preservation of a mutually consistent system that some members of the section should add to their monetary holdings, and this they will do, unless $q=0$. But, if $q=0$, the *whole* increment of money $x$ will be required by the business section to make good the excess of disbursements to income receivers over receipts from them.

Let the amount of saving in the unit period be $s$. Income receivers disburse in the purchase of securities $s-(1-q)x$ in the unit period. If the business community wishes to increase its holding of real capital by $s$ it must pay out to income receivers (including interest receivers) $s$ units more than it receives from them by the sale of consumable goods. It therefore needs to 'raise' $s$ units by the sale of securities. But it needs to raise more than this. For its capital assets consist not only of real capital but also of such monetary stocks as it needs to hold. Therefore, if it is to increase its holding of real capital by $s$ units, it must 'raise' by the sale of securities not only $s$ units but $s+qx$ units. But from the sale of securities to income receivers it will only get $s-(1-q)x$ units. Therefore it must 'raise' $x$ units in addition to what it gets from this source. And this is what it gets by the additional credits $(x)$ granted by the banks. If the banking system keeps its rates at such a level that the business community borrows $x$ units from it, it will enable the business community to increase its real capital by $s$ units, which is precisely equal to the difference between the income receivers' income and their expenditure on consumable goods. Therefore if the banking system keeps its rates at such a level that the business community is led to secure $x$ units of additional loans from it, it is maintaining rates at their natural level. The whole system is perfectly self-consistent.

The belief that disturbances of the sectional price level will follow on the infusion of new money appears to be due to the omission in this system of national book-keeping of an important cross-entry, viz. the addition to their monetary stocks that both sections or at least one section of the community will require to make. It need hardly be observed that if the velocity of circulation was rising at the same rate as national income, this cross-entry would not be required, but then the further consequence would also follow that no additional loans would be necessary for the maintenance of a stable price level.

It may have been observed that in computing the addition to the real capital of the community, which it is required to equate to savings, the increase of monetary stocks was excluded. And this was perfectly correct. The increase of mutual indebtedness which a rising aggregate of outstanding bank credit implies is not an addition to the real capital of the community. Far different would be the case in which the medium of exchange consisted of gold. In this case the addition to the monetary stock would have to be reckoned in as part of the addition to real capital, and the natural rate of interest would be that which equated the saving of the community to the increase of other forms of real capital plus the increase in its monetary holding. It may be well to trace out what happens in this case.

Suppose that the new supplies of gold $(x)$ accrue to the business community either by foreign exchange arbitrage operations or gold-mining. On the monetary side in any unit period it receives from income receivers $(1 - q)x$ less units than it pays to them; and it requires to add to its own gold holdings by $qx$ units. The new supplies of gold $(x)$ are disposed of in this way. On the capital side, it can sell securities to income receivers worth $s - (1 - q)x$; and of this sum it has to use $qx$ to build up its own monetary holdings; consequently, since it receives no loans from the banking system, only $s - x$ is available for additions to its real capital other than gold.

If an intermediate system is employed, in which the banks hold a fixed proportion of their assets in the form of gold and only banking obligations are used by the community as money, then the natural rate of interest is the one which equates the increase of real capital excluding gold to the savings of the community, as defined above, minus the addition to the banks' stock of gold. Thus with a given rate of saving, the addition to the aids to production consistent with equilibrium is diminished more, the more that gold stocks are increased. The increment of prosperity that may be obtained by dispensing with a gold backing has been explained long ago by Ricardo.

If these arguments are correct, it follows that new money can be injected by producers' credits at a steady rate without producing sectional price disturbances, and that we are free to choose whatever price policy the considerations of the first part of this essay indicate as best.

# KEYNES AND TRADITIONAL THEORY [1]

In this paper I do not propose to ask or answer the question, has Keynes succeeded in establishing the propositions which he claims to have established? nor again, what kind of evidence is required to establish or to refute those propositions? I shall confine myself to a narrower question, namely, what are the propositions which Keynes claims to have established? And in order to restrict my subject matter still further, I propose to confine myself to those propositions, which he claims to have established, that are in conflict with the theory of value in the form in which it has hitherto been commonly accepted by most economists. In other words, my question is, what modifications in the generally recognised theory of value would acceptance of the propositions that Keynes claims to have established entail?

In order to clarify the issues involved it may be well to divide commonly accepted theory into the general theory and its specialised branches. The general theory consists primarily of a number of functional equations expressing individual preference schedules and a number of identities, such as that supply must be equal to demand, and the elucidation of such questions as whether there are as many equations as there are unknowns and whether the solutions are single or multiple. The result of these enquiries should make it clear whether the equilibrium of the system as a whole is stable or unstable or undetermined, whether there are alternative positions of equilibrium, etc. There may be some clues as to the general form of some of the functional equations, provided by such principles as the Law of Diminishing Utility, to use old-fashioned terminology, which may make it possible to predict the direction of changes in the

[1] *Econometrica*, January 1937.

values of the various unknowns due to a given change in one of them. More precise prediction can only be achieved if or when it becomes possible, as a result of the labours of such investigators as Dr. Schultz, to write down the actual terms of the functional equations. Within the corpus of this general theory may be included the formulation of the market conditions that are required for the realisation of some kind of maximum. Thus if one individual A is indifferent whether he produces commodity X or commodity Y for a certain consideration, and another individual B prefers X to Y, the maximum is not realised if the market so operates that A normally produces Y and not X for B. On this condition the maxim of Free Trade is fairly securely founded, the more general maxim of *laissez-faire* much less securely so.

In contrast with the theory of value in this very general form may be set the special theories formulated to deal with specific problems such as interest, profit, joint production, discriminating monopoly, etc. The normal method used in dealing with these departmental studies is to assume that certain terms, which appear as variables in the general system of equations, may be treated as constants for the special purpose in hand. For instance, in studying the behaviour of duopolistic producers of a given commodity, it may be assumed that the duopolists can obtain the services of factors of production at rates the determination of which in the market will not be appreciably affected by the duopolists' behaviour. Such methods constitute short cuts to the unravelling of particular problems and they are often perfectly legitimate. In the minds of most economists, other than those who stand, so to speak, at the philosophical end of the economic array, the conclusions reached by these short-cut methods constitute the main findings of economic theory.

I may say at once that in my opinion Keynes's conclusions need not be deemed to make a vast difference to the general theory, but that they do make a vast difference to a number of short-cut conclusions of leading importance. Thus to those whom I may perhaps call without offence the ordinary working economists they ought, if accepted, to appear to constitute quite a revolution. Whether they entail a substantial modification of the more general theory depends on how that is stated. I need hardly observe that there is no authorised version. Those whose main interest is in the general theory, may, if they have laid their foundations well and carefully, be able to look down with a smile of indifference on the fulminations of Keynes. Pavilioned upon their Olympian fastness, they are not likely to show much irritation.

It is convenient to take Keynes's theory of interest as the starting point of this exposition. In the commonly accepted short-cut theory there are two unknowns and two equations. The two unknowns are the volume of saving (= the volume of investment) and the rate of interest. Of the new-fangled view, sponsored by some out-of-the-way definitions in Keynes's *Treatise on Money*, that the volume of saving may be unequal to the volume of investment, it is not necessary to say anything, since it has played no part in the standard short-cut formulations of interest theory (although it has figured in recent writings concerned with practical monetary problems). The commonly accepted interest theory from the time of the early classical writers onwards entails that saving is always and necessarily equal to investment.

The two equations in the traditional theory of interest correspond to the demand and supply schedules relating to a particular commodity. First there is the demand equation $y = f(x)$, $y$, the marginal productivity of capital, depending on $x$, the amount of capital invested per unit of time. So much capital will be invested that its marginal productivity is equal to the rate of interest; that is, $y = y'$, where $y'$ is the rate of interest. Since both the traditional theory and Keynes hold that investment is undertaken up to the point at which the marginal productivity of capital is equal to the rate of interest, $y'$ may be suppressed, and $y$ made to stand for the rate of interest which is equal to the marginal productivity of capital.

Then there is the supply equation $x = \phi(y)$; $x$, the amount which individuals choose to save, which is equal to the amount of investment, depends on the rate of interest. Thus there are two unknowns, the rate of interest and the volume of saving, and sufficient equations to determine them. It is not necessary for the present purpose to consider controversies concerning the forms of these equations, such as whether a rise in the rate of interest tends to cause people to save more or less.

This treatment of interest and saving is analogous to that of the price of a particular article and the amount of it produced. The treatment depends on the short-cut assumption of *ceteris paribus*. This is often legitimate in the case of particular commodities, although it is recognised that in certain cases it is idle not to bring in certain other variables, for instance the prices of close substitutes. Among the 'other things' which are supposed to be 'equal' is the level of income in the community under discussion. In many cases it may be true that when we are trying to determine how much of a particular commodity a producer is likely to produce, his decision to produce a little more or a little less will not have a sufficiently large effect on the total income of the community to react on the market for his goods in such a way as to make an appreciable difference to him. This particular short-cut is in that case justified. I suggest that the most important single point in Keynes's analysis is the view that it is illegitimate to assume that the level of income in the community is independent of the amount of investment decided upon. No results achieved by the shortcut of such an assumption can be of any value.

How does Keynes's analysis proceed? His first equation is substantially the same as that of the traditional analysis $y = f(x)$. The marginal productivity of capital is a function of the amount of investment undertaken. The marginal productivity of capital appears in Keynes's book under the title of marginal efficiency. It does not appear that there is a difference of principle here. It is true that Keynes makes an exhaustive and interesting analysis of this marginal efficiency and demonstrates that its value depends on entrepreneurial expectations. The stress which he lays on expectations is sound, and constitutes a great improvement in the definition of marginal productivity. This improvement, however, might be incorporated in traditional theory without entailing important modifications in its other parts.

When we come to the second equation the level of income must be introduced as an unknown term, giving $x = \phi(y, i)$, where $i$ is the level of income. The amount of saving depends not only on the rate of interest, but on the level of income in the community.

It might be thought that to introduce the level of income as an unknown at this point is tantamount to abandoning all attempt to have a departmental theory of the volume of saving, since the level of total income appears in all the equations of the general theory and it is impossible to determine its value without taking all factors into account. This would mean that we should have to leave the ordinary working economist without any departmental theory of saving and interest which he could grasp, and to let him flounder in the maze of $n \times r \times s$, etc., equations governing the whole system. Keynes has, however, come to the rescue and carved out a new short-cut of his own. In his view the value of the unknown level of income can be determined in a legitimate and satisfactory manner by the departmental equations relating to saving and interest only. To the legitimacy of this assumption it will be necessary to return presently.

Meanwhile, since there are three unknowns and but two equations in the savings/interest complex, another equation is needed. Before proceeding to that, it may be well to recur to the second equation, $x = \phi(y, i)$. This may be transposed into the form $i = \psi(x, y)$. The level of income depends on the amount of investment ($=$ that of saving) and the rate of interest. In this form the second equation shows itself as the doctrine of the multiplier. The multiplier is the reciprocal of the fraction expressing the proportion of any given income, which, at a given rate of interest, people consume. If the value of the multiplier is known for any given rate of interest and level of income, the actual level of income can be deduced directly from the volume of investment. Those to whom the doctrine of multiplier seems an alien morsel in the corpus of economic doctrine should remember that it is merely a disguised form of the ordinary supply schedule of free capital, but with the level of income treated as a variable.

In discussing this doctrine, for the sake of a still shorter cut, Keynes is inclined to let the rate of interest drop out of sight. Thus the equation becomes $i = \psi(x)$; the level of income depends on the volume of investment. The justification for this procedure is that whereas the relation of the level of income to the amount of investment is in the broadest sense known — it may be assumed that people save a larger absolute amount from a larger income — the relation of the amount which people choose to save to the rate of interest is a matter of controversy. Moreover in Keynes's view the level of income has a more important effect on the amount which people choose to save than the rate of interest. However, there is no need to pick a quarrel here. The rate of interest may be brought back into this part of the picture without affecting the main argument. The propensity to consume may be regarded as depending on the rate of interest, although for the sake of brevity and clarity mention of this need not be insisted on at every point in an exposition of the doctrine of the multiplier.

What of the third equation? We have $y = \chi(m)$, where $m$ is the quantity of money, a known term, depending on banking policy. This is the liquidity preference schedule. Probably $i$, the level of income, ought to be inserted in this equation, thus: $y = \chi(m, i)$, since the amount of money required for active circulation by consumers and traders depends on the level of income. Ought not the price level to come in also? That may be taken to be subsumed under $i$, the level of income, in a manner that I shall presently explain. The residue of money, not required for active circulation, is available for ordinary people who are discouraged by their brokers from immediate investment, and, more important, for firms, who may want cash for capital extensions or similar purposes within six months or a year or two, and are unwilling to hold their reserves in the form of securities to which some risk of depreciation within the prescribed period is attached. Since the amount of money available for liquid reserves is strictly limited and cannot be increased by the mere desire on the part of firms to hold more money than that, the prospective yield of less liquid reserves must be sufficient to confine those who insist on a money reserve to the amount of money available for that purpose. The less the amount of money available the higher the rate of interest will have to be, both because the high rate is a *quid pro quo* against the risk of depreciation of the capital and also because the higher the present rate the less probability is there of depreciation within the prescribed period.

It is not necessary to give a final pronouncement on the significance of the liquidity preference equation. It appears that even if some modification is required in this third equation, which determines the rate of interest, a type of analysis similar in its general structure to that of Keynes may be maintained.

We now have three equations to determine the value of the three unknowns, level of income, volume of saving (= volume of investment) and rate of interest (= marginal productivity of capital).

For the working economist these results may be set out in still briefer shorthand as follows. The amount of investment (= amount of saving) depends on the marginal productivity of capital and the rate of interest; the level of income is connected with the amount of investment by the multiplier, *i.e.* by the propensity to consume; and the rate of interest depends on the desire for liquid reserves and the amount of spare cash in the community available to satisfy that desire. The amount of this spare cash depends on the policy of the banks in determining the quantity of their I.O.U.s that are outstanding and on the level of income (the higher this, the more money will be taken away into active circulation).

Thus if the schedules expressing the marginal productivity of capital, the propensity to consume and the liquidity preference are known, and the total quantity of money in the system is known also, the amount of investment, the level of income and the rate of interest may readily be determined.

The next topic for consideration is the legitimacy of the assumption that the level of income may be regarded as determined by the complex of considerations expressed in the savings/interest equations rather than by the whole system of equations. In general the level of activity is traditionally conceived as depending on the preference schedules of the various factors expressing their willingness to do various amounts of work in return for income, and on the schedules expressing the relation between the amount of work done and the income accruing from it (Laws of Returns). In considering the former schedules we have to take into account all the factors of production. Now in Keynes's system the supply of capital has already been dealt with by the savings/interest equations. For the supply of risk-bearing we may provisionally content ourselves with the elegant device which he provides in his footnote to page 24. He writes: 'by his (the entrepreneur's) expectation of proceeds I mean, therefore, that expectation of proceeds, which, if it were held with certainty, would lead to the same behaviour as does the bundle of vague and more various possibilities which actually makes up his state of expectation when he reaches his decision'. Thus considerations affecting the supply of risk-bearing are subsumed in the equations which determine the volume of investment.

There remain the factors other than those covered by the category of investment. Of these we are only concerned with those the supply of which can be varied. Thus we are left with those which may roughly be designated prime factors. What is the nature of their supply schedule? What is the form of their preference for income in relation to the work required to obtain it?

In this field Keynes's argument is vitally dependent on his observation of real conditions. The work/income preference schedule exerts its power upon the economic system through the terms on which the prime factors are willing to sell their services. The contracts or bargains of the entrepreneurs with prime factors are normally fixed in money, with no proviso regarding the general level of prices. In the exceptional cases in which there is such a proviso, it is none the less usually the case that a rise in prices involves *some* fall in real rewards to prime factors and conversely. It is true that in a time of rising prices the factors may press for a rise in rewards, but, even if they achieve this, there is still no proviso to safeguard them against a further rise of prices, and prices may, for all the new bargains lay down, and indeed are very often in fact observed to, run on ahead of rewards. Conversely in a time of falling prices. This gives the supply schedules of the prime factors a very special kind of indeterminacy which undermines their power to determine the general level of activity. Keynes discusses this matter in Book I and its importance in his logical edifice justifies him in giving it pride of place.

Consider next the second set of schedules determining the general level of activity, namely those expressing the relations between the amount of work done and the income accruing from it (Laws of Returns). Since the bargains with prime factors are expressed in money, the returns due to their employment should be expressed in money also. But the money value of these returns depends on the level of prices. The general price level might be regarded as determined by the Quantity Theory of Money; Keynes does not so regard it for reasons which will be explained below. On the contrary he regards the general price level as completely malleable and determined by the equations in the general field without reference to the quantity of money.

The consequence of the conclusions yielded by the interest/savings equations, if these are accepted, is, that the level of income and activity is determined. Now suppose the entrepreneurs decide to produce more than the amount so determined. Owing to a deficient propensity to consume, they will find deficient purchasing power, and either accumulate stocks or sell at a loss. If they do the former the accumulation of stocks will constitute an additional (involuntary) investment on the part of the community, which when added to the intended investment, makes the total investment of the community such as to be consistent, in accordance with the interest/savings equations, with the higher level of activity which entrepreneurs are choosing to indulge in. But such a position is unstable. So long as stocks are accumulating, they will reduce activity and continue to do so, until it reaches the point indicated by the interest/savings equations. If on the other hand they sell at a loss, they will be dis-saving; the propensity to consume will be temporarily raised, so that the higher level of activity which they are choosing to indulge in becomes consistent with that required by the interest/savings equations. But again the position is unstable. The marginal propensity to consume will not be permanently sustained at an abnormally high figure by these means. To avoid losses, entrepreneurs will restrict and continue to do so, until activity and income are reduced to a level which satisfies the interest/savings equations, with the marginal propensity to consume normal for that level of income. Converse arguments would apply in the case of entrepreneurs deciding to produce too little.

Now if the level of activity so determined is indeed the equilibrium level of activity, the price level must be appropriate to it. Let us suppose that the price of each commodity is determined by the marginal money cost of production, in the crude way that a tiro might describe erroneously supposing himself to be explaining the true classical theory of cost of production. If the law of diminishing returns prevailed on balance, as Keynes supposes that it does anyhow in the short period, the general price level would be expected to rise with increases of output and to fall with decreases. To make the matter still more crude and common, suppose prices to vary not merely in proportion to changes in the number of units of factors required per unit of output, as output varies, but also in proportion to changes in rates of reward to the factors. In this case we should find, as output rose and diminishing returns came into play, that the rise of prices would just sufficiently exceed the rise of wages, etc., if any, to cover the increased real marginal cost of production per unit. Factors might press for a rise of rewards, but though they might gain on balance in *some* trades, they would always be beaten by the price level in the system as a whole.

Now this is precisely what Keynes supposes actually to

happen. It is, however, 'subject to the qualification that the equality (between marginal cost and price) may be disturbed, in accordance with certain principles, if competition and markets are imperfect' (page 5). The objections to this view which upholders of the Quantity Theory of Money might raise must be considered. But first observe its relation to the determination of the level of activity.

Take a period within which prime factor bargains do not change. The supply of each of these in money terms may then be represented by a horizontal straight line. But if prices vary in proportion to costs (cost variations including allowance for overtime rates, the employment of less efficient labour, etc.), then the money value of the marginal net product of each factor must be represented by a coincident horizontal straight line. Therefore on these conditions the two sets of schedules leave the level of output entirely indeterminate. If the matter is expressed in real terms both sets of schedules are downward sloping to the right; they are still coincident. If money rewards to factors are raised or lowered in response to changes in the level of employment *and* prices are adjusted accordingly, the same result ensues. Thus this complex of equations does *not* determine the level of activity; therefore it leaves that level free to be determined by the savings/interest complex. Q.E.D.

Thus the crux of the matter seems to have shifted to the Quantity Theory of Money. The essence of the difference between the traditional theory and Keynes's theory can be put thus : In the traditional theory the supply and demand schedules of all the factors stand on the same footing; the level of activity is an unknown, but the price level is determined by the monetary equation. This determination of the price level enables the level of activity to be determined by the factors' money supply schedules, and by their marginal productivity schedules. In Keynes's theory the level of activity is determined by the equations governing the savings/interest complex. In the general field, in which we are now only concerned with the demand and supply of prime factors, the level of activity is conceived as determined *ab extra*. It is a known quantity. But the price level is conceived to be completely malleable. If it were not, the system in the general field would be over-determined. Thus the monetary equation is shorn of its former powers. The level of activity being a known quantity, the price level is determined by the money cost of production, with suitable modifications for imperfect competition.

What right has Keynes to gut the monetary equation in this way? Has, then, the banking policy no power to influence the situation? Yes, certainly it has. The fact is that the power residing in the monetary equation has already been used up in Keynes's system in the liquidity preference equation and it cannot therefore exert any direct influence in the general field. To make it do so would be to use its determining influence twice over. In fact in Keynes's system all the old pieces reappear, but they appear in different places.

Explanation is necessary. It will be remembered that according to the liquidity preference equation, the rate of interest is determined by the desire of people for liquid reserves and the quantity of money available for that purpose. The quantity of money available for that purpose is equal to the total quantity of money in existence less that required for active trade.[1] Now if the quantity required for active trade were perfectly indeterminate, as it must be by the Quantity Theory — for according to that the price level depends on the quantity of money available for active trade, and therefore it is unknown what quantity of money any given amount of active trade will absorb — the residue would be indeterminate also. But if the $m$ in $y = \chi(m)$ is indeterminate, there are too many unknowns in the interest/savings set of equations. Thus it is necessary to the validity of Keynes's solution of the problem of investment and

---

[1] In his liquidity preference equation Keynes includes the demand for money for whatever purpose, and the quantity of money that appears in it is the total quantity of money in the community. It has appeared simpler in this part of the exposition to divide this total into two parts, the amount required for active circulation and the residue, to define the quantity of money which appears in the liquidity preference equation as that residue, and the demand which the equation expresses as the demand for purposes other than those of active circulation. This re-definition of terms is merely an expository device and does not imply any departure from Keynes's essential doctrines.

interest that the amount of money available for liquid reserves should be determinate, and that involves that the price level should be determined otherwise than by the monetary equation. And so in Keynes's system it is.

The matter may be put thus: The savings/interest equations suffice to determine the level of activity, subject to the proviso that the quantity of money which appears in the liquidity preference equation is a known quantity; and this will be known if the price level and therefore the amount absorbed in active trade is known. The equations in the general field suffice to determine the price level, subject to the proviso that the level of activity is known. Thus there is after all mutual dependency. The level of activity will be such that so much money is absorbed in active trade that the amount left over enables interest to stand at a rate consistent with that level of activity.

The mutual interdependency of the whole system remains, but the short-cuts indispensable to thinking about particular problems, as Keynes has carved them out, remain also.

The amount of investment depends on the marginal productivity of capital and the rate of interest. The level of income and activity is related to the amount of investment by the multiplier, that is by the marginal propensity to consume, the price level is related to the level of activity by the marginal money cost of production (which depends on the amount of activity undertaken), the amount of money absorbed in active trade depends on the volume of trade and the price level, the amount of money available for liquid reserves is equal to the total amount of money in the system less that required for active trade, and the rate of interest depends on the amount of money available for liquid reserves and the liquidity preference schedule.

It may be well to do some exercises. Suppose the banks to increase the total amount of money available by open market operations. The increment may eventually be divided between active circulation and liquid reserves. An increase of money available for liquid reserves will tend to reduce the rate of interest; and so to increase investment.

This will increase the level of income through the multiplier in accordance with the marginal propensity to consume. If the fall in the rate of interest increases the marginal propensity to consume, the increase of income will be *pro tanto* greater, but it is not certain that it does so. The increase of income involves an increase of turnover, and of prices in accordance with the law of diminishing returns. This involves an increased use of money in active circulation. Thus the fall in the rate of interest will not be so great as it would be if all the new money went into liquid reserves. The money will be divided between the two uses, but there is no reason whatever to suppose that the increments in each use will be in proportion to the amounts of money previously employed there, as is assumed in a Quantity Theory using a compendious index number. The comparative size of the increments will depend on the current elasticity of the liquidity preference schedule and the current elasticity of the marginal productivity of capital schedule (which involves expectations).

Suppose a fall in rewards to prime factors. The price level will drop. Money will be released from active circulation for liquid reserves. This will tend to make the rate of interest fall and to react on the level of investment and activity accordingly. Thus the stimulus to activity is very indirect and its effectiveness depends on the same factors as that provided by an increase in the quantity of money. This is very different from the view that a reduction of rewards will stimulate activity because costs fall while prices are sustained by the quantity of money remaining the same.

It appears to me that the achievement of Keynes has been to consider certain features of traditional theory which were unsatisfactory, because the problems involved tended to be slurred over, and to reconstruct that theory in a way which resolves the problems. The principal features so considered are : (i) the assumption that the level of income could be taken as fixed in the departmental theory of interest and saving ; (ii) the peculiar nature of the supply schedules of the prime factors which arises out of their bargains being fixed in money without proviso as to the price level ; and

(iii) the failure of monetary theory to explain how the total stock of money is divided between liquid reserves and active circulation, or, in other words, the unsatisfactory character of the theory of velocity of circulation.

I stated above that the old pieces in the traditional theory reappear, but sometimes in new places. It might at first be thought that the liquidity preference schedule is a new piece, and that therefore either the new system is over-determined or the traditional writers must have been wrong in supposing that their system was determined. But it is not really a new piece. The old theory presupposed that income velocity of circulation was somehow determined. But precisely how was something of a mystery. Thus the old theory assumed that there was a piece there but did not state exactly what it was. Keynes's innovation may thus be regarded as a precise definition of the old piece.

By placing it where he does, he overcomes a difficulty which has been assuming an alarming prominence in recent economic work. In monetary literature the rate of interest has been treated, and increasingly so, as an influence of vital importance in the monetary situation. But in traditional theory, neither in the general system of equations nor in the departmental theory of interest does it appear that the rate of interest is more intimately connected with the *numéraire* than the price of any other factor of production. This is a striking discrepancy. Keynes introduces the liquidity preference schedule at a point which makes it a vital link between the general system of equations and monetary theory. His treatment is in harmony with recent literature in that he justifies the special connexion of the price of this particular factor with monetary problems. It is an immense advance on recent literature because it removes the discrepancy between the treatment of interest in the two branches of study.

In my judgment Keynes has not affected a revolution in fundamental economic theory but a readjustment and a shift of emphasis. Yet to affect a readjustment in a system which in its broad outlines, despite differences of terminology, has received the approval of many powerful minds, Marshall,

Edgeworth and Pigou, the Austrian School, the School of Lausanne, Wicksell, Pantaleoni, Taussig and Clark, to mention but a few, is itself a notable and distinguished achievement. And in the sphere of departmental economics and short-cuts, which are of greatest concern for the ordinary working economist, Keynes's views constitute a genuine revolution in many fields.

The foregoing account has attempted to expound, not to appraise. The only criticism of Keynes which I venture to offer is that his system is still static. Note has been taken of the fact that at certain important points, *e.g.* in his definition of the marginal efficiency of capital, Keynes lays great stress on the importance of anticipations in determining the present equilibrium.

But reference to anticipation is not enough to make a theory dynamic. For it is still a static equilibrium which the anticipations along with other circumstances serve to determine; we are still seeking to ascertain what amounts of the various commodities and factors of production will be exchanged or used and what prices will obtain, so long as the conditions, including anticipations, remain the same. But in the dynamic theory, as I envisage it, one of the determinands will be the rate of growth of these amounts. Our question will then be, what rate of growth can continue to obtain, so long as the various surrounding circumstances, including the propensity to save, remain the same?

Saving essentially entails growth, at least in some of the magnitudes under consideration. No theory regarding the equilibrium amount of saving can be valid, which assumes that within the period in which equilibrium is established, other things, such as the level of income, do not grow but remain constant.

I envisage in the future two departments of economic principles. The first, the static theory, will be elaborated on the assumption that there is no growth and no saving. The assumption that people spend the whole of their income will be rigidly maintained. On this basis it will be possible to evaluate the equilibrium set of prices and quantities of the various commodities and factors, excluding saving. In the second department, dynamic theory, growth and saving will be taken into account. Equilibrium theory will be concerned not merely with what size, but also with what rate of growth of certain magnitudes is consistent with the surrounding circumstances. There appears to be no reason why the dynamic principles should not come to be as precisely defined and as rigidly demonstrable as the static principles. The distinguishing feature of the dynamic theory will not be that it takes anticipations into account, for those may affect the static equilibrium also, but that it will embody new terms in its fundamental equations, rate of growth, acceleration, de-celeration, etc. If development proceeds on these lines there will be a close parallel between the statics and dynamics of economics and mechanics.

But to develop this theme further would take me too far from my subject.

# AN ESSAY IN DYNAMIC THEORY[1]

1. THE following pages constitute a tentative and preliminary attempt to give the outline of a 'dynamic' theory. Static theory consists of a classification of terms with a view to systematic thinking, together with the extraction of such knowledge about the adjustments due to a change of circumstances as is yielded by the 'laws of supply and demand'. It has for some time appeared to me that it ought to be possible to develop a similar classification and system of axioms to meet the situation in which certain forces are operating steadily to increase or decrease certain magnitudes in the system. The consequent 'theory' would not profess to determine the course of events in detail, but should provide a framework of concepts relevant to the study of change analogous to that provided by static theory for the study of rest.

The axiomatic basis of the theory which I propose to develop consists of three propositions, namely : (i) that the level of a community's income is the most important determinant of its supply of saving ; (ii) that the rate of increase of its income is an important determinant of its demand for saving ; and (iii) that demand is equal to supply. It thus consists in a marriage of the 'acceleration principle' and the 'multiplier' theory, and is a development and extension of certain arguments advanced in my *Essay on the Trade Cycle*.[2]

---

[1] *Economic Journal*, March 1939.

[2] Especially in ch. 2, secs. 4-5. The 'Acceleration Principle' was there designated the 'Relation'. There is an objection to the use of the term acceleration in this connexion. The study of the condition in which demand and supply are flowing at an unaltered rate has long been known as Static Theory : this implies that the equilibrium of prices and quantities resulting therefrom is regarded as analogous to a state of rest. By analogy, therefore, a steady rate of increase of demand, which is our first matter for consideration in dynamic theory,

2. Attempts to construct a dynamic theory have recently been proceeding upon another line — namely, by the study of time lags between certain adjustments. By the introduction of an appropriate lag the tendency of a system to oscillate can be established. In these studies there is some doubt as to the nature of the trend on which the oscillation is superimposed. Supposing damping measures could be introduced, to counteract the oscillation caused by the lag, would the system be stationary or advancing? And at what rate? Dynamic theory in my sense may throw some light upon this.

Moreover it is possible, and this the following argument seeks to establish, that the trend of growth may itself generate forces making for oscillation. This, if so, would not impair the importance of the study of the effect of lags. But it may be that the attempt to explain the trade cycle by *exclusive* reference to them is an unnecessary *tour de force*. The study of the operation of the forces maintaining a trend of increase and the study of lags should go together.

3. The significance of what follows should not be judged solely by reference to the validity or convenience of the particular equations set forth. It involves something wider : a method of thinking, a way of approach to certain problems. It is necessary to 'think dynamically'. The static system of equations is set forth not only for its own beauty, but also to enable the economist to train his mind upon special problems when they arise. For instance, an economist may pose to himself the question, What would be the effect on the system of an increase of exports or of a labour-saving invention? By reference to the static equations, he then proceeds to work out the new equilibrium position supposing the new higher level of exports to be maintained in perpetuity or the labour-saving invention to be incorporated in the productive technique once for all.

and a major effect of which is expressed by the 'Relation', should be regarded as a velocity. Acceleration would be a rate of change in this.

However, the use of the expression Acceleration Principle in the sense of my relation is rapidly accelerating in current literature, and I reluctantly bow to the *force majeure* of usage.

But let the question be : Suppose the level of exports begins and continues to increase steadily, or suppose its rate of increase to increase, or suppose labour-saving inventions begin to be made in a steady or growing stream ; then the static method will not suffice. The static theorist may hope to reduce this supposed steady increase to a succession of steps up, each having the same effect. But if the following argument is correct, the effect on the moving equilibrium of advance may often be in the opposite direction to the effect on the static equilibrium produced by each of the steps considered singly. A new method of approach — indeed, a mental revolution — is needed.

Once the mind is accustomed to thinking in terms of trends of increase, the old static formulation of problems seems stale, flat and unprofitable. This is not to deny to static theory its own appropriate sphere. It will become apparent which kind of problem belongs to each branch of study.

4. I now propose to proceed directly to the Fundamental Equation, constituting the marriage of the acceleration principle and the multiplier theory. This probably gives too much importance to the acceleration principle, and the necessary modification is introduced subsequently.

Let G stand for the geometric rate of growth of income or output in the system, the increment being expressed as a fraction of its existing level. G will vary directly with the time interval chosen — *e.g.* 1 per cent per annum $=\frac{1}{12}$ per cent per month. Let $G_w$ stand for the warranted rate of growth. The warranted rate of growth is taken to be that rate of growth which, if it occurs, will leave all parties satisfied that they have produced neither more nor less than the right amount. Or, to state the matter otherwise, it will put them into a frame of mind which will cause them to give such orders as will maintain the same rate of growth. I use the unprofessional term warranted instead of equilibrium, or moving equilibrium, because, although every point on the path of output described by $G_w$ is an equilibrium point in the sense that producers, if they remain on it, will be satisfied, and be induced to keep the same rate of growth in being, the equilibrium is, for reasons to be explained, a highly unstable one.

If $x_0$ is output in period 0 and $x_1$ output in period 1, $G = \frac{x_1 - x_0}{x_0}$. Since we suppose the period to be short, $x_0$ or $x_1$ may alternatively stand in the denominator.

$x_0$ and $x_1$ are compounded of all individual outputs. I neglect questions of weighting. Even in a condition of growth, which generally speaking is steady, it is not to be supposed that all the component individuals are expanding at the same rate. Thus even in the most ideal circumstances conceivable, G, the actual rate of growth, would diverge from time to time from $G_w$, the warranted rate of growth, for random or seasonal causes.

Let $s$ stand for the fraction of income which individuals and corporate bodies choose to save. $s$ is total saving divided by $x_0$ or $x_1$. This may be expected to vary, with the size of income, the phase of the trade cycle, institutional changes, etc.

Let C stand for the value of the capital goods required for the production of a unit increment of output. The unit of value used to measure this magnitude is the value of the unit increment of output. Thus, if it is proposed in month 1 to raise the output of shoes, so that in month 1 and all subsequent months output is one pair higher than in month 0, and if the machine required to do this — neglecting all other capital that may be required — has a value 48 times the value of a pair of shoes, C per month = 48. The value of C is inversely proportional to the period chosen. C per annum = 4 in this case.[1] The value of G is directly proportional to the period chosen. The value of C depends on the

---

[1] If a month is the unit, the number of shoes added per period is 1, if a year 144. The value of G per annum is 12 times as great as that of G per month, since the numerator of G per annum is 144 times as great and the denominator 12 times as great as the numerator and denominator respectively of G per month. The number of machines added per month is $1 \equiv 48$ shoes $\equiv 48$ units of increment of output. C per month = 48. The number of machines added per year is $12 \equiv 48 \times 12$ shoes. Thus the value in shoes of the annual increment of capital required to produce an annual increment of 144 shoes is $48 \times 12$ units. Therefore C per annum $= \frac{48 \times 12}{144} = 4 = \frac{1}{12}$ of C per month.

state of technology and the nature of the goods constituting the increment of output. It may be expected to vary as income grows and in different phases of the trade cycle; it may be somewhat dependent on the rate of interest.

Now, it is probably the case that in any period not the whole of the new capital is destined to look after the increment of output of consumers' goods. There may be long-range plans of capital development or a transformation of the method of producing the pre-existent level of output. These facts will be allowed for in due course. For the moment let it be assumed that all new capital goods are required for the sake of the increment of output of consumers' goods accruing.

Reserving proof for the next paragraph, we may now write the Fundamental Equation in its simplest form:[1]

$$G_w = \frac{s}{C}. \qquad \cdot \qquad \cdot \qquad \cdot \qquad \cdot \qquad 1$$

It should be noticed that the warranted rate of growth of the system appears here as an unknown term, the value of which is determined by certain 'fundamental conditions'—namely, the propensity to save and the state of technology, etc. Those who define dynamic as having a cross-reference to two points of time may not regard this equation as dynamic; that particular definition of dynamic has its own interest and field of reference. I prefer to define dynamic as referring to propositions in which a rate of growth appears as an unknown variable. This equation is clearly more fundamental than those expressing lags of adjustment.

5. The proof is as follows. Let $C_p$ stand for the value of the increment of capital stock in the period divided by the increment of total output. $C_p$ is the value of the increment of capital per unit increment of output actually produced. Circulating and fixed capital are lumped together.

$$G = \frac{s}{C_p} \qquad \cdot \qquad \cdot \qquad \cdot \qquad 1(a)$$

is a truism, depending on the proposition that actual saving

---

[1] Since the value of $G_w$ varies directly and that of C inversely with the unit period chosen, and the value of $s$ is independent of the unit, the validity of the equation is independent of the unit period chosen.

in a period (excess of the income in that period over consumption) is equal to the addition to the capital stock. Total saving is equal to $sx_0$. The addition to the capital stock is equal to $C_p(x_1 - x_0)$. This follows from the definition of $C_p$. And so,

$$sx_0 = C_p(x_1 - x_0),$$

$$\therefore \frac{s}{C_p} = \frac{x_1 - x_0}{x_0} = G. \quad [1]$$

G is the rate of increase in total output which actually occurs; $C_p$ is the increment in the stock of capital divided by the increment in total output which actually occurs. If the value of the increment of stock of capital per unit increment of output which actually occurs, $C_p$, is equal to C, the amount of capital per unit increment of output required by technological and other conditions (including the state of confidence, the rate of interest, etc.), then clearly the increase which actually occurs is equal to the increase which is justified by the circumstances. This means that, since $C_p$ includes all goods (circulating and fixed capital), and is in fact production minus consumption per unit increment of output during the period, the sum of decisions to produce, to which G gives expression, are on balance justified — *i.e.* if $C = C_p$, then $G = G_w$, and (from 1(a) above) $G_w = \frac{s}{C}$. This is the fundamental equation, stated in para. 4, which determines the warranted rate of growth. To give numerical values to these symbols, which may be fairly representative of modern conditions: if 10 per cent of income were saved and the capital coefficient per annum (C) were equal to 4 the warranted rate of growth would be $2\frac{1}{2}$ per cent per annum.

It may be well to emphasise at this point that no distinction is drawn in this theory between capital goods and consumption goods. In measuring the increment of capital, the two are taken together; the increment consists of total production less total consumption. Some trade-cycle

[1] [It would be preferable to define total saving as $sx_1$. The conclusion is the same, since $\frac{x_1 - x_0}{x_1} = G$. 1952.]

theorists concern themselves with a possible lack of balance between these two categories; no doubt that has its import-ance. The theory here considered is more fundamental or simple; it is logically prior to the considerations regarding lack of balance, and grasp of it is required as a preliminary to the study of them.

6. To use terminology recently employed by distinguished authorities, $C_p$ is an *ex-post* quantity. I am not clear if C should be regarded as its corresponding *ex-ante*. C is rather that addition to capital goods in any period which producers regard as ideally suited to the output which they are under-taking in that period. For convenience the term *ex-ante* when employed in this article will be used in this sense.

The truism stated above, $1(a)$, gives expression to Keynes's proposition that saving is necessarily equal to investment — that is, to *ex-post* investment. Saving is not necessarily equal to *ex-ante* investment in this sense, since unwanted accretions or depletions of stock may occur, or equipment may be found to have been produced in excess of, or short of, requirements.

If *ex-post* investment is less than *ex-ante* investment, this means that there has been an undesired reduction of stocks or insufficient provision of productive equipment, and there will be a stimulus to further expansion of output; conversely if *ex-post* investment exceeds *ex-ante* investment. If *ex-post* investment is less than *ex-ante* investment, saving is less than *ex-ante* investment. In his *Treatise on Money* Keynes formulated a proposition which has been widely felt to be enlightening, though experience has led him subsequently to condemn the definitions employed as more likely to be misconstrued than helpful. He said that if investment exceeded saving, the system would be stimulated to expand, and conversely. If for the definitions on which that pro-position was based, we *substitute* the definition of *ex-ante* investment given above, it is true that if *ex-ante* investment exceeds saving, the system will be stimulated, and conversely. This truth may account for the feeling of satisfaction which Keynes's proposition originally evoked and the reluctance to abandon it at his behest. In many connexions we are more interested in *ex-ante* than in *ex-post* investment, the latter including as it does unwanted accretions of stocks. Keynes's proposition of the *Treatise* may still be a useful aid to thinking, if we substitute for 'Investment' in it *ex-ante* investment as defined above.

7. Two minor points may be considered before we proceed with the main argument.

(i) It may be felt that there is something unreal in this analysis, since the increase in capital which producers will regard as right in period 1 is in the real world related not to the increase of total output in period 1, but to prospective increases in subsequent periods. This objection may be divided into two parts. (*a*) In view of the fact that much of the outlay of capital is connected with long-range planning, it may be held that the fundamental equation gives too much weight to the short-period effect of the acceleration principle. This objection is freely admitted and allowed for in the subsequent modification of the equation. (*b*) It may further be objected that even in the sphere in which the acceleration principle holds there must be some lag between the increased provision of equipment (and stocks?) and the increased flow of output which they are designed to support. There may be some force in this. But the point is deliberately neglected in this part of the argument, along with all questions of lags. The study of these lags is of undoubted importance, but a division of labour in analysis is indispensable, and in this case the neglect is necessary in order to get the clearest possible view of the forces determining the trend and its influence as such. Moreover, the lag referred to in this subheading (*b*) may properly be regarded as unimportant, since, in the event of a *steady* advance (G) being maintained, the difference between $x_1 - x_0$ and $x_2 - x_1$ will be of the second order of small quantities. In other words, it matters not whether we regard the increment of capital as required to support the increment of total output in the same period or in the one immediately succeeding it.

8. (ii) In the demonstration given above (paras. 6 and 7) reference was made to the distinction between the *ex-post* and the *ex-ante* increase of capital goods. No reference was made

to the distinction between *ex-post* and *ex-ante* saving.[1] Suppose that G is not equal to $G_w$; might not the discrepancy show itself on the other side of the equation, not in any divergence of $C_p$ from C, but in *ex-post* saving not being equal to *ex-ante* saving?

I have no very clear view as to possible causes likely to operate in a systematic way to distort *ex-post* from *ex-ante* saving, or of the probable importance of such distortions. It is said, for instance, that in a time of rising prices, fixed-income classes will not adapt their modes of life simultaneously, and so may save less than they would be disposed to do had they clearly foreseen the impending rise. *Per contra* variable-income classes may not foresee their own rise of income, and so spend less than they would have been disposed to do.

This question of the possible divergence of *ex-post* from *ex-ante* saving must be kept entirely distinct from that of the variations in *s* in the different phases of the trade cycle, which not only are admitted, but also play a part in the argument. *s* may vary because the level of income or of profit is abnormally swollen or depressed.

The neglect of these possible divergences has no importance for the argument, since they will have the same effect on growth as the divergences of $C_p$ from C for which they may serve as substitute. Thus if G exceeds $G_w$, the right-hand side of the equation must exceed $s/C$. If the whole of this effect is found in $C_p$ it will be *less* than C, and this is a stimulus to expansion.[2] Firms finding themselves short of stock or equipment will increase their orders. If, on the other hand, the whole of this effect is found in a divergence of *ex-post s* from *ex-ante s*, *ex-post s* will be *greater* than *ex-ante s*. Savers will find that they have saved more than they would have done had they foreseen their level of income or the level of prices correctly. Consequently they will be stimu-

---

[1] Be it noted that *ex-ante* is here used of saving in a sense analogous to that defined in the expression *ex-ante* investment; it is the saving which savers would choose to make in any period, were they able to adapt expenditure simultaneously with the changing circumstances of the period.

[2] The reader who is surprised that an excess of G over $G_w$ is stimulating will find the explanation in the next paragraph.

lated to expand purchases, and orders for goods will consequently be increased. Throughout the following pages the reader, whenever he finds a reference to the excess or deficiency of $C_p$ compared with C, may substitute, if he prefers it, a supposed deficiency or excess of *ex-post* saving compared with *ex-ante* saving, without affecting the course of the argument.

9. We now come to a point of major importance, constituting the difference between the dynamic equilibrium (warranted rate of growth) and the static equilibrium. Normally the latter is stable and the former unstable. This gives a *prima-facie* reason for regarding the dynamic analysis as a necessary propaedeutic to trade-cycle study.

Some recent writers have been disposed to urge that the static equilibrium is not so stable as is sometimes claimed. Suppose that an increased output of a commodity, constituting a departure from equilibrium, is tried, so that its supply stands at a point at which the supply curve is above the demand curve. It is argued that, instead of a relapse at once occurring, reducing supply to the point of intersection of the supply and demand curves — this showing the stability of the old equilibrium — the upshot depends on how all parties now proceed. It is suggested that there may be a tendency to waltz round the point of intersection or, more broadly, that in the backward adjustment there may be wide repercussions disturbing the whole system. It is even held that the whole question of the stability of the static equilibrium, in the sense of the tendency of a relapse to it when a random departure occurs, is itself a dynamic problem, which cannot be looked after by the system of static equations. I have the impression that this type of criticism exaggerates the importance of this problem, and constitutes to some extent a failure to see the wood for the trees, and that on its own ground the theory of static equilibrium is well able to hold its own.

But when we look at the dynamic equilibrium, new vistas are opened. The line of output traced by the warranted rate of growth is a moving equilibrium, in the sense that it represents the one level of output at which producers will feel in the upshot that they have done the right thing, and which will induce them to continue in the same line of advance. Stock in hand and equipment available will be exactly at the level which they would wish to have them. Of course what applies to the system in general may not apply to each individual separately. But if one feels he has over-produced or over-ordered, this will be counterbalanced by an opposite experience of an equal importance in some other part of the field.

But now suppose that there is a departure from the warranted rate of growth. Suppose an excessive output, so that G exceeds $G_w$. The consequence will be that $C_p$, the actual increase of capital goods per unit increment of output, falls below C, that which is desired. There will be, in fact, an undue depletion of stock or shortage of equipment and the system will be stimulated to further expansion. G, instead of returning to $G_w$, will move farther from it in an upward direction, and the farther it diverges, the greater the stimulus to expansion will be. Similarly, if G falls below $G_w$, there will be a redundance of capital goods, and a depressing influence will be exerted; this will cause a further divergence and a still stronger depressing influence; and so on. Thus in the dynamic field we have a condition opposite to that which holds in the static field. A departure from equilibrium, instead of being self-righting, will be self-aggravating. $G_w$ represents a moving equilibrium, but a highly unstable one. Of interest this for trade-cycle analysis!

Suppose an increase in the propensity to save, which means that the values of *s* are increased for all levels of income. This necessarily involves, *ceteris paribus*, a higher rate of warranted growth. But if the actual growth was previously equal to the warranted growth, the immediate effect is to raise the warranted rate above the actual rate. This state of affairs sets up a depressing influence which will drag the actual rate progressively farther below the warranted rate. In this as in other cases, the movement of a dynamic determinant has an opposite effect on the warranted path of growth to that which it has on its actual path. How different from the order of events in static theory.

The reader may have some difficulty in the expression 'stimulus to expansion'. What is the significance of this, in view of the fact that some growth is assumed as a basic condition? It must be remembered that the value of G depends on aggregates $x_0$ and $x_1$. These are sums of numerous quantities for which individuals are responsible. It must be supposed that at all times some individuals are jogging on at a steady level, others are risking an increase of orders or output, others are willy-nilly curtailing. G is the resultant of their separate enterprises. Some are in any event likely to be disappointed. If G is equal to $G_w$, it is to be supposed that the general level of enterprise undertaken in period o, including in sum a certain increase over that in the preceding period, is found to be satisfactory. Those running short of stock balance those with surpluses. This justifies further action on similar lines, though the individuals increasing orders for stock in trade or planning new equipment in period 1 may not be identical in person with those doing so in period o. If an expansive force is in operation, more individuals, or individuals having greater weight, will be induced by their trading position to venture increases than did so in the preceding period. Conversely if a depressing force is in operation.

The dynamic theory so far stated may be summed up in two propositions. (i) A unique warranted line of growth is determined jointly by the propensity to save and the quantity of capital required by technological and other considerations per unit increment of total output. Only if producers keep to this line will they find that on balance their production in each period has been neither excessive nor deficient. (ii) On either side of this line is a 'field' in which centrifugal forces operate, the magnitude of which varies directly as the distance of any point in it from the warranted line. Departure from the warranted line sets up an inducement to depart farther from it. The moving equilibrium of advance is thus a highly unstable one.

The essential point here may be further explained by reference to the expressions over-production and under production. The distinction between particular over-production and general over-production is well known. In the event of particular over-production, there will normally be a tendency to reduce production of the particular line, and so equilibrium will be restored. We may define general over-production as a condition in which a majority of producers, or producers representing in sum the major part of production, find they have produced or ordered too much, in the sense that they or the distributors of their goods find themselves in possession of an unwanted volume of stocks or equipment. By reference to the fundamental equation it appears that this state of things can only occur when the actual growth has been *below* the warranted growth — *i.e.* a condition of general over-production is the consequence of producers in sum producing too little. The only way in which this state of affairs could have been avoided would have been by producers in sum producing more than they did. Over-production is the consequence of production below the warranted level. Conversely, if producers find that they are continually running short of stocks and equipment, this means that they are producing above the warranted level.

But the condition of over-production, or, as we should perhaps call it, apparent over-production, will lead to a curtailment of production or orders, or a reduction in the rate of increase on balance, and consequently, so long as the fundamental conditions governing the warranted rate are unchanged, to a larger gap between actual and warranted growth, and so to an intensification of the evils which the contraction was intended to cure.

It must be noted that a rate of growth lying on either side of the warranted rate is regarded here as unwarranted. If the actual rate exceeds the warranted rate, producers on balance will not feel that they have produced or ordered too much; on the contrary, they will be running short of stocks and/or equipment. Thus they will not feel that they have produced the warranted amount plus something; on the contrary, they will feel that everything which they have produced has been warranted, and that they might warrantably have produced something more. None the less, we define their production as unwarrantably large, meaning by that that they have produced in excess of the unique amount which would leave them on balance satisfied with what they had done and prepared to go forward in the next period on similar lines.

10. The foregoing demonstration of the inherent instability of the moving equilibrium, or warranted line of advance, depends on the assumption that the values of $s$ and $C$ are independent of the value of G. This is formally correct. The analysis relates to a single point of time. $s$ is regarded as likely to vary with a change in the size of income, but a change in the rate of growth at a given point of time has no effect on its size. $C$ may also be expected to vary with the size of income, *e.g.* owing to the occurrence of surplus capital capacity from time to time, but the same argument for regarding it as independent of the rate of growth at a particular point of time applies.

It may be objected, however, that this method of analysis is too strict to be realistic, since the discovery that output is excessive or deficient, and the consequent emergence of a depressing or stimulating force, takes some time, and in the interval required for a reaction to be produced an appreciable change in $s$ or $C$ may have occurred.

Consider this with reference to an experimental increase in G above a warranted level. According to the theory of instability, any such experiment will be apparently over-justified, stocks or equipment running short in consequence of it. Is it possible that if resulting changes in the values of $s$ or $C$ are taken into account, this doctrine will have to be modified?

In order to justify modifying the doctrine, it would be necessary to show that, in consequence of the experimental increase, $s$ was substantially increased or $C$ reduced. It is unlikely that $C$ would be reduced. The capital coefficient may often stand below the level appropriate to the technological conditions of the age, owing to the existence of surplus equipment. If this were so, the higher rate of output consequent upon the experimental increase would tend to raise $C$. A smaller proportion of firms would come to find their capacity redundant, and a larger proportion would have to support a greater turnover by ordering extra equipment.

With saving, the case is different. An expansion of activity might increase the proportion of income saved. What increase of saving is required for a modification of the instability theory?

This can be shown simply. Let $x_e$ be an experimental increase of output above the warranted level. Let $s_m$ stand for the fraction of the consequential income saved. The instability principle requires that $Cx_e > s_m x_e$,

*i.e.* that
$$s_m < C$$
$$< \frac{s}{G_w}.$$

This condition needs interpretation. Since C and $G_w$ do not both appear in the equation, it is necessary to define the period by which $G_w$ is measured. This should be done by reference to the reaction time mentioned above — namely, the time required for an undue accretion or depletion of capital goods to exert its influence upon the flow of orders. If this reaction time is six months, then $G_w$ must be measured as growth per six months.

Thus the instability condition requires that the fraction of marginal income saved shall not be more than the fraction of total income saved multiplied by the total income and divided by the increment of warranted income per six months. Thus if the warranted growth is $2\frac{1}{2}$ per cent per annum, or $1\frac{1}{4}$ per cent per six months, the instability principle requires that the fraction of marginal income saved must be less than eighty times the fraction of average income saved. Supposing that the high figure of 50 per cent is taken as the fraction of marginal income saved, the fraction of total income saved must be greater than five-eighths of 1 per cent. Thus for any normal warranted rate of growth and level of saving, the instability principle seems quite secure.

The force of this argument, however, is somewhat weakened when long-range capital outlay is taken into account. It will then appear that the attainment of a neutral or stable equilibrium of advance may not be altogether improbable in certain phases of the cycle.

11. It should be noticed that the instability theory makes the empirical verification of the acceleration principle more arduous. For it leads to the expectation that in the upward phase of the cycle the actual rate will tend to run above the warranted rate, and the accretion of capital to be less than that required by the acceleration principle; and conversely in the downward phase. Thus a finding that the volume of investment fluctuates less than is required by direct computation from the acceleration principle is consistent with the theory here set forth, in which, none the less, the acceleration principle is presented as a leading dynamic determinant.

12. It is now expedient to introduce further terms into our equation to reduce the influence of the acceleration principle. Some outlays of capital have no direct relation to the current increase of output. They may be related to a prospective long-period increase of activity, and be but slightly influenced, if at all, by the current increase of trade. Or they may be induced by new inventions calculated to cheapen production or change consumers' modes of spending their income, so that they are not related to increments of output, but are designed to revolutionise the methods for producing some portion of already existing output or to substitute one line of goods for another in the consumers' budget. There are doubtless numerous factors, including the state of confidence and the rate of interest, affecting the volume of such outlay. It may suffice for the purpose in hand to divide it into two parts.

One part, K, is conceived to be quite independent both of the current level of income and its current rate of growth. The other, expressed as a fraction of income, $k$, is conceived to vary with the current level of income, as distinct from its rate of growth. This seems a reasonable assumption. Long-period anticipations are bound to be influenced by the present state of prosperity or adversity: even public authorities are apt to reduce the volume of public works in a slump. Companies may relate their expenditure on long-range plans to the current state of their profit account.

Having regard to the principle that the total increase of capital is equal to the total saving in the period, our fundamental equation may be modified as follows :

$$G_w = \frac{s - k - \dfrac{K}{x}}{C}. \qquad \qquad . \qquad . \qquad . \quad (2)^1$$

It must be noticed that C and $C_p$ now stand not for the total increase of capital (desired and actual, respectively) per unit increment of output, but only for the net increase of capital after the capital represented by $k$ and K has been subtracted.

It may be noticed that the larger the volume of outlay which will be sustained independently of the current rate of growth, the *smaller* is the warranted rate of growth. A larger part of savings being absorbed in such outlay, there will be a smaller part to be looked after by the acceleration principle.

13. In the following pages the expression long-range capital outlay will be used for the magnitude denoted by $xk + K$. This must not be supposed to cover all investment in durable fixed equipment; for much of that is related to, and directly governed by, the current output of consumption goods. It refers only to that part of the output of fixed equipment the production of which is not governed by the current demand for consumption goods.

If long-range capital outlay were large by comparison with that required to support the current increase in turnover of consumable goods, the peculiar conditions defined in para. 10 for the invalidity of the instability principle might in certain circumstances be realised. For the fraction of total income saved *and* devoted to the finance of the increase of current output might be very small compared with the fraction of marginal income saved. It is not, however, to be supposed that it would normally be small enough to invalidate the instability principle. For, with normal

---

$^1$ $sx_0 = C_p(x_1 - x_0) + kx_0 + K.$

$$\therefore \frac{s - k - \dfrac{K}{x_0}}{C_p} = \frac{x_1 - x_0}{x_0} = G\,;$$

$$\therefore G_w = \frac{s - k - \dfrac{K}{x_0}}{C}.$$

growth at $2\frac{1}{2}$ per cent, saving at 10 per cent, marginal saving at 50 per cent and the reaction time six months, this would mean that fifteen-sixteenths of capital would normally be devoted to long-range capital outlay and only one-sixteenth would be directly associated with the current increase of output (cf. para. 10). But such a situation might well arise in certain phases of the trade cycle, especially when capital capacity was redundant and saving low. In that case a stable equilibrium of advance might for a time be achieved.

14. To complete the picture, foreign trade must be taken into account. It is reasonable to measure exports, including invisible exports and the earnings of foreign investments, in absolute terms. The value of income which may be earned in this way may be conceived to be independent both of the level of activity at home and of its growth (though in so far as the trade cycle is world-wide, its value will be *de facto* related to income). Let E stand for this value. Imports, on the other hand, are better taken as a fraction, $i$, of the current level of income. We then have, by parity of reasoning,

$$G_w = \frac{s + i - k - \dfrac{K}{x} - \dfrac{E}{x}}{C}. \qquad \qquad (3)[1]$$

$i$ need not be equal to $\dfrac{E}{x}$; the difference represents an international movement of capital. The influence of the various magnitudes on the warranted rate of growth is shown by the equation.

15. The fundamental dynamic equation has been used to demonstrate the inherent tendency of the system to instability. Space forbids an application of this method of analysis to the successive phases of the trade cycle. In the course of it the values expressed by the symbols on the right-hand side of the equation undergo considerable change. As actual growth departs upwards or downwards from the

[1] The principle now is that saving plus income expended on imports must be equal to the increase of capital in the country plus income derived from abroad. This is deducible from the fact that income derived from the sale of home-made goods to consumers at home is equal to the income devoted to their purchase. Thus: $sx_0 + ix_1 = C_p(x_1 - x_0) + kx_0 + K + E$.

warranted level, the warranted rate itself moves,[1] and may chase the actual rate in either direction. The maximum rates of advance or recession may be expected to occur at the moment when the chase is successful.

For the convenience of the reader who may be tempted to experiment with this tool, it must be observed that C is always positive. Being the total quantity of capital required in connexion with increments (or decrements) of current output divided by the increment (or decrement) of that output, when the latter is negative the former is negative also, and the coefficient remains positive. $C_p$, on the other hand, may be negative; it is not negative whenever there is a depletion of capital goods, but only when the amount of capital goods outstanding is moving in the opposite direction to the level of total output.

The formula is not well adapted to dealing with the case of zero growth. But that matter is quite simple. Zero growth is only warranted when the amount of saving is equal to the amount required for long-range capital outlay. If the amount of saving exceeds this, there will be a tendency for output to decline, and conversely.

It may be well to make one point with regard to a downward departure from the warranted position of sufficient importance to outlive one reaction time and bring the system within the field where the centrifugal forces have substantial strength. The downward lapse will then continue until the warranted rate, determined by the values on the right-hand side of the equation, itself moves down. This will happen when the numerator falls or the denominator rises. But in a phase of declining rate of growth the capital coefficient is not in general likely to rise. And so long as there is still some positive growth, albeit at a declining rate, the fraction of income saved is not likely to fall. Therefore, once the rate of growth is driven downwards from the warranted level, the warranted level is not itself likely to fall, or the downward movement therefore to be checked, until the rate of

[1] This idea is analogous to that propounded by Mr. D. H. Robertson that the 'natural' rate of interest may be expected to vary in the different phases of the trade cycle. Cf. *Economic Journal*, December 1934.

growth becomes negative and the level of income recedes. Now, if the actual rate is standing below the warranted rate, 'the centrifugal force will continue to operate, driving the actual rate progressively downwards, unless or until the warranted rate itself falls to a level as low as the actual rate. But, since the actual rate is now negative, this cannot happen until the numerator of the right-hand side of the equation becomes negative — that is, until saving falls below the level required for long-range capital outlay.

16. Alongside the concept of warranted rate of growth we may introduce another, to be called the natural rate of growth. This is the maximum rate of growth allowed by the increase of population, accumulation of capital, technological improvement and the work/leisure preference schedule, supposing that there is always full employment in some sense.

There is no inherent tendency for these two rates to coincide. Indeed, there is no unique warranted rate; the value of the warranted rate depends upon the phase of the trade cycle and the level of activity.

Consideration may be given to that warranted rate which would obtain in conditions of full employment; this may be regarded as the warranted rate 'proper' to the economy. *Prima facie* it might be supposed healthier to have the 'proper' warranted rate above than below the natural rate. But this is very doubtful.

The system cannot advance more quickly than the natural rate allows. If the proper warranted rate is above this, there will be a chronic tendency to depression; the depressions drag down the warranted rate below its proper level, and so keep its average value over a term of years down to the natural rate. But this reduction of the warranted rate is only achieved by having chronic unemployment.

The warranted rate is dragged down by depression; it may be twisted upwards by an inflation of prices and profit. If the proper rate is below the natural rate, the average value of the warranted rate may be sustained above its proper level over a term of years by a succession of profit booms.

Thus each state of affairs has its appropriate evils. There is much to be said for the view that it is better that the proper warranted rate should be lower rather than higher than the natural rate.

17. In order fully to grasp the dynamic principle, it is necessary to bear in mind that changes in fundamental conditions have opposite effects on the actual rate and the warranted rate. An increased amount of long-range capital outlay, an increase in the capital coefficient, an increase in the propensity to consume, and an increase in the active balance on international account, or a decline in the passive balance, are all properly thought to have a stimulating effect on the system. But they all tend, as may readily be seen from the equation, to reduce the warranted rate. This paradox may be readily explained.

Suppose that one of these stimulants begins to operate when the actual rate is equal to the warranted rate. By depressing the warranted rate, it drags that down below the actual rate, and so automatically brings the actual rate into the field of centrifugal forces, driving it away from the warranted rate — that is, in this case, upwards. Thus the stimulant causes the system to expand.

It must not be inferred that these stimulants are only of temporary benefit. For it may be healthy for an economy to have its proper warranted rate reduced. This is likely to be so when its proper warranted rate is tending to be above the natural rate.[1] The long-run value of the stimulant can only be assessed if it is known whether, in its absence, the proper warranted rate is running above or below the natural rate.

It is often felt that a high propensity to save should warrant a great increase in the output of wealth and this induces an extreme aversion to accept Keynes's view that excessive saving in the modern age is hostile to prosperity. The feeling is justified to the extent that higher propensity to save does, in fact, *warrant* a higher rate of growth. Trouble arises if the rate of growth which it warrants is greater than

---

[1] This may be the most fundamental rational explanation of the common view that it is dangerous for an old country to be a large importer of capital. For this involves a high warranted rate of growth, and it is dangerous to have a high warranted rate when the natural rate is low. *Per contra* for a young country, whose natural rate is high, it is considered healthy and proper to have a large import of capital.

that which the increase of population and the increase of technical capacity render permanently possible. And the fundamental paradox is that the more ambitious the rate *warranted* is, the greater the probability that the actual output will from time to time, and even persistently, fall below that which the productive capacity of the population would allow.

18. Policy in this field is usually appraised by reference to its power to combat tendencies to oscillation. Our demonstration of the inherent instability of the dynamic equilibrium confirms the importance of this. But there are two points to be noticed in this connexion. (i) The nature of the measures suitable for combating the tendency to oscillate may depend on whether the natural rate is above or below the proper warranted rate. (ii) In addition to dealing with the tendency to oscillation when it occurs, it may be desirable to have a long-range policy designed to influence the relation between the proper warranted rate of growth and the natural rate.

If, in the absence of interference, the proper warranted rate is substantially above the natural rate, the difficulties may be too great to be dealt with by a mere anti-cycle policy. In the first place, there is the probability of a slump occurring before full employment is reached, since during the revival the warranted rate may be dangerously near the actual rate, and liable at any time to overpass it, thus generating depression. Secondly, there is an acute problem if the actual rate reaches the ceiling of full employment and is depressed to the natural rate, and therefore below the warranted rate. An attempt may then be made to drag down the warranted rate below its normal level by increasing public works (K). But the difficulty of the proper warranted rate being above the natural rate will be chronic, and this means that only by keeping in being a large and growing volume of public works can the slump be prevented. In fine, the anti-cycle policy has to be converted into a permanent policy for keeping down the proper warranted rate.

19. The ideal policy would be to manipulate the proper warranted rate so that it should be equal to the natural rate.

If this could be achieved — but in fact only a rough approximation would be possible — an anti-cycle policy would none the less be an indispensable supplement. For the warranted rate is bound to be disturbed by the varying incidence of inventions and fluctuations in the foreign account. An anti-cycle policy would be necessary to combat the runaway forces which come into being as soon as a substantial change occurs in the warranted rate.

20. A low rate of interest makes for a low warranted rate of increase, by encouraging high values of K and C and, possibly also, by having a depressing influence on $s$. Since the effects of changes in the rate of interest are probably slow-working, it may be wise to use the rate of interest as a long-range weapon for reducing the warranted rate of growth, and to reserve *suitable* public works for use against the cycle. It is not suggested, however, that a low rate of interest has sufficient power of its own to keep down the warranted rate without the assistance of a programme of public works to be kept permanently in operation.

If permanent public works activity and a low long-term rate availed to bring the proper warranted rate into line with the natural rate, variations in the short-term rate of interest might come into their own again as an ancillary method of dealing with oscillations.

21. This essay has only touched in the most tentative way on a small fraction of the problems, theoretical and practical, of which the enunciation of a dynamic theory suggests the formulation. In the last paragraph it was implicitly hinted that our present situation is one of a relatively high proper warranted rate. The evidence for this comes from inside and outside the dynamic theory itself. According to the dynamic theory, the tendency of a system to relapse into depression before full employment is reached in the boom suggests that its proper warranted rate exceeds its natural rate. Outside evidence includes the known decline in the growth of population, which involves a decline in the natural rate. More controversial points are the tendency of a more wealthy population to save a larger fraction of its income (high value of $s$ involves high warranted rate), and

the tendency of modern progress to depress rather than elevate the value of C (low value of C involves high warranted rate).

The main object of this essay, however, is to present a tool of analysis, not to diagnose present conditions.

# SUPPLEMENT ON DYNAMIC THEORY

THE ideas contained in the foregoing essay were expanded and set against a background of more general dynamic theory in my *Towards a Dynamic Economics*. It must suffice here to add certain supplementary notes.

1. I draw attention to para. 11 of the essay. There has been some tendency to cast doubt on the part played by the 'acceleration principle' in the trade cycle, on the ground that statistical studies do not reveal investment as varying as much as the acceleration principle would require. According to my theory investment would not be expected to vary so much. Indeed my theory might be succinctly put by stating that the cycle takes place precisely because investment does *not* show the variation required by the acceleration principle. It is the non-fulfilment of the principle *ex-post* that provides the driving force making activity move upwards or downwards.

2. I have drawn the distinction between *ex-post* investment, viz. that which actually occurs, and an ideal amount of investment, being an amount, neither more nor less, which is deemed to be justified by the course of events as they occur. I suggested (para. 6) that by a stretch of language one might apply the familiar expression *ex-ante* investment to this ideal amount. I think that thereby one does violence to language, *ex-ante* essentially relating to what was intended in some prior period. Except on the warranted line of advance, justified investment, *ex-ante* investment and *ex-post* investment will, all three, have different values.

It may be convenient, in this connexion, to draw a distinction between circulating and fixed capital. It is of the essence of the former that in its various specific forms it is destined either for transformation by further processing or for consumption. Thus an *ex-post* deficiency of circulating capital may be due to the fact that some items of output intended to maintain or increase existing stocks may have passed more quickly than was anticipated into the next stage of processing (or distribution) or into consumption.

If the expansion of the economy is greater than that warranted, the *ex-post* accumulation of circulating capital will be less than the *ex-ante*, the difference being due to the fact that the expansion has pulled the stuff on into its next stage or into consumption. The ideal amount of accumulation that would be considered justified is likely to be somewhat greater than the *ex-ante* amount; for the unexpectedly large turnover is likely to be deemed to require a larger circulating capital to support it than was previously envisaged as needed. Thus the *ex-post* amount will be the least, the *ex-ante* amount intermediate and the justified amount the greatest of the three quantities. Conversely on a downward movement.

In the case of fixed capital it does not appear that *ex-ante* investment will differ much, if at all, from *ex-post* investment in amount. The building of a factory implies *ex-ante* investment in that factory; but, if it is built, there it will be. There will be an *ex-post* factory as well as an *ex-ante* one. By a refinement one might say that, in the event of a recession, the *ex-post* investment was slightly greater than the *ex-ante*; it may have been intended *ex-ante* that the new factory should be subjected to wear and tear immediately, so that its value would at once begin to decline on this account, whereas, *ex-post* it has not been put into commission owing to the recession, or, being put into commission, has caused another factory to be put out of commission and thus not subjected to wear and tear. These are small points. But there will be a great difference between the justified investment, on the one hand, and the *ex-ante* and *ex-post* investments on the other. In the circumstances envisaged the factory will be deemed not to have been justified at all, and justified investment falls short of *ex-ante* and of *ex-post* investment by the full amount of the factory.

3. In his *Theory of the Trade Cycle* Mr. Hicks has made a

crucial distinction between 'induced' and 'autonomous' investment. The former corresponds to my C (in the formula on page 270) and the latter to my K, my *k* being intermediate.

I now hold that in my original essay too sharp a distinction was drawn between C and K and that Mr. Hicks's contribution suffers from a similar defect. Those who make the decisions and give the orders, the sum-total of which actuates economic effort and determines the level of activity, are determined partly by current and recent experience and partly by other considerations. The acceleration principle summarises and reduces to a formula the influence of current and recent activity It may supply too rigid a formula; the schematism involved in *any* general theory is apt to be too rigid, and the wise statistician or practitioner of applied economics habitually makes allowance for this. Thus the acceleration principle governs what Mr. Hicks calls induced investment; in my theory it governs the rate of growth, since it determines whether realised investment (including circulating capital) is greater or less than what would be judged desirable by the current out-turn of events. Autonomous investment (my K )may be regarded as the investment flowing from orders that would be given whatever the current out-turn. Autonomous investment is decided upon in consequence of considerations of longer range. It also embodies part of the investment that is due to technological improvement. If some method is devised for producing something in common use much more cheaply, installations will be made for putting that method into effect, regardless of fluctuations, upwards or downwards, in the marginal demand for the article; induced investment *per contra* is precisely that part of investment that is influenced by those marginal fluctuations.

Now the distinction between the two kinds of investment depends in part upon the period during which 'recent' experience is taken; it is analogous to the distinction between Marshall's long- and short-period costs; indeed it may be regarded as an aspect of that distinction. In a sufficiently short period all investment is 'autonomous' investment; a firm may experience a decrease of sales during one day, or even during a whole week, without decreasing its orders or changing its plans in any way; all investment due to those orders and plans may be regarded as autonomous in relation to very short-period declines in its put-through; this gives our economy a day-to-day stability. On the other hand, it is hard to think of any investment which will not be made subject to reconsideration if a depression is sufficiently prolonged and intense. Thus, as a depression continues, the various items of long-term investment will successively be brought under review, and swing over from the category of autonomous to that of induced. The shift of items from autonomous to induced is one element in the self-aggravating character of a slump. Any such shift reduces the level at which the slump will be arrested, and the longer it takes to reach the bottom the more items are likely to be shifted over.

This was one reason for making me doubt whether Mr. Hicks can be right in attributing revival to the long-run upward slope of the autonomous investment curve, since it is in the period just prior to revival that the shift of items out of the autonomous category is likely to be greatest. The revival may be accounted for by the fact that, once a bottom is reached, orders on replacement account will very soon begin to expand. In the same connexion I would register a note of dissent from Mr. Hicks's view that the ultimate actuating force in the expansion of an economy is autonomous investment working through a super-multiplier. There is no doubt that the concept of a super-multiplier is an ingenious invention and should have a part to play in theory. But autonomous investment, like all investment, is in the long run governed by the rate of expansion of the economy.

In a small slump K may be stationary and large; $\dfrac{K}{x}$ will clearly increase; that is most helpful for bringing the slump to an end. But in a larger slump more and more items will be displaced from K; these must reappear elsewhere, either in $k$ or C. The latter is the more injurious.

4. Mr. S. Alexander has spot-lit the fact that my theory implies a certain behaviour in regard to induced investment,

which may not accord with the facts.[1] He correctly interprets it as implying that if an entrepreneur finds at any time that his equipment and stocks are satisfactory, being neither redundant nor short, he will increase his order by the same amount that he increased it last time he gave one. I should hold that to be quite a reasonable postulate; but it is by no means safe.

In order to probe this matter more deeply it is necessary to frame the concept of an entrepreneur, who is representative in two respects, namely: (i) demand for his output must expand at the same rate that the economy as a whole is expanding; and (ii) he must be psychologically representative, in the sense that his reaction to recent experience is an average one. He must be average in his make-up of courage and prudence, of optimism and pessimism. He may be defined more precisely in this second respect as one whose orders in response to a given current out-turn are such that the sum of the excesses of orders by all entrepreneurs in the economy who would order more in a precisely similar situation over what he would order is equal to the sum of the shortfalls of all those who would order less. The formula that correctly describes the behaviour of this representative entrepreneur may be applied to the macro-economy.

I assume that some part of his ordering is induced, that is, dependent on the current out-turn of events. I further assume, and this I take to be safe, that the smaller his equipment and stocks in relation to his current activity the larger his order will be. One might draw an aggregate demand or order curve, where the amount ordered ($x$) has two components, one the autonomous orders, and the other the induced orders, which will be larger the smaller the ratio of stocks and equipment in hand to current put-through. If we measure the ratio of stocks and equipment in hand to current put-through on the $y$ axis, the aggregate demand curve will have a conventional shape.

Secondly, the value of $y$ at any date $t_1$ which we call $y_1$ will be already determined by the value of previous orders

[1] Cf. 'Mr. Harrod's Dynamic Model', by S. Alexander, *Economic Journal*, December 1950, and my reply, June 1951.

and by the rate of growth between $t_0$ and $t_1$. The larger the rate of growth the smaller $y_1$ will be. Therefore the larger the rate of growth between $t_0$ and $t_1$ the larger the orders at $t_1$ will be. Therefore the larger the rate of growth between $t_0$ and $t_1$, the larger the rate of growth between $t_1$ and $t_2$ will be. I call the rate of growth between $t_0$ and $t_1$ which is such, neither less nor greater, as to cause the rate of growth between $t_1$ and $t_2$ to be equal to it, the warranted rate of growth. *If the rate of growth between $t_0$ and $t_1$ is greater than this there will be an acceleration between $t_1$ and $t_2$, and if it is less, there will be a deceleration.* This is my basic proposition.

In this account of the matter I have freed myself from the particular assumption made in the foregoing essay in regard to the reaction of the representative entrepreneur and replaced it by a more general assumption. The particular assumption has been pronounced by Mr. Alexander to be unsafe, and I agree. The more general assumption is simply that the entrepreneur will order more the lower the ratio of his stocks and equipment to his current put-through, and this I take to be safe.

I take the foregoing argument to prove that on the more general assumption, no less than on the particular assumption of my previous article, there will be a unique warranted rate of growth surrounded by centrifugal forces; but the precise formula for the warranted rate of growth supplied in that article depended on the particular assumption. I am not able to supply a formula of sufficient generality to match the general assumption. At any time the actual behaviour of entrepreneurs, and thereby that of the representative or mean entrepreneur, must conform to some particular variant of the general assumption. The general assumption we take as axiomatic, but which particular variant of it governs behaviour is unknown.

In the foregoing article I deduced a warranted rate of growth by assuming that a particular variant of the general assumption operated. In what follows I have chosen an alternative variant, rather widely different from the previous one, and deduced a warranted rate of growth from it. The fact that the two warranted rates of growth, deduced respectively from two rather widely different assumptions, are very near each other is encouraging. A similar exercise could be done for other particular variants of the general assumption.

I call the particular assumption used in the foregoing essay postulate A, which is as follows : *If investment ex-post is justified in any period, the representative entrepreneur will (unless prevented by physical limitations) in the succeeding period increase production in the same proportion as it has just been increased. If in a period investment ex post is less than justified investment, entrepreneurs will in the next period increase the rate of growth of investment and vice versa.*

I now substitute postulate B as follows : *Let the representative entrepreneur on each occasion of giving an order repeat the amount contained in his order for the last equivalent period, adding thereto an order for an amount by which he judges his existing stock to be deficient, if he judges it to be deficient, or subtracting therefrom the amount by which he judges his stock to be redundant, if he does so judge it. Let him judge his stock to be neither redundant nor deficient when it consists of a certain fraction, C, of his intended order.*

Some adjustment of wording is required to cover the case of orders for fixed equipment. It is assumed that the entrepreneur replaces at a steady rate if he finds his equipment used to convenient capacity, but reduces his replacement order by the full amount of any redundant capacity or increases it if and to the extent that he finds that at the existing rate of working it would be convenient to have more. This postulate B is also reasonable but betokens a more cautious temperament than A. The actual representative entrepreneur may well have a behaviour line intermediate between A and B.

On postulate B also a line of steady advance exists, but it is achieved in a slightly different condition. Under postulate A the amount of capital on hand remains continuously satisfactory; under postulate B there must be a chronic shortage. The entrepreneur must judge his stock to be deficient by a certain amount $x_r$, which has to be determined.

Let $x$ stand for the amount by which he judges his stock

to be deficient at any time. According to postulate B he will order on order day one the amount that he ordered on order day nought plus $x_1$. It is to be remembered that the entrepreneur, as well as being representative as regards his attitude of mind, as explained above, is also representative in that his activity varies in direct proportion with total national income. If $y_0$ stands for his order on day nought, $x_1 = Gy_1$ $\left(\text{since } x_1 = y_1 - y_0 \text{ and } G = \dfrac{y_1 - y_0}{y_1}\right)$.

On order day one his order was $y_1$. He will repeat this order on order day two if on that day his stock stands at $Cy_1$.

In order that a regular advance may be maintained, it is 'required' that he should increase his order on order day two in the same proportion that he increased it on order day one. On order day one he increased his order by $Gy_1$; it is 'required' that on order day two he should increase his order by $Gy_2 = \left[\dfrac{(Gy_1)^2}{y_0}\right]$. If he is to increase his order by this amount, it is 'required', in accordance with postulate B, that his stock on order day two should stand below the convenient level defined above, viz. $Cy_1$, by the amount $Gy_2$.

Therefore it is 'required' that his stock on order day two should stand at $Cy_1 - Gy_2$.

On order day one it stood at $Cy_0 - x_1 = Cy_0 - Gy_1$.

Therefore in order that his stock stand at the 'required' level on order day two, it is necessary that it should increase between order day one and order day two by

$$(Cy_1 - Gy_2) - (Cy_0 - Gy_1) = C(y_1 - y_0) - G(y_2 - y_1).$$

Assuming that the representative entrepreneur's sales stand in the same proportion to consumer expenditure that his orders stand to national income, his stock will increase between order day one and order day two by an amount $= sy_1$. Thus for a steady growth to be maintained, it is necessary that $sy_1 = C(y_1 - y_0) - G(y_2 - y_1)$. This means that under postulate B a higher growth rate is conjugated with given values of $s$ and $C$.

But the difference is only slight when compared with the regular rate of advance under postulate A, viz. $\frac{s}{C}$, since the stimulus required is a small fraction from stocks and equipment being insufficient is of small amount only, compared with C. Thus the more cautious attitude of entrepreneurs as defined by postulate B makes a very slight difference only to the warranted growth rate.

5. I should claim for the basic principle, as distinct from the alternative variants, that it has as wide a generality and as high a deductive status as any of the 'laws' of static economics.

Interesting further results can be obtained by comparing the slope of this line of 'warranted' advance with the 'natural' line of advance, as defined in the foregoing article, and also in relation to the trade cycle. In the latter connexion it is to be observed that it does not yield a complete account of the course of the cycle and in that differs from certain so-called 'complete models' that have been set up for study. These complete models require special postulates and assumptions in regard to lags and coefficients, which can only be accepted subject to statistical verification. While it is interesting and satisfactory to have such complete models for comparison with the phenomena of the real world, it is clear that the 'theories' of the cycle based on them have a greatly inferior authority, since their logical status is precarious, while mine rests, like the 'law of demand' itself, on assumptions of the utmost simplicity and generality. But mine makes no pretension to giving a complete explanation of the cycle.

A few words may be said, none the less, about its relation to the successive phases of the cycle. If output proceeds at a greater rate than the warranted line, shortages of circulating and fixed capital tend to develop. What then happens to the relation between the actual line of output and the warranted line? The former can be charted as a historic curve, the $x$ axis representing the progress of time. The latter cannot be so charted, since the equation does not determine the $y$ value of the curve at any point, but only $\frac{dy}{dx}$. As the curve of actual output moves up, the whole warranted line should be deemed to slide up with it, retaining its slope; the upward propulsion remains in being so long as the *slope* of the actual line is greater than that of the warranted line. The centrifugal force subjects the slope of the actual line to successive increase, so long as the slope of the warranted line remains the same. There is then the theoretical possibility of an unlimited expansion. This is clearly impossible in practice. The check to expansion may come in one of two, and probably both of two, ways.

(i) The general theory assumes that the wish to expand and the orders which reflect that wish can be effectuated without hindrance. This may not be so. The slope of the actual curve depends not on the amount of orders given but on the amount of activity resulting from those orders. Strong impediments to an increase of activity may in due course depress the slope of the actual line, so that it ceases to be greater than that of the warranted line. If this happens the upward propulsion dies a natural death, and if the slope of the actual line becomes less than that of the warranted line, expansion will automatically give place to depression. In this connexion it is not necessary to suppose that the 'ceiling of full employment' is reached. As activity expands after a period of depression, it may be easy to bring additional productive factors into play. On the side of labour this will be specially so if there are pools of unemployed in most places and trades. At a later stage it may become more difficult to mobilise more labour, or other resources, for additional activity. The difficulty will be greater, the greater the immobility of labour and the greater the change in the pattern of demand since the economy was last in a state of equivalent activity. The slowing down in the practicable rate of expansion may reduce the actual rate of growth below the warranted rate, with an affect similar to hitting the ceiling of full employment.

(ii) The slope of the warranted line is not stationary, depending as it does on the values of $C$ and $s$. We are not now concerned with chance variations in these, but we have to consider whether a rapid expansion will cause a systematic variation. A rapid forward movement may cause a sizable increase in *s*, owing to the receipts of firms rising more rapidly than their currently paid-out expenses. If there is an inflation of prices, the marginal propensity to save may rise well above unity. This tilts the warranted line upwards and may make its slope greater than the maximum practicable rate of advance.

It is of interest in this connexion to consider how an economy may react to a situation in which orders cannot be met in full. If inflation is 'suppressed' by the establishment of waiting lists and the lengthening of delivery dates, the effect on *s* will be less strong than if prices are pushed up with a view to clearing order books. It seems that 'suppressed' inflation is likely to keep a boom in being longer than open inflation. In both cases the actual rate of expansion is kept down by what is physically possible and the centrifugal forces are not allowed full play; this may by itself bring the boom to an end in either case. But in the case of open inflation there is a second cause tending to bring the boom to an end, namely the strong upward movement of the line of warranted advance. Open inflation may cause the boom to peter out rather quickly.

A few words may also be said about the downward movement. For this purpose it is convenient to revert to a simple version of my equation, viz. :

$$G = \frac{s - \dfrac{K}{x}}{C_p}.$$

If G becomes negative, $C_p$ must be negative, so long as $\left(s - \dfrac{K}{x}\right)$ is positive. A negative value for $C_p$ means that the stock of capital is moving in the opposite direction to the level of activity; if $C_p$ is negative in a depression, this means that capital is still increasing; it is required to decrease. So long as capital (other than K) is increasing while activity is decreasing, the downward propulsion remains in being; thus the slump can only find a bottom when $\left(s - \dfrac{K}{x}\right)$ becomes negative. The mere movement of recession by raising the value of $\frac{K}{x}$ reduces that of $\left(s - \frac{K}{x}\right)$. $s$ is likely to decline owing to business losses or, anyhow, owing to receipts falling more rapidly than paid-out expenses. If $\frac{K}{x}$ is large, that is helpful for securing an early termination to the downward movement; and, by the same argument, it is most unhelpful if K proceeds to decline, as is only too likely if the depression is protracted and severe. (cf. page 281 above).

Only when $\left(s - \frac{K}{x}\right)$ becomes negative can there be any hope of reaching bottom; when it first becomes negative, it will only have a small arithmetic value, which means that C will have a small value also; capital (other than that represented by K) has at length begun to move in the same direction as the general level of activity, but it may not yet be moving enough.

Mr. Hicks has, rightly in my judgment, stressed the importance of the fact that in a slump there is a maximum physically possible rate of disinvestment.[1] To illustrate the working of this, the equilibrium equation may be re-written:

$$G_w = \frac{s - \dfrac{K}{x}}{_cC + _fC},$$

where $_cC$ is circulating capital and $_fC$ fixed capital. If the recession has reached a point at which capital (other than K) has begun to decline *ex post* and the maximum possible rate at which fixed capital can decline is less than the rate at which total capital (other than K) is declining, the rate at which circulating capital declines is *pro tanto* greater. The value of $(_cC_p + _fC_p)$ is determined by the other terms in the equation. The smaller $_fC_p$, the greater must be $_cC_p$. Anything which tends to raise the (arithmetic) value of $_cC_p$ expedites the bottom of the slump; when $_cC_p = _cC$, the impetus to reduce the orders for circulating capital comes to an end.

[1] For an anticipation of this proposition see my *Towards a Dynamic Economics*, p. 90.

The foregoing paragraph implied that all orders for fixed capital (other than K) are in suspense during the slump. This will not be so in fact, since even in a severe slump it is usual to find some particular demands continuing to expand and some investment in fixed capital (viz. 'investment in fixed capital over and above K) proceeding. This will make the decline of *ex-post* investment in all other forms of capital, fixed and circulating, greater than it would otherwise be. But the decline in other fixed being physically limited, the decline in other circulating will be increased by this factor also.

Once a bottom is reached and there is no further decline in the orders for circulating capital, the orders for fixed capital will rise in due course, since the economy will not be able to carry on at a given level, however low, without a revival of orders for fixed capital on replacement account.

# IV
# GENERAL

# PROFESSOR F. A. VON HAYEK ON INDIVIDUALISM

PROFESSOR VON HAYEK's *Road to Serfdom* had a combination of qualities — sincerity, passion, fine English writing, acute and subtle logic, wisdom and appositeness — which may well cause it to take its place as a classic. It will probably long be read with both pleasure and advantage. In a work of this character, which may be called a polemic, or perhaps, with greater precision, a tract, some over-emphasis is in place; it adds a spice, and at the same time reveals the sources of the author's inspired mood, thereby helping the understanding of what he has to say, and it can easily be allowed for by the reader of sense when he makes his final assessment. There are some, it is true, including some who are sympathetic to Professor Hayek's main position, who felt that he took just a little too much of the licence properly accorded to inspiration, thereby impairing the cogency of the tract. This excess, if indeed it was there, consisted not so much in the ruthlessness with which he pushed his arguments to their logical conclusion — a procedure appropriate in the context — as in a certain tendency to dogmatism and exclusiveness which cannot be validly maintained in the field of political studies. The subject-matter is too complex, elusive and mysterious.

In the present lecture,[1] which may be regarded as a pendant to the larger work, the inspiration flags and the dogmatism is more prominent. As there is a clear danger that Professor Hayek may let this tendency to dogmatism assume the mastery in his intellectual make-up — as illustrious writers on politics have done before him — and as this

[1] *Individualism: True aud False.* Finlay Lecture, University College, Dublin, December 1945. B. H. Blackwell, Oxford, 1946.

might obscure his other lights, which are capable of being of such great service in these harassed times, it may be well to examine the work before us with exceptionally critical scrutiny.

Dogmatism is implicit in the title itself — *Individualism: True and False*. This seems to serve notice of a heresy hunt. One would have thought that in these days of sadly waning individualism, one should be reluctant to cast out of the canon interesting and influential 'individualist' thinkers, even although their work contained certain impurities. Anyhow, if there is to be a purge, let us be quite sure that our criterion is correct.

First it is necessary to examine, much more strictly than Professor Hayek seems to have done, the meaning of the words 'true' and 'false' in this context. As an opening move I suggest six possible meanings, without claiming exhaustiveness.

1. It may be held that in the history of thought certain writers have so clearly established the title to be the expounders of individualism that the doctrines of other lesser writers may be tested by their agreement or disagreement with the ideas of these master minds. (Historical criterion.)

2. Instead of certain writers, the word itself may be made the criterion. Presumably, individualism entails stressing the importance of the individual. Doctrines may be tested according as whether they do or do not genuinely do this. (Etymological criterion.)

3. Individualism may be regarded as comprising a number of propositions about the working of society. Propositions may be true or false. True individualism could be said to consist of all those 'individualist' propositions which are true and false individualism of those which are false. (Scientific criterion.)

4. Individualism may be regarded as comprising not a set of sociological laws, but a statement of aims or ends or values. Individualism might be deemed true, if the aims or values set out are things which mankind does in fact value, and conversely. (Value criterion : ends.)

5. Alternatively, individualism may be regarded as

prescribing not ultimate values, but the means to achieving certain more fundamental aims commonly accepted by mankind. True individualism would then prescribe a set of maxims which do in fact tend to the achievement of those aims, while the maxims of false individualism would be those which have plausibly been taken to do so, but do not in fact do so. (Value criterion : means.)

6. True individualism might be taken to state the values men ought to aim at whether they do so or not and false individualism values which men ought not to aim at. (Moral criterion.)

Professor Hayek certainly does not make plain which of these or which combination of these criteria he has in mind. His citation of certain authors suggests the first. By this he cannot be deemed to have established his case. He attaches himself firmly to Burke, Adam Smith, de Tocqueville and Acton. He stretches out tentacles towards Locke and Hume. But Locke, his claim on whom he makes no attempt to substantiate, must definitely be denied him, for reasons which will be explained. Among the false we have by his admission the Encyclopaedists, much of the work of the Benthamites and of J. S. Mill and Herbert Spencer. When we examine the doctrine expounded by Professor Hayek, we have to class Locke and Bentham among the false. Clearly then in this appeal to authority, as manifested in the history of political thought, the verdict is indecisive. It may be noticed in passing that Professor Hayek's four favourites, while very sagacious men, were not, except Adam Smith, moral philosophers who dealt with first principles. Professor Hayek hints at the second criterion when he argues that individualism ought to mean something that is the opposite of socialism. When he says emphatically that individualism is 'a *theory* of society, an attempt to understand the forces which determine the social life of man, and only in the second instance a set of political maxims derived from this view of society', he seems to point to the third criterion, and away from those numbered 4 to 6. None the less the general drift of his argument suggests that he has the fifth also in mind.

It seems difficult to dispense with the first and second

criteria altogether. If we concentrate attention on the third (or on any of the last four, for that matter), individualism seems to become identical with sociology. Perhaps Professor Hayek would say that it is. Yet it seems more natural to suppose that what is true or wise in individualism constitutes some important part or aspect of sociology, not the whole. And if we ask which part, we are driven back to the first or second criterion. But when one considers his argument on these, one cannot escape the notion that Professor Hayek is not seeking to apply them strictly, but that he has quite a different approach, that he thinks that there is some absolute doctrine laid up, so to speak, in Heaven, a Platonic idea of individualism, which mundane writers may or may not have succeeded in grasping. This is a common error of the man in the street when he discusses Liberalism, Socialism, etc. For him there is some absolute doctrine, a true Liberalism, for instance, which is not on the one hand merely truth itself nor on the other a rescript or conflation of what Liberals have expounded. This of course opens the door for the prophet, for the man who claims to have seen the invisible Text. And this is the danger. I am reminded of a book I once read by an American lady, the whole of which was devoted to proving, without reference either to the artistic intention of Shakespeare or any alleged facts of history, that Shakespeare had altogether failed to do justice to the moral character of Hamlet's mother.

The main characteristic ascribed by Professor Hayek to true individualism is respect for 'spontaneous social products' which promote a good social end but were not deliberately devised for the purpose they serve. One detects at once the economist's reference to Adam Smith. But Professor Hayek wishes to broaden the basis of respect for property and markets, by assimilating the economic doctrine of harmony to the more far-reaching conceptions of Burke on the utility of established institutions and quotes a notable tribute by Adam Smith to Burke.[1] He contrasts this doctrine with the

[1] It should be noticed, however, that Adam Smith severely condemns another of Professor Hayek's favourites — de Mandeville (*Moral Sentiments*, Pt. 6, sect. 2, ch. 4).

rationalist approach which assumes that Reason can provide blue-prints which will solve all human problems; the reference to our modern planners is obvious. Now much of what he says in this passage concerning the imperfect rationality of human beings and the power of social processes to achieve more than the highest individual human reason could devise is wise and true. But it is not at all clear what this has to do with the doctrine of individualism. What Professor Hayek seems to be doing here is roughing in a philosophical defence not of individualism, but of the best type of conservatism. The antithesis to the doctrine he is expounding in these passages is not socialism or collectivism, but radicalism, which is prepared to tear down established institutions and build quite afresh in the light of reason or first principles. Such a radical was Bentham, who wished to test all establishments by the greatest happiness principle. That surely is a characteristically rationalist procedure. It is not merely the Benthamite school but Bentham himself who stands condemned of rationalism and thereby of false individualism. But is not this a little absurd? We cannot really have a definition of individualism that excludes Bentham. Furthermore, Locke was a thoroughgoing rationalist in this sense. So he too would have to be excluded.

In the eye of truth there is much to be said both for conservatism, a disposition to ascribe hidden values to customs and institutions that have grown up, and for radicalism, the urge to sweep away all the old rubbish. The social value of each disposition depends on time and circumstance. No formula can exempt us from the difficult intellectual task of deciding which way we should incline from time to time, seeking the golden mean, recognising both the weakness and fallibility of human reason, and also its amazing power. This lecture adds point to Mr. Durbin's spirited plea for reason in his review of Professor Hayek's previous volume.[1] But what has all this to do with individualism? In many societies, perhaps most, time-honoured institutions have been exceedingly cramping to the individual. The radicals or rationalists of to-day may incline to centralist

[1] *The Economic Journal*, December 1945.

planning, but at other times they have sought to release the individual from despotic power or unduly cramping laws or customs.

Surely the American constitution may be regarded as an individualist blueprint, and therefore, according to Professor Hayek, as a type of 'false' individualism. It is true that British people have for many years poured some scorn on its rigidity, preferring their own more flexible system, which has evolved or been patched from time to time in a way that should commend it to Professor Hayek. Yet it is possible that a man of to-day, who really valued individual liberty, would feel more secure of his freedom if living in the United States under the aegis of that piece of rationalist planning than he would under our own régime.

The attempt to link Smithian economics to Burke's conservatism is not a happy one. It is true that they are both inimical to centralist planning and rely on the un-fettered working of existing institutions. But whereas Burke was anxious to make us look to the hidden virtue in estab-lished things, Smith's system was fully rationalist. Professor Hayek is right in urging that this does not imply that each individual is fully rational; but the *raison d'être* of the system as a whole and its parts can be demonstrated by argument. This is quite in contrast to the emotional foundations of loyalty on which Burke builds.

This confusion between two separate issues shows itself in a number of ways, for instance in the treatment of Rous-seau, who is lumped in with the Encyclopaedists, despite the fact he was in sharp conflict with them on most points. Profes-sor Hayek treats this great man in altogether too cavalier a way; he is assigned the role of a power for evil. Rousseau has two very different, and indeed in some sense opposed, strains, neither of which Burke 'commonly (and rightly) represented as the main opponent of the so-called "individu-alism" of Rousseau' (page 7), was capable of understanding.

In his strict political theory Rousseau should probably be classed as a collectivist. He stated the case for the general will. The power of incisive logic shown in the *Le contrat social* places Rousseau in the ranks of political philosophers concerned with first principles — Hobbes, Locke, Hume. When Rousseau refutes the doctrine of 'might is right' in a few limpid and immortal sentences, he is as far beyond the range of Burke in theoretical philosophy as Burke is beyond Rousseau's range in practical wisdom. Burke had not the power of precise logic which would have enabled him to meet Rousseau at all on the high philosophical plane. As a political theorist Rousseau should not be classed as an individualist, true or false. Presumably the reason why Professor Hayek classes him as the latter is that he was a radical, prepared to sweep away the old rubbish.

In his attitude to other matters, in his temperament, in his emotions, Rousseau was no doubt a strong individualist. As such he is regarded as father of the Romantic Movement — and was a man of great influence and genius. And about that aspect too Burke, albeit for totally different reasons, was quite unqualified to pass comment. As a romantic Rousseau probes deep into the human heart, lifts the veil, turns our attention back to elemental and universal passions, stirs, moves, shocks. That was not at all Burke's *milieu*. For all his poetic imagination, Burke was essentially a man of business, State papers, bustle and conventionality. It is not to belittle Burke's greatness in his own field to say that it showed a considerable narrowness that he could see in Rousseau only a perverted egoist. Perhaps that was typically English ; for, if we give to Ireland Burke's oratory, we should probably accede to Burke's own claim to be of English stock, when we seek the national source of his political wisdom — and his philistinism as regards the deeper emotions. Not all Englishmen are like that, however. We have our Shelley. Before closing his list of individualists, Professor Hayek would do well to examine the case of Shelley carefully. He was an individualist and a rationalist, prepared to pull down the pillars, and yet an object of great veneration in prim Victorian England.[1]

This brings me to the later pages of this lecture. Professor Hayek has so much of value to contribute to the thought of

[1] I may be allowed to bring Shelley into the argument, since Professor Hayek cites Goethe.

the country of his adoption that I hesitate to discourage him by joining those who would warn him about the difficulties of summarising the typically English point of view. He thinks that the Germans are 'rationalist' and thereby 'falsely individualist' in insisting on the development of 'original' personalities. He contrasts this with the 'voluntary conformity' of the English Public School system. There is much confusion in this. In many respects the English are fundamentally non-conformist, and this country has been singularly rich in 'original' personalities. One has only to examine the literature from Shakespeare to Dickens. It is a well-known dictum of literary criticism that our imaginative writers show their best genius in the portrayal of secondary characters, who are commonly eccentric, while their heroes and heroines are a little lacking in depth. The most notable exception to this dictum, Hamlet, illustrates the point.

The question of the essential characteristics of the English Public School is notoriously a treacherous one. The English themselves have not been able completely to unravel it. There is a typically English concept, much older and of far greater importance than that of old Public School boy, perhaps of waning influence now, but historically of great moment, the gentleman. It is well known that the criterion for distinguishing a gentleman is something other than income or even heredity. For centuries English gentlemen have been famous for their frequent eccentricity. Enthusiasts might claim that no class in recorded history has been so rich per head in 'original personalities'. The conformist tradition of Public Schools, referred to by Professor Hayek, is comparatively modern and its cause is readily explainable. To be a gentleman is (or used to be) an ideal near the heart of many Englishmen. Public Schools came to establish the claim that they had a secret patent for manufacturing gentlemen artificially. Parents of means naturally sought this advantage for their sons. Conformism has no connexion with the concept of gentleman as such but was necessary to the process of artificial manufacture. In the broad picture of English social life through the centuries it is a phenomenon of minor importance. None the less some hold that the increasing predominance of this rather more uniform Public School product in recent decades has weakened our national character. It is possible also that the amount of conformism often ascribed to these schools is exaggerated. At my own school, an ancient one, the most influential masters were certainly very eccentric characters, and their influence to some extent lay precisely in that. They were odd ; but it was not thought in the least odd that they should be so ; on the contrary, their oddness was accepted and admired as being essentially in the British tradition. There is no need for Professor Hayek to look beyond British experience for the stress that J. S. Mill lays in his *Liberty* on the value of variety in individual self-expression. This is something deeply rooted in British individualism. 'Voluntary' conformity is more characteristic of American Main Street; and there, according to report, it is not so much superior to legal restraint, in the point of oppressiveness, as Professor Hayek suggests.

It is of course quite true that there is something very un-English in the quest for self-expression that one finds in Werther, Faust and Wilhelm Meister. But what is un-English there is not the originality of the protagonists, but their self-conscious quest for it. It is the craving for something that they feel themselves to lack. When Faust is confronted with Euphorion he perceives an inborn freedom and natural waywardness of spirit that are quite beyond his range. I may remind Professor Hayek that Euphorion was an Englishman.

This lecture contains much that is wise, much that is well said and much that is worthy of Professor Hayek at his best. I have concentrated my notice on his heresy hunt. The doctrine of individualism needs nourishment from many sources and will flourish only by an interplay of opinion as free and varied as the mode of life which it seeks to secure in practical affairs. If any one, even someone so distinguished as Professor Hayek, ever succeeds in establishing himself as its S. Athanasius, that will be the death of it.

## ESSAY 16

# INCREASING RETURNS

*The Theory of Monopolistic Competition*[1] is a magisterial work. It opened up a new subject that constitutes a branch of economics as it is now recognised, research into which is still flourishing. The book is written in a distinguished style which maintains clarity through difficult passages. In its description of industrial organisation it is realistic and sensitive as regards the motives likely to play on the minds of entrepreneurs. At the same time it is an abstract work, an essay in pure theory in the fullest sense; and as such it contains many elegant constructions.

When asked to write in honour of its illustrious author, I had it in mind to try to make a reappraisal of his thinking, eliminating all traces of the ego. This ego was apt to come in, as I involved myself at the outset in attempts to formulate a theory of this subject; and I have made one contribution since. Despite my good resolution, I found that it was humanly impossible to fulfil my programme. The ego was irrepressible.

In 1952 an article of mine on monopolistic theory appeared in a book of my essays,[2] and Professor Chamberlin's attempted refutation of its argument appeared in 1957.[3] Subsequently I had a correspondence with him, in which I affirmed that I could deal with his queries and rebut his criticisms, and he expressed a strong desire that I should publish my views. Some time after that he had dinner with me in Christ Church, and over the port the question of a possible article by me recurred. It so happened that at that time he was editor of the

---

[1] Hereafter simply denoted *Monopolistic Competition*.

[2] R. F. Harrod, Essay 8, 'The Theory of Imperfect Competition Revised', in *Economic Essays*, Macmillan, London, 1952, pp. 139–87.

[3] E. H. Chamberlin, *Towards a More General Theory of Value*, Oxford University Press, New York, 1957.

*Quarterly Journal of Economics*, while I was editor of the *Economic Journal*. The question was raised in which journal the projected article should appear. We decided to spin a coin, and I drew in my colleagues around the table as witnesses of this solemn event. The coin fell in favour of the *Quarterly Journal of Economics*.

But, alas, the article was never written. Perhaps the present contribution may be considered as a substitute, *longum post intervallum*, for that unwritten article. But it is written in a spirit less controversial than might have been present during the excitement of debate in those days.

Although my 1952 essay asked for the rejection of a certain doctrine that appeared in *Monopolistic Competition* as well as in my own earlier work—Professor Chamberlin accordingly characterised it as a 'recantation'—I like to think of it, rather, as a continuation and confirmation of Chamberlin's main work. In recent years there have been widespread doubts about the validity of certain doctrines that were considered to be part of the theory of monopolistic competition, as explained in classrooms and textbooks in the 'thirties. Much work of an empirical character has since been done on the subject, and empirical work is absolutely essential in this field. On the theoretical front there has been some disintegration, and the results of research have not been embodied in conclusions that form so good an intellectual background as was furnished by *Monopolistic Competition*. Certain generalisations may have been achieved; but generalisations, as such, do not have the same status as principles that can be regarded as integral to the theory of value. My article, although in part destructive, claimed to furnish new principles worthy of taking their place alongside earlier doctrines as part of a general theory. And thus, although Chamberlin was displeased with my essay, I should like to think that it was a contribution in the tradition that he established.[1]

[1] This 1952 essay has, I believe, been little studied. It did not appear in a journal. The book in which I, perhaps injudiciously, published it, contained articles about quite different topics, such as dynamic theory and population theory, so that specialists in monopolistic competition may not have seen any need to acquire it.

It may be helpful to go back to the origins of this topic. When *Monopolistic Competition* appeared I had already written a number of articles on its subject,[1] and, of course, any discussion of the intellectual origins of this subject must include the work of Professor Joan Robinson.

I have reread *Monopolistic Competition* and *The Economics of Imperfect Competition* during the last fortnight, and I was struck again, as I so vividly remember being struck 33 years ago, by the fact that two independent minds, working in two different countries against somewhat different intellectual backgrounds, should have written books that, taken separately, deserved to establish a new and important subject of study, possessing so many doctrines in common. There were also, of course, very serious differences in their treatment and in some of their opinions. Chamberlin has thought it right to stress the differences, and he has been perfectly entitled to do so, because these differences have implications that should be taken carefully into account. However, this is not an appropriate place to attempt to compare the rival merits (and demerits) of these two great works.

[1] See 'Notes on Supply', *Economic Journal*, 1930, pp. 232–41; 'The Law of Decreasing Costs', *Economic Journal*, 1931, pp. 566–76; and 'Further Note on Decreasing Costs', *Economic Journal*, 1933, pp. 337–41.

In the first of these I devised the concept of 'increment of aggregate demand', which has subsequently become known, at the suggestion of Professor E. A. G. Robinson, as 'marginal revenue'. Chamberlin uses the expression 'marginal receipts', with a footnote reference to me and to Professor Erich Schneider, whose article 'Drei Probleme der Monopoltheorie', *Zeitschrift für Nationalökonomie*, 1931, appeared the following year.

On the rather boring question of priorities, I may mention that I composed this 1930 article in 1928 and submitted it for the *Economic Journal* during that year. Keynes referred it to Frank P. Ramsey, a philosopher of the highest repute, and also author of 'A Contribution to the Theory of Taxation', *Economic Journal*, 1927, pp. 47–61, and the very famous, still-discussed 'A Mathematical Theory of Saving', *Economic Journal*, 1928, pp. 543–59. Ramsey recommended rejection, and, as I was heavily pressed at that time with administrative duties and also in rather poor health, I did not take the matter up with my good friend, Ramsey, until the following year. I have in my possession a letter received from him in 1929, dated 6 July, in which he wrote 'you are quite right; I am sorry I cannot have understood the point before. I think I even had a muddled notion that you came to the opposite conclusion . . . I must have been very stupid.' In an eight-page letter, Ramsey had his own shot at supplementing my views, introducing the question of what Chamberlin later called 'oligopoly'. It is possible that this letter from so distinguished a pen is worthy of publication.

One difference consists in Mrs. Robinson's omitting to treat the subject of oligopoly. She wrote:

> Thus if one 'firm' raises its price the demand curves for the others will be raised. This may cause them to raise their prices also, and the rise in their price will react upon the demand for the commodity of the first firm. In drawing up the demand curve for any one firm, however, it is possible to take this effect into account. The demand curve for the individual firm may be conceived to show the full effect upon the sales of that firm which results from any change in the price which it charges, whether it causes a change in the prices charged by the others or not. It is not our purpose to consider this question in detail. Once the demand curve for the firm has been drawn, the technique of analysis can be brought into play, whatever the assumptions on which the demand curve was drawn up.[1]

It is a merit of Chamberlin's book that it makes an analysis of this question in detail. And his conflation of the theory of oligopoly with his theory of product differences is an especially fine piece of work.[2]

If I understand him aright, Chamberlin holds that, if oligopolists do their stuff fully and properly, the oligopoly price will be equal to the monopoly price. He writes in *Monopolistic Competition*, 'If sellers have regard to their *total* influence upon price, the price will be the monopoly one' (p. 54). At that time I did some work on oligopoly (duopoly) and reached a somewhat different conclusion: that the oligopoly price will lie between the monopoly price and that of perfect competition. This result, achieved with some

---

[1] J. Robinson, *The Economics of Imperfect Competition*, Macmillan, London, 1933, p. 21.

[2] I have used the word 'differences' here. There are two quite distinct phenomena, for which we need two words. There are the differences that occur almost inevitably in the case of manufactured goods, including processed foods, as distinct from primary products that can be made subject to complete standardisation. Second, there are the differences deliberately introduced by wicked producers with a view to creating monopolistic positions for themselves. My sense of our language suggests that 'differentiation' should be used with an active meaning. If this is right, it should be reserved for the second of the two phenomena mentioned.

mathematical apparatus, seems to commend itself to common sense.[1]

## The Tangency Solution

Among the striking points of resemblance in the work of Chamberlin and Mrs. Robinson was the doctrine of the tangency of the demand and cost curves in equilibrium in conditions of monopolistic competition (the large-group case). There is a great elegance in this doctrine of tangency. It is truly remarkable that in this position it is possible to combine monopoly and competition in a radical manner, by showing that the equilibrium would have the characteristic of monopoly—that price was above the competitive level—and the characteristic of competition—that profit was no more than normal.

This doctrine of tangency went with the view that a downward sloping particular demand curve would in itself have a tendency to generate excess capacity. There were, indeed, certain technical differences between the two theories: the methods by which the tangential curves were drawn were not quite the same, as Chamberlin pointed out in his criticism of Mrs. Robinson.[2] Nonetheless, the fact that two separate authors independently reached this tangency solution was so striking that the technical differences seemed to be a minor point.

The articles of mine cited in the footnote on page 304 reached a number of the conclusions that subsequently appeared in the works of Chamberlin and Mrs. Robinson, but not the tangency solution. Indeed, in the 1931 paper I drew the average cost and demand curves as intersecting at a point at which they should have been tangent, because the marginal revenue and marginal cost curves cut each other vertically below this point. When this article was republished in my *Economic Essays* I inserted a lame footnote (p. 96) apologising for this inaccuracy.

[1] See my 'The Equilibrium of Duopoly', *Economic Journal*, 1934, pp. 335-7. This article also, I believe, has not been much studied.
[2] Chamberlin, *Towards a More General Theory of Value*, p. 308.

I was so impressed with the convergence of two minds on the doctrine of tangency that when I endeavoured in 1934 to summarise the position I went some way toward endorsing the tangency position as of important significance.[1] How far I actually went is for readers of that article to judge. They will thereby judge whether, in later repudiating the account of the tangency position that occurs in Chamberlin and Mrs. Robinson, I have indeed made what Chamberlin has called a 'recantation'. In this respect there is a difference between Chamberlin and Mrs. Robinson. In the latter's work the tangency position appears to be more necessary to equilibrium than in the former's, and this springs from Mrs. Robinson's definition of normal profit—a matter on which I argued against her.[2] For her a normal profit is defined as one that neither attracts outside firms into the business nor repels others now in it. Thus this dispenses her from entering into details about the question of free entry, which are discussed by Chamberlin, and by myself in the paper cited in footnote 2 below, but more cogently in the 1952 essay. But Chamberlin did hold that if there is free entry the position of tangency, as defined by me, will necessarily be reached—a doctrine that, since 1952, I have continued to condemn.

## New Entrants and Excess Capacity

Allied to this tangency doctrine is the logical necessity for excess capacity to come into existence whenever there is free entry and particular firms are confronted by downward sloping demand curves. As the latter condition is almost universal, except in the case of primary products, it follows that there is a very prevalent tendency for excess capacity in industry to be generated—a doctrine that strikes me as extremely unrealistic. I would submit that it was the remarkable and independent concilience of the two authors in the same year that inclined too many to accept the tangency doctrine uncritically. It is a curious fact that Chamberlin, who

[1] See 'Doctrines of Imperfect Competition', *Quarterly Journal of Economics*, 1934, pp. 442–70.
[2] In my 'Further Note on Decreasing Costs'.

was so very appreciative of the many facets of the problems of entrepreneurs, did not ask himself whether producers would not hesitate to set prices likely to attract new competitors into their field of business. Would they not, rather, cautiously say 'we had better not set so high a price as that'?

There are two points to be considered here. One is that if a producer sets a lower price in order to avoid provoking fresh competition he may actually be making a loss at the margin, in the sense that his current marginal revenue will be below his marginal cost. This does not, of course, mean that he will be making a loss over-all. Still, the objector may argue that if he is making a calculable loss at the margin he will pull in that margin so as to avoid that marginal loss. Even if he is making a profit over-all, it is better not to make a (theoretical) loss at the margin. But if he raises the price above the level at which he is making a marginal loss currently he will make another kind of loss, a *future* loss, through attracting fresh competitors, which he would certainly take into his calculations. I deal with this more fully later.

Professor Chamberlin has charged[1] that my argument concerning the danger of attracting future competitors implies oligopoly, whereas his general argument is independent of whether there is oligopoly or not. (But in the analysis of *Monopolistic Competition* I believe that the tangency position can be reached even if there is oligopoly.) I would argue, on the contrary, that prudent action against the attraction of fresh competitors is independent of whether oligopoly exists or not. The argument against me is that if there are many producers the action of one by himself will have no effect in attracting or not attracting fresh competition. I do not agree. The essence of imperfect competition is that the market is broken up by product difference, location, and so forth. However many producers there may be in a large region, each and every producer will have particular regard to the region close to himself by product type and location. He will seek to pursue a policy that does not attract fresh competition against himself in particular. If other competitors are foolish enough to charge high prices, so as to attract fresh competition, that

[1] *Towards a More General Theory of Value*, pp. 286–7.

is their funeral. Of course our particular competitor may be adversely affected by that, but to a far lesser extent than if fresh competition is attracted into his immediate vicinity by product type or location. It is the essence of imperfect competition that each man thinks of his own particular affairs. Therefore I would suggest that whether, in a wider field, there is oligopoly or not, each particular producer will be at pains not to make himself vulnerable to fresh competition in his close vicinity. Accordingly, he will not charge a price that stimulates such competition, even if by not charging such a price it can be shown that he is allowing his current marginal revenue to fall below his marginal cost.

Therefore I hold that there is no general tendency for producers faced by downward sloping demand curves, which means almost all producers of manufactured things, to charge prices such that fresh competition is attracted and they are pushed back to the point of tangency of price and average cost, with excess capacity and too many firms operating. I do not rule out the possibility that such a situation may occasionally occur.

A side point must be made here. The doctrine that excess capacity will not normally arise from excessive profits attracting fresh competition has nothing to do with the point that, where increasing returns obtain owing to markets being restricted by downward sloping demand curves, firms will build plants with a view to producing $x$ units, the optimum point of exploitation of which would be an output of $x+a$ units. This follows from the long period cost curve being an envelope of the short period curves.[1] This should not be called excess capacity, because to have a plant the optimum output of which was $x+a$ units would be the optimum way of producing $x$ units; if we actually intended to produce $x+a$ units, we would have a bigger plant still (assuming, of course, this level of output falls on the declining portion of the envelope).

There is one further point to be made about the tangency solution, in which price is above the competitive level although the profit is normal. It is only on recent reconsideration of this whole matter that I have raised to myself the

[1] See my *Economic Essays*, p. 119.

question whether there will necessarily, or normally, be any such point of tangency. It appears to me that although there may be such a point there may equally well be no such point —in which case the elegant tangency solution falls to the ground. Chamberlin does explicitly argue in favour of such a point of tangency. The demand curve, $DD'$,

> . . . must either intersect $PP'$ [the average cost curve] in two places or be tangent to it. . . . It is bound to cut across $PP'$, i.e., lying below it at either extremity, by the nature of the two curves. It lies below it to the left because, whereas the demand will characteristically become zero at a finite price and at a fairly low one on account of substitutes, the necessity of covering overhead or supplementary costs (including the minimum profit of the entrepreneur), no matter how small the production, defines the cost curve as meeting the $y$-axis at infinity.[1]

This strikes me as profoundly unsatisfactory. For the long period, in any event, supplementary costs should fall *pari passu* with prime costs, in proportion to diminished production. There is no need for the total cost to rise to infinity, except at points so near the $y$-axis (on account of the entrepreneur's indivisibility) as to be of no practical importance. I see no reason whatever why the demand curve, as it is pushed to the left by the incursion of fresh competitors, should not continue to intersect the cost curve downwards, for as far as you like to make it go. This sole argument of Chamberlin is too weak to sustain the view that there must be, or even normally will be, any point of tangency. I have searched Mrs. Robinson's pages in vain to discover any reason why there must be a point of tangency. She merely says that only at such a point can full equilibrium be realised: that at which there occurs the equation of marginal cost and marginal revenue on the one hand, and the establishment of a normal rate of profit on the other. But perhaps in many, or even in most, cases, no such total equilibrium is possible. This, if correct, would seem to give the quietus to the tangency solution as a general one. But I disfavour it also on the wider grounds already stated.

[1] Chamberlin, *Monopolistic Competition*, p. 76.

## A Suggested Solution

If we ask how a producer can fail to adjust his position when he is not maximising his current rate of profit and, in the strictest sense, is making a loss at the margin—there is of course no visible loss—I suggest that we should introduce into his profit-maximisation calculation the present value of future receipts, to the extent that these are affected by current policy. If a producer charges a price that is likely, on the best judgement, to attract fresh competitors, then his income prospect over the years ahead is reduced. The fresh competitor or competitors will take part of the market that our producer would otherwise have kept for himself and thus reduce his profit-earning capacity. Doubtless it is impossible to calculate this reduction precisely; but we might have some rough idea of its magnitude. Our producer will in any case be dealing with rough magnitudes only, because the current slope of the demand curve confronting him is something usually quite impossible to assess even within wide limits. If we take the quantity of output that would seem to maximise profit *this year*, and if we suppose that that involves a price high enough to attract fresh competition, then we must subtract from current income the present value of the consequent loss of future income. If this is done the result is likely to show a point of profit maximisation considerably to the right of the point that takes into account current net income only.

I have constructed a figure that brings into the picture once more a tangency condition. I am not suggesting that the presence of a tangency is necessary for equilibrium; it is necessary only if we postulate absolutely free entry in the fullest sense. The following diagram rests on a hypothesis, which may not be true in all, or even most, cases, but is the simplest hypothesis to make and is a suitable basis for an initial theoretical construction of this type.

That hypothesis is that if the producer charges more than full cost, this will damage his future position; that if he charges less than full cost this may even improve it, being a sort of sales-pushing device; and that charging full cost will be neutral in relation to future prospects. This seems a sufficiently reasonable hypothesis. The curve entitled 'average net proceeds (long-period)' in Fig. 1 shows what, for any given price charged, is the value of present proceeds per unit (i.e., price) plus or minus the present value of the increase or decrease of future proceeds, also per unit of output. The consequence of this hypothesis is that, for the amount at which price equals average cost, the price will also be equal to the average net proceeds (long-period) per unit of output. That is to say, because the producer is charging his full cost price he is neither damaging nor improving his future prospects by his current policy; consequently the present value to be added or subtracted from his demand curve is zero. It is to be noted that in the diagram the demand curve is *not* tangential to the average cost curve, but intersects it in a downward direction.[1]

Only at the point at which price is equal to average cost are average net proceeds (long-period) equal to the price and present value of future gain or loss equal to zero. Hence the average net proceeds curve *must* pass through this point of intersection. In Fig. 1 it is the average net proceeds curve, not the demand (equals current average revenue) curve, that is tangential to the cost curve. And this is how it should be. It is the average net proceeds (long-period) that the producer is trying to maximise.

It will be noted that in the early range the average net proceeds (long-period) curve slopes upwards. This is because, although the current average revenue per unit will be greater the smaller the output, if a very high price is charged, the large magnitude of the negative present value due to loss of future sales outweighs the greater current average revenue. The average net proceeds curve (long-period) rises to its own maximum, but has already begun to decline (owing to the effect of the decline in the current average revenue curve) when it reaches the point of tangency with the average cost curve. Owing to the tangency, the marginal cost curve will intersect the marginal net proceeds (long-period) curve upwards at a point vertically below the point of tangency. The other curves in the figure are self-explanatory.

[1] I am indebted to Mr. R. Hamond, marine biologist, for constructing these diagrams from my original freehand drawings.

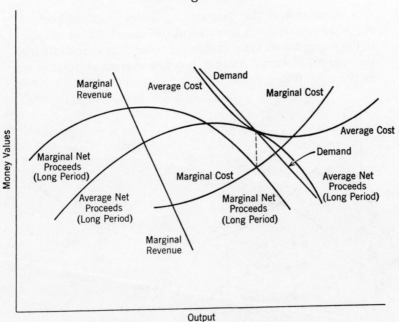

Fig. 1  A tangency equilibrium.

This diagram gives us a fit and proper equilibrium. Price is equal to average cost. Average net proceeds (long-period) are also equal to price because if this price is charged there will be no tendency to attract fresh competition or to drive out existing competitors. The marginal cost curve intersects the marginal net proceeds (long-period) curve upwards, for this same level of output. There is no excess capacity because at the tangency point average cost is equal to the cheapest possible way of producing the output in question.

In Fig. 2 we have a diagram in which this full equilibrium is not realised. The average net proceeds (long-period) curve is not tangential to the average cost curve, but intersects it twice. The amount of output is determined by the intersection of the marginal cost curve and the marginal net proceeds (long-period) curve. The demand curve (not shown in

Fig. 2) intersects the average net proceeds (long-period) curve downwards at a point vertically above the intersection of the marginal curves. It may be noted that in both figures the current marginal revenue is below current marginal cost at the equilibrium point.

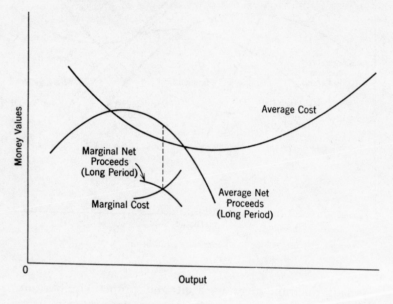

Fig. 2   A non-tangency position.

If the second diagram is to represent an equilibrium, this means that the producer believes that he can safely charge a price above the average cost without attracting fresh competition. This would be so in cases in which there is some obstacle to the freedom of entry of competitors. Of course if the impediment to entry was serious the segment of the average net proceeds (long-period) curve lying above the average cost curve would be much greater, and a correspondingly higher price could safely be charged. But even in that case a sufficiently high price would damage future prospects and the average net proceeds (long-period) curve should always be shown as sloping upwards in its early range.

A word may be said on the question of distortion away from the welfare optimum. I argued in my 1952 essay, to which Chamberlin took exception, that the downward slope of the particular demand curve would not by itself cause distortion if there was absolute freedom of entry. Fig. 1 shows no distortion because the price is equal to the average cost. The monopoly element and its accompanying distortion is to be associated with some impediment to the freedom of entry. I also argued in the aforementioned essay in favour of the Marshall-Pigou position that increasing returns would in and by itself cause distortion. Increasing returns can, of course, only occur if competition is less than perfect. But competition can be less than perfect even when there are constant returns. The traditional doctrine seems to make the presence of a downward sloping particular demand curve necessitate increasing returns; but this is surely not right. I hold that when there are constant returns and freedom of entry a downward sloping demand curve will not by itself cause distortion. Professor Chamberlin complained that I did not show long-period demand (here called average net proceeds (long-period)) in the diagram supplied.[1] The reason was that for the purpose of elucidating the relations set out in the figure I assumed that in each case the producer charged a price equal to average cost. Thus the present value of damage to future prospects would be zero in all cases and the long-period curve would be coincident with the short-period curve as shown.

### The Genesis of the Original Analysis

On this retrospective occasion I may be permitted to refer to a question that was not a matter of controversy with Chamberlin. I have in mind the impulse that originally caused me to spend my time considering these relations. The impulse actuating Chamberlin is clear enough: he was dissatisfied with the applicability of the traditional theory of perfect competition to the real world, and accordingly aspired to be the architect of a more comprehensive and realistic and thorough-going theory.

[1] *Economic Essays*, p. 180.

For me the matter was more of a sideline. I was particularly concerned with the subject of increasing returns. During the 'twenties many of us were deeply interested in Keynes's advocacy of measures to promote fuller employment. According to the traditional theory, success in this would entail higher marginal costs and lower real wages. And yet there was a great paradox. If an academic economist left his ivory tower and mingled a little with industrialists in the field, he could not help being impressed with the fact that the great majority of these industrialists affirmed that they could produce at lower cost, both in the long *and* in the short period, if only they had a bigger demand to satisfy. There seemed to be a stark contradiction between the views of the industrialists and the theory of perfect competition. And, of course, if the industrialists were right, this would be helpful for Keynesian policy. On the theoretical plane the matter was brought to a head by Sraffa's oft-cited article.[1]

My 1934 article cited in the footnote on page 307 contained a third section in which the significance of the widespread prevalence of increasing costs for trade cycle theory was underlined. As my original interest in the whole subject had sprung from my concern with the trade cycle and with Keynesian policy, it was natural for me to stress this matter. When Professor F. H. Knight had that article mimeographed for his seminar at Chicago, he omitted this third section, presumably because he thought it irrelevant to the main theme. I was working towards the view that a full employment policy would not necessarily have an inflationary tendency, because it would enable goods to be produced at lower real cost. I also made the point that, whereas Pigou's psychological explanation of the trade cycle depended on the periodic presence of *errors* of optimism or pessimism, if increasing returns were generally prevalent a psychological explanation would be valid, even if there were no errors present at all.

All these considerations were somewhat lost sight of when Keynes's *General Theory* appeared. In that book he seemed to accept—lock, stock, and barrel—the assumption that dimin-

[1] P. Sraffa, 'The Laws of Returns under Competitive Conditions', *Economic Journal*, 1926, pp. 535–50.

ishing returns normally applied, at least in the short period. I recall being disappointed about this, but such a minor disappointment was overlaid by the great intellectual excitement and enthusiasm generated by that volume. He had his own partial explanation of the trade cycle which sprang from his general doctrines and this seemed enough to go on with, so to speak, other matters being then forgotten. In my book on the trade cycle,[1] which appeared a year later, and attempted to give a dynamised version of Keynesian doctrine, I think that I may be said to have succumbed to diminishing returns. But enough of my old thoughts remained for me to have introduced a passage (pp. 39–41) stressing that it was quite paradoxical that prices should move upwards when output was increasing, and conversely.

Although I did then assert that the paradox was a truth, and although it is universally assumed that this is the case, I have been inclined in recent years to believe that it ought to be regarded as an unsettled question. The rule certainly applies to primary products, which are probably on the whole subject to diminishing returns, especially in the short period, and in the cases of many of which there are rather long supply lags. But in the case of manufactured products, which becomes more important decade by decade, the matter seems more doubtful. In England, for instance, there does not appear to have been any correlation in recent years between the movement of manufactured prices and the intensity of manufacturing activity. The overwhelming influence of the traditional view, which is taken for granted, may have been a barrier to systematic investigation of the facts of the case.

Chamberlin's desire was to establish a system of ideas that would be more applicable to the real world than the theories that he found prevalent. Although certain elements in his system may be subject to criticism, we may affirm that on the whole he succeeded in what he set out to do. Teaching and research in this branch of economics have been radically changed by his work, and the effects of that change will remain.

[1] *Trade Cycle*, Clarendon Press, Oxford, 1936.